DEMCO-M

The CONSTITUTION:
ITS STORY AND BATTLES

By

F. DUMONT SMITH
of the HUTCHINSON, KANSAS, BAR

KERR - JEFFERSON COMPANY
Law-Book Publishers and Law-Book Sellers
SECOND AND BROADWAY
LOS ANGELES, CAL.

Dedication

To former Senator Chester I. Long of Wichita, Kansas, in remembrance of a friendship that has endured for more than a third of a century, without whose first suggestion and sympathetic interest it would not have been written, this volume is affectionately dedicated.

CONTENTS

V

CONTENTS

CONTENTS

CONTENTS

VIII

CONTENTS

PART I.

PART I.

INTRODUCTION
CHAPTER I.

PREFATORY

The decisive battles of Constitutional Law were first published in the Journal of the American Bar Association and are reprinted here by the courtesy of its editors. They are not intended in any sense as a text-book on the Constitution. It is a popular error that the Constitution is complete in itself, that it is sufficient to learn the details of that instrument. Of course, lawyers know better. To understand that great instrument, a knowledge of its application by the Supreme Court of the United States is essential. Nor is it undertaken to explain all the cases which have applied the Constitution to the various relations of American life and business.

The attempt is to make familiar to the readers, those great decisions that have vitally affected American history, American government, and American lives. Many cases of great interest and importance are omitted. The central idea of these papers may be best understood by considering some of the cases. If the decision in Marbury vs. Madison had been other than it was, Congress would have been left as omnipotent as the British Parliament. All of its legislation would have been valid regardless of constitutional limitations. It would have been within the power of Congress to disregard, change or completely destroy the constating instrument. If the decision in Cohen vs. Virginia had been other than it was, each state Supreme Court would have been the final judge of state enactments that would conflict with the national Constitution and we should have had today a different interpretation of the Constitution in every state. If the decision in Bank vs. Maryland had been other than it was, any state hostile to a particular function of the national government could by local taxation cripple or destroy it. If the decision in Gibbons vs. Ogden had been other than it was, each state would have assumed control over interstate commerce with conflicting and hostile regulations against other states, leaving us in the utter chaos of the pre-Constitutional period.

Enough has been said to denote the purpose of the articles, which are intended not only for the lawyer, but for the general reader who is interested in the institutions of the government. These great decisions are enormously voluminous. In the aggregate, with the citations of related cases necessary to their understanding, they cover thousands of pages. The gist of the cases which I have endeavored to set down is lost in lengthy briefs and copious discussions, much of whose learned verbiage is now archaic and the main points are obscured by this immense verbosity. Few lawyers are as familiar as they should be with these great decisions, and still fewer laymen.

CHAPTER II.

THE SUPREME COURT

Section 1 of Article 3 of the Constitution vests the judicial power of the United States "in one Supreme Court and such inferior courts as the Congress may from time to time ordain and establish." The second section, after describing the cases to which "the judicial power" shall extend, thus defines its original jurisdiction: "All cases affecting ambassadors, other public ministers, or consuls and those in which a state shall be a party."

In Marbury vs. Madison the court held that these words of inclusion were exclusive, that the court had no original jurisdiction except as explicitly set forth, *supra,* and denied its power to issue a writ of mandamus because this power was not specifically mentioned. Appellate jurisdiction is given to all of the cases mentioned in the first paragraph of Section 2, "both as to law and fact with such exception and under such regulations as the Congress shall make." Under this clause the Supreme Court has uniformly held that it has no appellate jurisdiction except as is conferred by acts of Congress. The first Judiciary Act, that of 1789 which remained practically unchanged until 1875, set forth

6

the matters in which the court had appellate jurisdiction derived from the Act of Congress, these Acts being held to be the regulations mentioned in the above section by which the Supreme Court is strictly bound.

The number of judges is entirely within the control of Congress. The first court had six justices, in the 60's it had ten, in 1867 was reduced to seven and then increased to nine, and has so remained. This is a weak point in the Federal Judiciary. Congress can play politics with the court by reducing or increasing its numbers. In 1867, there being three judges about to retire, Congress reduced the number from ten to seven in order that Andrew Johnson might not have the appointment of the successors and as soon as a Republican President was elected, increased the number to nine. And so a radical Congress and President could at any time increase the number of Judges and by radical appointments entirely reverse the policy of the court and previous decisions. This is one of the ways the other two departments of the government can affect its decisions, powers that may some time be very dangerous. The other way is the control of Congress over the appellate jurisdiction of the court. To what extent the court would submit to have its appellate jurisdiction curtailed and restricted by Congress is of course unknown. Judging from past decisions it would probably not veto by its decisions any such restrictions so long as any appellate power is left. This was strikingly shown in the decision in the McArdle case. McArdle had been arrested for trial before a military tribunal under the Reconstruction Acts. Denied a writ of habeas corpus by the Circuit Court, he appealed to the Supreme Court under a statute authorizing such appeal. The appeal would have drawn in question the validity of all the Reconstruction Acts. The radical Congress, fearing the decision, repealed the statute allowing the appeal after the case had been argued, submitted and was under consideration, and the court promptly dismissed the appeal. This subserviency showing the length to which the court may go in submitting to Congressional curtailment of its appellate jurisdiction, affords another dangerous Congressional power over the court.

As soon as the Judiciary Act of 1789 had been adopted, providing for a Chief Justice and five Associate Justices, Washington made the appointments with John Jay as Chief Justice. Jay was a distinguished statesman but not a profound lawyer. He wrote five numbers of the Federalist and had been very active in politics. No one at the outset, not even the members of the court, seemed to have any conception of the vast importance it was to attain under Marshall, as we shall see.

The most important case that came before the court during Jay's term was Chisholm vs. Georgia,[1] in which

1. 2 U.S. (2 Dall.) 419, 1 L. ed. 440.

8

the court held that a state might be sued by a citizen. This decision created great dissatisfaction, especially in the South, and led to the adoption of the 11th Amendment. In Calder vs. Bull,[2] the doctrine was laid down which was to be followed for more than a hundred years, that the decision of a state court interpreting its own constitution and statutes would be followed by the Supreme Court, where no question of the Constitution, laws or treaties of the United States was involved.

Jay resigned to become the Governor of New York. Nothing could better show the esteem in which this great court was then held. When he was again, without his knowledge, appointed by Adams, to succeed Ellsworth, he declined in a letter to Adams and declared that the court under its defective system could never obtain the energy, weight and dignity which was essential to it. Ellsworth, who had been an Associate Justice from the beginning, was appointed to succeed Jay. He was a great lawyer, one of the leading figures in the Constitutional Convention, and probably the author of the Judiciary Act of 1789. So little did the court have to do that Jay had spent a year abroad during his term in service in a diplomatic position. Ellsworth, too, while Chief Justice, in October, 1799, had been commissioned one of the Three Envoys Extraordinaries to France and he remained on the mission for more than a year. In November, 1800, he resigned his

2. 3 U.S. (3 Dall.) 386, 1 L. ed. 642, affg. 2 Root (Conn.) 350.

office and on January 31, 1801, a little over a month before Adams' term expired, John Marshall was appointed Chief Justice, one of the most fortunate events that ever happened in American politics.

Had Ellsworth withheld his resignation till Adams' term had expired, Jefferson would have appointed Spencer Roan, Chief Justice of the court of appeals of Virginia, a very able lawyer and the bitterest States Rights advocate in the Union. Had he been appointed, no decision like Cohen vs. Virginia would have been pronounced. On the contrary, every state would have been given full power to interpret the Federal Constitution, laws, and treaties as it saw fit and its decisions made final. This exaggeration of the centrifugal force of the federal system would have speedily destroyed it.

The administration of Washington, who was unanimously elected and re-elected, was non-partisan and non-political in the sense that he represented no political party. He made Hamilton, the leader of what came to be the Federalist Party and an advocate of a strong central government, his Secretary of Treasury, and Jefferson, who was entirely opposed to centralization and the first protagonist of the rights of the States under the federal Union, Secretary of State, because of his diplomatic service abroad. Very speedily the ideas of these two great leaders, each the founder of oppugnant schools of American political thought, came in collision on the question of the United States Bank.

Hamilton insisted that the public credit was a sacred thing, that every promise to pay issued by the Continental Congress or the Confederation, whether currency, scrip or bonds, should be paid in full. All of these were refunded and by the operation of the new government, enabled to levy adequate taxes and import duties, were soon redeemed. To carry on fiscal operation of the government and especially to issue bills backed by a gold reserve which should be as good as gold everywhere in the country, Hamilton wished to establish the United States Bank, patterned after the Bank of England in which the federal government should be a stockholder and have a controlling interest. Jefferson bitterly opposed this as unconstitutional. Washington asked each of them for a written opinion. Jefferson's was hasty, ill-considered and set forth the doctrine upon which he founded the Republican party which later became the Democratic party, whose fundamental doctrine was that the federal government was a government of limited powers, that it took nothing by implication and could do nothing except what was expressly granted to it by the strict letter of the Constitution, entirely ignoring Section 7 of Article 1. Hamilton's brief was clear, logical and set forth that application of the implied powers that Marshall was later to apply with such tremendous and far-reaching effect. Hamilton's argument convinced Washington and the bank was established and continued for twenty-five years successfully and with great benefit not only to the

11

government, but to trade commerce and general prosperity. Thus it gave the country a sound currency as good as gold. Its benefits under its second incorporation are set forth in Marshall's decision in Bank vs. McCulloch.

This division of political ideals made a breach in the cabinet that could not be healed. Jefferson soon left the cabinet and from that time was the bitterest enemy of Washington and his administration. Anonymously and through hired scribblers, he assailed Washington in the most scurrilous manner.

The administration of Adams following Washingtion, gave Jefferson his opportunity. Adams had rendered priceless service to the cause of the revolution, but like all the Adams family was a profound and selfish egotist, domineering, arrogant and jealous. This jealousy led to a fatal breach with Hamilton, who was the real head of the Federalist Party. That party committed political suicide by the passage and drastic enforcement of the Alien and Sedition Laws, which, abhorrent to American ideals, destroyed the Federalist Party which ceased to exist except in New England. On its wreckage Jefferson rode into power, a power that the Republicans held for twenty-four years until John Quincy Adams was elected President by Congress, the electoral college being unable to give a majority to any candidate. The last and most noteworthy act of Adams' administration was the appointment of Marshall, a Federalist, as Chief Justice.

12

Jefferson throughout his administration and during the sixteen years of the administration of Madison and Monroe, who were completely under his tutelage, formed, developed and guided the doctrine of popular sovereignty, the Rights of the States, and strict construction of the Constitution. Marshall, a Federalist, by his position as Chief Justice of the Supreme Court, which by the overwhelming power of his intellect he made supreme, established the contrary doctrine of the liberal construction of the Constitution and the supremacy of the Federal government in national concerns, and this brings us to the first decisive battle—as given in Part III, Chapter I.

PART II.

PART II.

THE STORY OF THE CONSTITUTION

CHAPTER I.

FOREWORD

I trust it will not be thought that in the following pages I praise the Anglo-Saxon too much. I have merely set down the facts of history. The race has many faults. Other nations surpass it in many ways— in music, painting, sculpture, and the finer arts of civilization. The distinction of the Anglo-Saxon is his capacity for self-government, his creation of permanent free institutions, but this development is partly due to chance, his isolation in the Isle of Britain and later in America. From the time of the Norman Conquest no foreign foe has ever set foot on the soil of England. Here in America we have been free from foreign invasions and largely free from foreign wars, and so in both situations we have been able to work out, undisturbed, our impulses and instincts for self-government.

On the other hand, our Germanic cousins who were

17

left behind, as well as the other races on the continent, have been continually at war, and war requires a strong government. War and Democracy are enemies. The Hundred Years War left the greater part of France a desert. The thirty years religious war in Germany destroyed more human lives than the Great War. Every yard of the soil of Europe has been soaked with blood. It was impossible for these nations to found or maintain free institutions. It has been the happy lot of the Anglo-Saxon to work out his problems undisturbed by foreign invasion and the despotic influences that overwhelmed his brethren on the continent.

CHAPTER II.

THE ANGLO SAXON

The story of the American Constitution really began two thousand years ago. It is the story of the Anglo-Saxon race. While there are some things in the American Constitution that were new, the greater portion of it is a growth developing gradually as the Anglo-Saxon race increased in civilization, culture, and knowledge of government. Nearly all political institutions are things of slow growth, starting with crude beginnings when manners and customs were simple, among a people mostly devoted to farming, hunting, fishing and war, and developing as they became civilized, built towns with manufactures and trade and commerce and increasing wealth. So to study the Constitution properly, we must know something about this Anglo-Saxon race, as it is called.

The people who conquered Great Britain and from whom the most of us are descended, were a part of one of the great divisions of mankind known as the Germanic. Some time, many thousands of years ago, the first wave of the Caucasian race, the Celtic, came from the East and occupied and settled Northern Europe. Later there came the Germanic race who pushed the

19

Celtic race west of the Rhine and settled in what is now Germany, Denmark, Sweden and Norway. Nowadays it is the fashion to call this race the Nordic or Northern race.

We get our first real glimpse of this race when the Roman Empire, having conquered nearly all the civilized world, including Gaul, which is now France, west of the Rhine, attempted to conquer Germany. In this they never succeeded. They made some settlements, won some victories, but in the long run they never permanently conquered any of the German territory. But we get a very life-like picture of these barbarian ancestors of ours from the Roman historians beginning with Julius Caesar and for the ensuing three hundred years, which were years of warfare between the Romans and the Germans.

These ancestors of ours were tall, large-boned, powerfully built, fair-haired, blue-eyed, and very light-skinned. Their heads were what we call "long-headed" as contrasted with the Southern people who were "round-headed." They were indomitable fighters, great eaters and drinkers who lived largely by hunting, for the forests in those days were full of game. They were divided into many different tribes under different leaders or chieftains. Frequently they warred among themselves, but against a common enemy they could be united under one great leader like Herminius, who won the great victory against the Roman General Varus when two Roman Legions were destroyed, the worst defeat that the Romans had ever suffered. Their lives were simple, their wants few, their homes of logs in villages surrounded by a palisade. They had none of the arts of civilization, there were no manufactures and very little trade, but they had one peculiarity that distinguished them from the rest of the world at that time. Rome was then the mistress of the world. She ruled from the Caspian Sea westward to the Atlantic and from the cataracts of the Nile to the Firth of Forth in Scotland. It was a despotic government. The people had no voice in it. The Empire maintained a great standing army of trained professional soldiers, paid by taxes wrung from the conquered provinces. These trained soldiers were considered invincible. Among the Germans every able-bodied man was a warrior trained from childhood to use such weapons as they had, the bow and the spear chiefly. There was little discipline among them, and except when they greatly outnumbered the Roman Legions they could never make a stand against them in the open field, but in the woods and defiles of Germany they were often successful, so the Romans were never really safe except in their fortified camps and were never able, as they were in Gaul, to conquer the whole country and impose Roman government and Roman law upon its people.

21

The Germans as contrasted to the people under the yoke of the Roman Empire were free men. Every man had his share of the land owned by his community. Their chiefs were elected. The headship by whatever name known was not hereditary. It did not descend from father to son. These chiefs were usually selected from certain families distinguished for ability, courage, and military skill. They had another peculiarity. Everywhere else in the world at that time, the position of woman was very low. She was practically a slave, but the German women were free and the equals of their husbands and brothers. They had the same vote in the tribal councils. They had the same voice in determining the question of peace and war, and when suffrage was granted to women in this country by the Nineteenth Constitutional Amendment, we merely restored woman to the same position she held among our ancestors in the German forests two thousand years ago.

The children of these free men and free women inherited the free spirit of their fathers and mothers. They bowed the knee to no human being. They followed their own leaders and made their own laws. It is from this free Germanic spirit with its democratic form of government that we mainly have descended and we derive from them our freedom of spirit, our independence and instinct for self-government. Very often and sometimes for considerable periods this spirit has been temporarily subdued by despotic kings and nobles, but never crushed. Sooner or later it has revived and overthrown its monarchs and restored its own government.

These people were heathens. They worshipped the old heathen gods Thor, Wodin and Freya, most of whom were gods of battle and bloodshed. It was long after they had conquered Britain before they accepted the Christian religion. We must regard them then as a very crude, barbaric people, cruel in many of their customs, warlike rather than peaceful, but honorable in their relations with each other, faithful to their obligations of kinship and the immediate ties of family, reverencing womanhood and above all, free men.

CHAPTER III.

THE INVASION OF ENGLAND

In the year 410 Rome, which had begun the conquest of England, or Britain, as it was known then, under Julius Caesar and completed it under Agricola, was compelled by the growing weakness of her government and the inroads of the Northern Tribes to withdraw her Legions from Britain, leaving it defenseless. During the three hundred years that Rome had occupied Britain she had largely civilized it according to the standards of that time. Towns had sprung up with manufactures and trade. Roads had been built over all the country. The Roman law and to some extent the Roman language had been introduced. It had become a settled and well, though despotically governed country.

In the year 449 two bands of the Germanic tribes crossed the English Channel and attacked Britain from the South, landing on the Isle of Thanet. While we call our people Anglo-Saxon and a majority of those who conquered Britain were Angles and Saxons, there were many other tribes, Jutes, Frisians and others, coming from the lowlands at the mouths of the Elbe, Weser and the shores of the North Sea, but they were all related, all of the Germanic blood. The term Anglo-Saxon probably comes from the fact that the invading tribes called themselves Angles, while the Celts seemed to have called them generally Saxons. Probably in that way came the term Anglo-Saxon.

This first invasion was led by two brothers, Hengist and Horsa. Horsa was killed very early but Hengist lived to found a small kingdom and was succeeded by his sons. Hengist had had a peculiar history. He was by birth a Dane who had taken service under the King of the Jutes. A party of Frisian soldiers in the pay of the Jute king treacherously killed his father, who was a petty king of the Danes. Under the customs of the time and their religion, it was the duty of Hengist to avenge his father's death by the slaughter of his murderers. The Jute king forced Hengist, who led a band of his soldiers, to promise to forego his vengeance against the Frisians, who were also soldiers of the Jute king. Hengist, convinced that his father's spirit would never be at rest until he had slain the Frisians, such was their religious belief, brooded over it until he was unable to restrain himself and with a band of his followers he attacked the Frisians in the night and would have killed them all had not the King of the Jutes come to their rescue. It was agreed that to save bloodshed, Hengist and the King of the Jutes should settle the matter in a single combat. If Hen-

25

gist won he was privileged to destroy the Frisians and if he did not he was to become the slave of the Jute king. Hengist won and killed the King of the Jutes. The nobility of character that shines out through all the bloody deeds of our ancestors is shown by Hengist's conduct after he had won. By agreement he could have slaughtered all of the Frisians and he was entitled to become King of the Jutes. He refused because he had broken his promise to the Jute king. For the same reason he would not return to his own country. He felt shamed and dishonored because of this broken promise. He persuaded the conquered Frisians and Jutes to take him as leader and with his brother, Horsa, led them to the conquest of Britain. Immediately there followed invasions of Britain by other Germanic tribes, the Saxons on the Southwest, the Angles on the North and East. The war lasted for more than a hundred years. Inch by inch the invaders fought their way forward, every foot of ground being stubbornly defended by the native Celtic inhabitants of the island, until finally these native inhabitants were all exterminated or driven into the highlands of Wales and North Scotland, and all the country from the North Sea to the Irish Channel and from the English Channel to the Firth of Forth was divided into seven small Germanic Kingdoms which after two hundred years more were united under Egbert into the Saxon Kingdom of England.

CHAPTER IV.

THE CONQUEST OF ENGLAND

To rightly understand the story of our race and its peculiar growth, we must note the difference between the conquest of England and the other conquests of the Germanic race which were taking place at the same time. When Constantine, Emperor of Rome, founded the city of Constantinople and made that the Capital of the Roman Empire, the vast extent of its territory compelled a kind of division into the Eastern and Western Empire. The Capital of the whole empire was at Constantinople which was the home of the Augustus or Emperor. The Caesar, a sort of sub-emperor, ruled the Western Empire from Rome. And while the Angles and Saxons were conquering England, other Germanic tribes, Goths, Vandals, Burgundians, and Lombards, were conquering the Western Empire. They broke through the Roman lines, over-ran Gaul, Spain, Italy, captured Rome and established a Vandal Kingdom in Northern Africa on the ruins of the Roman Province. In 476 the keys of Rome were sent to Constantinople as notice that the Western Empire had ceased to exist. These Germanic tribes who founded separate Kingdoms in France, Spain, Northern and Southern Italy and Northern Africa

27

simply subjected the inhabitants to their rule. They became the masters of these countries, the ruling class. There was of course a great deal of pillage and destruction but on the other hand Roman law, Roman customs, and the Roman language remained. Very soon the conquerors were to an extent subdued by the conquered. The German rulers adopted the customs, the laws and the institutions of the conquered country, more or less melted into the mass of people and the language of each country became a mixture of that of the Romans and the Germans and became what we call the Romance Tongues, from their Roman origin. The native inhabitants remained the majority of the people, but subject to rulers of German blood.

Quite the reverse of this happened in England. There the stubborn resistance of the native inhabitants resulted in their extermination. Some of them fled for refuge to the highlands of Wales and Scotland. Those who remained were wiped out. When the conquest was complete, scarcely a trace remained of the original inhabitants. Their laws, such as they were, their customs and their religion, together with all traces of Roman culture, had completely disappeared. England by this conquest became as completely Germanic as the territory from which the conquerors had come. These German tribes retained their language, customs, institutions and religion absolutely unchanged and untouched by contact with the early Britons. The blood

28

is absolutely the same because in all the years that have passed England has had a very small mixture of foreign blood by immigration except that brought in by the Norman conquest and that was Germanic blood. In effect the Germanic Tribes were transplanted from Northern Germany to England and there took root as though on vacant soil, an extremely rich and fertile soil. Naturally, separated from their kinsmen they began to change in every way, including their language.

CHAPTER V.

THE SAXON GOVERNMENT

The government of the Saxon Kingdom which finally united all England under Egbert in 815, was entirely the outgrowth of the free spirit and institutions that they had brought with them from the mainland of Europe. True, they had Kings instead of Chiefs and to some extent the crown had become heritable, that is, it descended from father to son, but this was not a fixed rule. The lineal heir was frequently set aside for some worthier candidate, nor was there any trace of the despotism and the claim to divine right of rule which rapidly grew up on the continent. The Kingship of Saxon England continued to be an office and not a property. He ruled within the law of his realm and was subject to it. The last King of the Saxons, Harold, was an elected king.

In the meanwhile, growing out of this free spirit, the political institutions of the kingdom had developed along free lines. They had the Folkmote, the assemblage of all the people to approve laws, the foundation of the English House of Commons. They had their Witenagemot, the assemblage of leaders and wise men who surrounded the king and gave him advice and counsel which amounted to a check upon the

30

royal will, and which was the foundation of the English House of Peers. Codes of laws were enacted, strikingly wise for their time and adapted to a rude and simple people. There was a crude beginning of the Jury trial, an institution that is one of the dearest treasures of our political institutions. At first when a man was accused of a crime a jury was called of those who knew the circumstances and they decided his guilt or innocence. Very gradually this developed into the modern jury system where the jurors are chosen because they know nothing of the facts, are impartial and hear the evidence of those who know the facts and from that determine the guilt or innocence of the accused. But the essential fact was that no man could be convicted without a trial according to the forms of law. No man could be deprived of his property except by lawful judgment. On the continent, on the contrary, the king had absolute power. He could kill or imprison his subjects or deprive them of their property by royal word without any trial. It is this which distinguishes the Anglo-Saxon from all the other peoples of that time and aside from the interval under despotic kings following the Norman conquest, has always distinguished him. He has always been a stickler for justice, for the orderly administration of law and opposed to every form of arbitrary power.

CHAPTER VI.

The English Language

Language is a living thing and has its growth like all other living things. All of the races of Europe, the Germans, the English, the French, the Spanish, the Italians, the Greeks as well as the Hindus of India, came from one common stock that we call the Aryan. The cradle of this race was somewhere in the highlands of Continental Western Asia. Philologists, those who make a study of language, discovered that in all of these different languages there were certain common root forms, about five hundred in all, that were the same for the same objects, in each country. The word Aryan comes from "Ar," the plow. We have it in the word arable, meaning able to be plowed, and many other forms.

When these Aryan people began their migrations some of them went east and conquered India, others in successive waves, Celtic, Germanic, and Slav, swept westward over all Europe. They traveled into different countries. They met and conquered or mingled with different peoples and very soon their own common tongue began to change with each of these migrating tribes so that in a few hundred or a few thousand years, we know not how many, these different tribes spoke different languages having the same root form of which they were ignorant and were unable to understand each other. It is the story of the Tower of Babel.

So it was with our Germanic ancestors when they conquered England. They brought with them the common tongue of their ancestors which forms very largely the basis of our language, and by coming in contact with different peoples and in different surroundings the language began to change until it became the Saxon tongue. The Norman conquest brought an infusion of Latin words derived partly from the Greek, and French words derived from the Latin, and out of all of these tongues has come the English language as we know it today.

Where people are isolated, the tendency is always towards dialects, to use different words to express the same idea, different names for the same object, and above all a different pronunciation. As late as one hundred years ago it was almost impossible in England for a native of Cornwall to understand a native of Yorkshire. Even to this day in this country, the native of Alabama or Mississippi uses a different pronunciation from a native of the North and the accent of the New Englander is different from that of the Westerner. It was not until the invention of printing that language began to assume a fixed form and the vast increase in the facilities of travel and inter-communication have tended to the elimination of dialects. Saxon England was almost entirely isolated and cut off from the rest of the world. It had at first no written language and so it grew with a separate form of speech, differing largely from its Germanic origin. It was not until the time of King Alfred, of whom I shall speak later, in the 9th Century, that any intelligent attempt was made to reduce the Saxon tongue to a written language, with a grammar of its own.

So to conclude these brief observations, we find the Saxon Kingdom of England cut off from the continent of Europe by the English Channel, developing a free and independent set of political institutions, a different language, and an entirely different idea of the relations between the people and their ruler; a people who had a more or less crude system of law, courts of justice, trial by jury and a monarchy that was more or less elective. There was no form of despotism such as existed everywhere else. Down to the Norman conquest we may fairly say that our ancestors were free men. They had no conception of a Republic like ours but they did in a large measure govern themselves and make their own laws.

CHAPTER VII.

Religion

It is not the purpose of this brief story to deal with the general history of the Anglo-Saxon Race further than it concerns its development as a free people. The conversion of these heathen ancestors of ours to Christianity had many important results on their character and institutions. Before the Roman forces left Britain, Rome under Constantine and his successors had become a Christian government and Britain before the Germanic invasion was largely Christianized.

The religion of the early Celtic inhabitants had been that of the Druids, a cruel supersition with human sacrifices to its gods. The Oak and the Mistletoe were worshipped and the pleasant Christmas custom of our day of hanging the mistletoe as an invitation to the young people to take the privilege of kissing each other is a survival of that old worship. Relics of that worship still survived when the Romans withdrew from England. Our forefathers wiped out both religions as entirely as they did the native inhabitants. Nothing remained of Christianity or the Druids. Churches and temples were destroyed and the Christian religion disappeared.

35

It is related that one of the greatest Popes of the Roman Church who afterward became Gregory the Great, while still a young Deacon, walking along the quay at Marseilles, saw a group of Saxons who had been captured by Danish pirates and were offered for sale as slaves. He noted their beautiful features, fair hair, blue eyes, and their white skins and asked of what nation they were. He was answered, "Angles." "Not Angles," said he, "but Angels." He inquired where they were from and he was told from England. He determined that such should not be heathens and when he became Pope one of his first missions in 597 was sent to convert England to Christianity. It landed in the Kingdom of Kent and speedily converted the king, whose wife was already a Christian, and from there the religion spread northward.

About the same time Columba (later canonized as a Saint), an Irish Priest, where the Catholic Religion had taken firm root, landed in northern England and began his labors. In less than a hundred years all of England was entirely Christianized. For a long time our heathen ancestors were reluctant to give up their old gods, Wodin, Thor, Freya and the rest of them. They were frequent backsliders. When fortune went against them they relapsed into worship of the old gods and when the old gods failed them they returned to the Christian God, and in their drunken revels swore indifferently by the old gods and the new God

36

of the Christians. There again was a strong distinction between the Anglo-Saxon and their kinfolk who remained at home. The Saxons on the continent were not Christianized until three hundred years later and then only by force, by the strong arm of Charlemagne, who gave them the choice of Christianity or death. It is related of one old Saxon who had reluctantly accepted the Religion and agreed to be baptized, that just as the ceremony was to take place and he had one foot in the baptismal font he stopped to ask the priest, "Where is my father who died a heathen as you call it?' "In Purgatory," said the priest. "Where are my brothers who died on the field of battle?" "In Purgatory." "Where are all my other kinfolk?" "In Purgatory." The old heathen withdrew his foot. "Heaven would be a lonesome place, I prefer to go where my kin have gone." And he refused to be baptized.

In England, on the contrary, our ancestors adopted the Christian religion by argument and persuasion and without force and it may be noted here that while in England in the next thousand years, and only after the beginning of the Protestant Revolt, Catholics sometimes persecuted Protestants and in turn Protestants persecuted Catholics, there never was in England a religious civil war such as desolated France, Germany and the other countries of the continent. Religious toleration seems to be in our blood and it was crystallized in the First Amendment to our Constitution;

"Congress shall make no law respecting an establishment of Religion or prohibiting the free exercise thereof." This is one of the precious privileges of our government, that every man may worship God in his own way according to his own conscience. Freedom of worship is a racial characteristic like self-government.

The coming of Christianity made a remarkable change in the character, customs and government of Saxon England. It softened the cruelties of the national character. From the very first the church worked to abolish slavery which was then a general condition over all the world. Prisoners captured in war, men convicted of crime or unable to pay their debts, were sold into slavery and the slave class was cruelly treated. The Church succeeded eventually in practically wiping it out. It brought learning and knowledge of the Roman Law to England. The long reign of the Roman government had built up a system of law unsurpassed in the history of the world. It outlasted the Roman government and the English law has borrowed from it many vital principles. The Romany clergy, in addition to founding churches, monasteries, and nunneries, established schools and seats of learning. They became advisers of the monarchs because they were educated on the continent, knew the Roman law, the customs of other countries and could read and write, a rare accomplishment in those days. The higher members of the clergy became the trusted advisers of the Kings of both the Saxons and the Normans from Dunstan down to Wolsey. English history is full of Archbishops and Cardinals who acted as Prime Minister to the Monarch and largely directed the affairs of government. The church gradually assumed jurisdiction over marriage, divorce, wills, the administration of property, and finally a separate legal jurisdiction was established under an Archbishop or Cardinal who was known as Chancellor, from whose decisions we derive an important branch of our law known as Equity. This ecclesiastical jurisdiction was changed under Henry VIII. when he quarreled with the Pope and separated the English church from the Roman See, and eventually the Chancellor became a secular officer.

CHAPTER VIII.

ALFRED THE GREAT

In writing this story of the Constitution, which involves the story of our race, there is a great temptation to wander. No racial history is more remantic or fascinating, but in this brief history, I must confine myself to so much of that story as concerns our political development and the growth of our free institutions. But no story of our race would be complete without some allusion to Alfred, or as the Saxons spelled it, Aelfred the Great. He became King at a time when the greater portion of England had been conquered by the Danes. At one time he was confined to the small territory of Athelney with a few followers.

One day as he was wandering in the forest, poorly clad, he stopped at a hut for food and found the housewife preparing some oaten cakes for baking. She supposed the King a peasant like herself and set him to baking the cakes for his dinner. Absorbed in sorrowful thoughts of the miseries of his Kingdom, Alfred let the cakes burn and the good wife boxed his ears soundly for his neglect. Alfred told the story with great glee to his followers. It is an index to his character. In all the long, bloody, cruel history of our race and indeed of the whole world up to then, Alfred shines out as the one thoroughly good king—the one King who believed that he derived his scepter from God, not as an absolute tyrant but as the true father of his people, representing God on Earth in his mercifulness, his pity for all of his people. To him the lowliest serf was as dear, as cherished, as the highest noble. Little by little be recovered his Kingdom, conquered the Danes, subjected all England to his rule and to the rule of law, built a great fleet that patroled the coasts of England and kept off the Northern pirates, enacted new and wise laws and above all was the patron of learning and art. He built churches, founded schools, made a study of the Anglo-Saxon language, had its grammar formulated in writing, himself wrote poems and composed music, but to the end of his days remained a common man cherishing the rights of the comon people. Down to our own Washington, he is the most perfect ruler that the world has ever known.

CHAPTER IX.

HAROLD

The last king of the Saxons was Harold, who perished and his Kingdom with him at the hands of William the Conqueror in the battle of Hastings, or Senlac, as the Normans called it.

He belonged to the semi-royal family of the Earl of Godwine. While Edward the Confessor was still King and Harold's father, the Earl of Godwine, stood next to the throne, Harold was shipwrecked on the coast of Normandy. William, the Duke of Normandy, who later became the Conqueror, forced Harold to swear that he would help him to the throne of England to which he claimed a shadowy title. On the death of Edward the Confessor, Harold, who had returned to England, although not of the Royal line, was elected King of England. Almost immediately his half-brother, Tostig, with a force of Danes landed in the north of England, claiming the Crown. Harold, by a hasty march, collecting such troops as he could, met Tostig at Stamford Bridge, defeated and slew him. In the hour of his victory he had word that William of Normandy had landed at Pevensey on the Southern coast, claiming the Crown, and was ravaging the southern countries.

The story of his battle with William comes later. Harold the Last was one of the best of the Saxon kings. He had the conspicuous virtues of his race; honesty, courage, tenacity and a love for his people. William's victory at Hastings would have availed him little if Harold had lived. He would have rallied the forces of his kingdom and ultimately won. His death left the Saxons without a leader.

CHAPTER X.

THE FEUDAL SYSTEM

An understanding of the Feudal System, which had grown up on the continent while the Saxon Kingdom was being formed in England, is essential to understand the Norman Conquest. The theory of the Feudal System was that all the land in the kingdom belonged to the King, not to the people. He leased the land to great nobles, not for a cash rental but in return for military service. Each of these great Nobles, Tenants in Chief as they were called, who held directly from the King, were bound to furnish, on the call of the King, a certain number of Knights and men at arms, or foot soldiers, and place them under the command of the King in time of war. They furnished their own horses, armor, military equipment and generally the supplies for the troops. These Tenants in Chief sublet portions of their lands to lesser nobles who became their tenants and as rental furnished a certain number of Knights and men at arms to their immediate landlord. Each tenant owed allegiance to his immediate superior or landlord and all to the King. So when there was a war the King called on his Chief Tenants for their allotment of warriors, they in turn called on their tenants and so the army was built up. The King

44

had a certain following of troops of his own, as did each of the nobles. The King depended for his cash revenue upon the crown lands, lands that were leased for a cash rental or a share of the crop and taxes levied on the towns and traders, on goods imported and exported and cash exactions in money sometimes levied from all the people which were always bitterly resented and resisted. The King was an absolute despot except so far as his power was checked or controlled by the great nobles, some of whom were almost as powerful as the King himself.

Beneath the military class were the farmers who tilled the soil and raised the food for all of these soldiers who lived in idleness and whose sole business was war. The farmers were ground under the heel of the military class. They farmed the lord's lands and paid him a share of the crops, the wheat, the corn, the live stock, the wine and the other products. In return they received protection from their over-lord, such as it was, but they had no rights that the King or the Lords were bound to respect. In effect they were mere serfs, living in wretched huts with just enough to keep themselves alive.

Between these two classes were the townsmen or burghers, the foundation of the present great middle class, as it is called. They lived in walled towns, carried on manufactures, trade and commerce. They had the only ready money in the country. Little by little, in consideration of money payments to the King, they were granted certain privileges of self-government. Some of these towns, like Paris, London, Nuremburg, and many Italian cities, became very powerful in the state. It was the growth of these cities and their independence which finally enabled Holland to throw off the yoke of Spain. London in this way became a very important factor in the politics of England. The citizens were trained to arms, trained to man the walls and resist invasion. Many of these merchants were very enterprising, importing luxuries from over the seas in exchange for their own commodities and always paid tribute to the King or overlord. The Feudal army, levied as I have described, was at best a very unsatisfactory military force. It felt its first allegiance to its own leaders. Quarrels were always breaking out between these great nobles and their followers. Frequently there were combinations of these nobles against the King himself. When such an army took the field there was little general discipline or obedience to orders.

The provisioning of the forces was haphazard and generally they relied for food upon ravaging the country where they were. There was very little difference so far as the poor farmers were concerned between the invading armies or the troops of their own country. All the food and animals were taken for the support of the army in either case and the poor people were left to starve.

46

Such an army was capable of tremendous but very brief exertion. In any long campaign it gradually melted away. In the Chronicles of Froisart, which I hope you will read, you will find a lively picture of such an army, its lack of discipline, its shortage of food, the utter absence of information by scouts of the whereabouts of the enemy, and many things that would seem ridiculous to the modern soldier. He tells of one instance where two armies set out to engage each other, the English against the Scotch. After wandering for a week within twenty miles of each other, each ignorant of the other's whereabouts, they finally melted away and disbanded without a battle.

Very gradually the system changed, the obligation of military service was commuted into money as rental and with this money the King hired his soldiers, in effect a standing army. The King was glad to do this because with a standing army he could bridle the power of the great Nobles. Before these Nobles realized what had happened the King with his mercenary troops had become strong enough to defy them and the result, eventually, on the continent was that the King became an absolute despot, decreasing constantly the power of the Nobles until he reigned supreme.

So when the Normans undertook to conquer England, it was the clash of two systems, the Norman, a military caste composed of professional soldiers, and the Saxon army composed of citizen soldiers who were

47

ordinarily farmers and only took up arms to defend their land from invasion or their homes from ravage. The Feudal army properly led was a terrible force for a brief period. The onset of its horsemen clothed in steel mail, that could turn an arrow or stroke of a sword, backed by men at arms with pikes and a force of bowmen, was usually irresistible against untrained troops and it was with such an army that William landed in England.

CHAPTER XI.

WILLIAM THE CONQUEROR

The Dukedom of Normandy had been carved out of the domain of France by bands of Scandinavian pirates of Germanic blood, kinfolk of the Saxons. Wearied with their constant pillage and destruction on his coast, the King of France, Charles the Bald, granted them lands in Northern France on the condition they would pay allegiance to him and out of this cession grew the Dukedom of Normandy, a part of the Feudal System of France. Nominally it owed allegiance to the King but in effect it was independent.

The father of Duke William, Duke Robert, saw his mother, Arletta, washing her linen in a stream and fell in love with her. She was the daughter of a tanner in the town and one of the taunts hurled at William by his enemies was that he was the grandson of a tanner.

His father died when he was little more than a child and surrounded by turbulent Nobles, his early career was stormy; he grew up practically sword in hand. He became and still remains one of the outstanding figures of history. He was of gigantic stature, enormous strength and unexcelled in arms. No man of his day could stand before him in single combat. He had the headlong courage of his race but mingled with it, even in the hour of battle, an unsurpassed coolness.

49

He was an unequalled fighter but also a great general. With all his rashness in battle, his fierce bursts of almost inhuman temper, he was wary. He could wait as well as charge and he was a master intriguer. He was capable of warm friendships and his friends were devoted to him. Some little touches show the contradictory points of his character. Besieging a town, the townsmen hung out hides on the battlements with a writing, "Welcome to the tanner's grandson." In revenge he had the eyes of some of the prisoners torn out, their hands cut off and flung over the battlements.

In his youth when he first obtained complete power in Normandy, he quarreled with Lanfranc, a Christian Bishop, and banished him from the Dukedom. After sending him out of the Kingdom, impatient to see that he was gone, he mounted and rode after him. Lanfranc was riding a lame mule. William burst out on him with abuse because he was not sooner out of the country. Lanfranc calmy replied, "Give me a good horse and I will get out quicker." William laughed and Lanfranc became his chief and wisest adviser. He was capable of great cruelty and great magnanimity, but he was the greatest soldier of his time. When the line of the Saxon Kings was set aside by the election of Harold who had sworn fealty to William, as William claimed, the latter set up a claim to the crown of England and with tremendous effort gathered a host, built a fleet and in 1066 landed on the coast of England.

CHAPTER XII.

THE BATTLE OF HASTINGS

What William feared was that Harold would play a waiting game retreating before him, laying the country waste so that he could secure no supplies until William's army, like all Feudal armies, should melt away. It would have been impossible for William to feed his army from France for any length of time. That would have been the wiser thing to do, for Harold had just fought a great battle with his half-brother Tostig and had marched the length of England to meet William. He was calling up his citizen soldiery, loath to leave the plow, but Harold's gallant spirit could not brook delay on William's defiance nor his ravages of Harold's country and his people. He took his stand on the hill of Senlac which compelled William to attack him or retreat.

The battle between these two contending systems of government, between William the Despot backed by his powerful army and Harold, the Constitutional King, backed by his citizen soldiery, half soldier, half farmer, began at daylight on October 14, 1066. Harold had strengthened his camp with palisades behind which stood his pikemen and bowmen. He had but a small force of Knights. The Norman Knighthood

51

attacked the palisade, hewing it down with their battle-axes, but were steadily repulsed. William raged like a lion from one part of the field to another but it was impossible to break the Saxon ranks. Finally a part of his force feigned a retreat and drew the right wing of the Saxons out of their entrenchment. The Normans turned and cut them down. In another part of the field, the Normans broke through. But Harold's iron ring of friends remained impenetrable. Finally William directed his bowmen to shoot their arrows into the air and one of these pierced Harold's eye and killed him. Still his followers fought on and when his body was found next morning it was covered deep with the bodies of his friends and foemen. So perished Harold and the Saxon Kingdom never to be revived. It had had a brief and stormy history, lasting hardly two hundred and fifty years, ravaged by foes from without and civil war from within, but it had established free institutions, the spirit of liberty and self-government which though submerged for a time by the Norman Conquest was never subdued and eventually conquered its conquerors.

CHAPTER XIII.

THE NATURE OF THE CONQUEST

Harold's death left the Saxon Kingdom without a leader. Southern and middle England, including the great city of London, speedily submitted. A Parliament was called which acknowledged William as King of England. In the North, the Earls of Umberland and Mercia speedily submitted. For the first two years William seems to have wished to reign as a Constitutional Monarch. He took his crown at the hands of the Saxon people, he recognized Saxon laws, Saxon institutions and the ownership of the land, and was a mild king. At the end of two years he returned to the continent to look after the affairs of Normandy. In his absence, the Norman nobles that he had left in control of England by their oppression roused the Saxons to revolt. When William returned two-thirds of the Kingdom was in rebellion against him. His greatness as a commander speedily manifested itself. He marched from one end of the land to the other, conquering wherever he went. His innate savage spirit showed itself in the bitter devastation of all Northern England. Castles were destroyed, towns pillaged and the countryside laid waste. From then on he ruled as a despot. Saxon titles were forfeited and the lands granted to his followers. He compiled the celebrated

53

Domesday Book in which was listed every land holding in England with its rental value, the sum it should
pay to the crown.   He established in England the
Feudal System of the continent, that all of the land
belonged to the King and those who occupied it were
merely his tenants.

For a time the Saxons were trodden under foot,
deprived of their lands or any voice in the government.   They were ruled by Norman over-lords who
treated them with the utmost cruelty and oppression.
At William's death he was succeeded by his son
William, surnamed Rufus (because he had red hair).
So speedily did the Norman conquest amalgamate itself
with the Saxon people that twenty-eight years after
the conquest, when Stephen's Norman nobles rebelled
against him, he subdued them with the aid of his
Saxon subjects whom he had called on for help.   From
that time on very gradually the Norman nobles were
curbed and the Saxon Thegn and Franklin were restored to their rights.   Very gradually the Norman-
French and the Saxon-English became one language.
Very gradually the old Saxon customs and laws were
revived, the Norman nobles began to join hands with
Saxon Thegn and Franklin against the despotic power
of the Norman King and when on the field of Runnymede the English people wrested from John the Magna
Charta (Great Charter), the forces of freedom were
led by a Norman Baron and a Saxon Archbishop.

CHAPTER XIV.

IMPORTANCE OF THE CONQUEST

Historians have paid too little attention to the Norman Conquest. In my opinion it was the greatest event of modern history. Our Germanic ancestors in the six hundred years after the conquest of England had become Christianized, had established and maintained a Constitutional Elective Monarchy with a civilized code of laws, courts, trial by jury, and a sort of Parliament with two branches, the first government of its kind in the history of the world, with the King as much subject to the law as his subjects were. They had become an indwelling, home loving, civilized, settled people tenacious of their rights, courageous in defending their firesides but with no desire for foreign conquest or the acquisition of territory from their neighbors. It is curious how this particular quality from thence on runs through all the history of our race. After the Norman Kings had given up their attempt to conquer France and acquire a continental dominion, our race has never waged an aggressive warfare, a war merely for the purpose of conquering some other people and seizing its territory. In fact I think if we carefully consider the history of our race we shall find that the Saxon traits of freedom, self-government, liberty of conscience, willingness to abide by the will

55

of the majority, the tendency towards peace except in self-defense, have been our dominant characteristics.

But the Norman Conquest did this. The infusion of Norman blood was small, but considering that for three hundred years it was the dominant governing race, it was powerful and engrafted upon the Saxon blood certain dominating traits. It engrafted upon those peaceful, home loving, indwelling Saxons the wild searoving, raiding, conquering spirit of the Scandinavian pirates, the Northmen who had become Normans, and the combination made a world conquering race. The Normans were seamen and the English who had been farmers became the masters of the sea. The Normans were always seeking new lands and the English became rovers. But there was this difference between the English and the old Scandinavian pirates. The Norman spirit reached out for new lands and conquered them; the Saxon spirit held them. The Normans conquered with the sword, the Saxons held the lands, settled, cleared the forests, planted, tilled and built towns. The Saxon plow followed the Norman sword. The Norman hand took; the Saxon hand held. In addition to that when the Norman-Saxon blending had become complete and the new English race started to colonize, these people carried with them the Saxon principles of self-government. When the old hive overflowed and the new swarm went forth to the new lands, they took with them their Codes of Laws, their principles of self-government, and these self-governing colonies flourished under the principles they took with them from their homes. I shall have occasion to allude to this later.

CHAPTER XV.

MAGNA CHARTA

William was succeeded by William Rufus, by Stephen and Mary, by Henry I and II, by Richard and then by his brother John, the weakest, most sensual, cruel, cowardly and wicked that ever sat on the English Throne. His exactions and cruelties finally aroused the English people, by that time pretty well melted into a common mass, and on the little Isle of Runnymede in the Thames, forced the beaten and baffled King to sign the Great Charter by which he agreed to a government by law instead of by his arbitrary will. He promised that he would no more "send upon, imprison, nor disseize any free man or deprive him of his life or liberty except by the judgment of his peers and the law of the land." This is a landmark in the history of the world. At that moment all the other peoples of the world were sunk in abject slavery at the foot of thrones stained with every crime, without a human right. Our ancestors, sword in hand, compelled the King to give up his despotic power, but note here something that I shall have occasion to refer to later: the Great Charter was a limitation on the power of the executor only; the English Parliament which was then coming into existence was unlimited in its power. Therein is a distinction between the English Government and ours.

CHAPTER XVI.

GROWTH OF THE ENGLISH CONSTITUTION

Constitutional government in England begins with the Great Charter. The Norman Kings and those who followed them continually fought for depotic power, but on the field of Runnymede the English people had learned the power of combination; Norman and Saxon became one, speaking a common language, the English tongue. The Nobles whom the King had attempted to crush joined with the common people and became their leaders. Little by little the English Parliament grew into its present proportions. At the first the Norman Kings followed the example of the Saxons, surrounded themselves with great Nobles and Ecclesiastics as advisers known as the Great Council, that eventually became the English House of Lords, hereditary, their title descending from father to son. The House of Commons was of slower growth, called into being by the King's Writ, summoning Knights of the Shires and Burgesses representing the towns, into a lower house that eventually became the House of Commons.

I have spoken before of taxes imposed by the Feudal Kings upon their subjects. Very early, the English people established the principle that no gen-

eral taxes could be levied upon the English people
without the consent of the Commons. They left the
sword, the power to declare peace and war, the right to
make treaties, to their King, but they held the purse
strings, and whenever the King demanded a tax or, as
it was called, a tenth, in return the Commons demanded new privileges and required that the King
renew the Great Charter. In addition, during all this
period from the Eleventh Century for more than three
hundred years the English Kings retained dominions
on the continent and were constantly seeking to extend
them. At one time the English Kings held Normandy,
Aquitaine, and other territories, a vast domain running through the center of France. Edward III practically conquered France, his successors losing most of
it. Henry V again completed the conquest and was
acknowledged King of France, a kingdom lost by his
feeble son Henry VI and it was not until the close of
the seventeenth century that the English lost their last
hold on the continent when Calais was surrendered to
the French King.

CHAPTER XVII.

The French Wars

The wars with France had an important influence on the Constitutional development of England. English blood and English money were spent on the continent in these vain attempts of the English Kings to establish and maintain a continental Empire. The expenses of these wars, together with the extravagance of the Court, compelled the English kings from year to year to call on their English subjects for money, and with each new grant of money, the English Commons demanded new rights and privileges. In fact they bought their freedom, cash down. The great cities that were growing up with manufactures and commerce, accumulating vast wealth by their trade with continental Europe, willingly gave their money to the King in return for charters that enlarged their franchises and their privileges. The English wars kept the martial spirit of England alive, the English bowmen. common citizens, became the most dreaded soldiery of Europe and won the battles of Crecy, Potiers, and Agincourt against the mailed chivalry of France. The invention of gunpowder destroyed the Feudal System, for the common soldier with his musket over-

matched the steel-clad knight. The old sturdy Saxon
spirit revived and very gradually the old Saxon laws
came to life. The Great Charter was not a new thing.
When Saxons and Normans aligned on the field of
Runnymede, their demand was not for something new
but for a return to "the laws of Edward the Confessor,"
the last but one of the Saxon Kings. The revival of
the English spirit and the old constitutional habit, was
simply a revival of Saxon law and a return to a Constitutional Monarchy.

CHAPTER XVIII.

THE FIRST PARLIAMENT

The first legal English Parliament was called by Edward I in 1295. Prior to that Simon de Montfort, who had led a successful rebellion against Henry III, the father of Edward I, because of his tyranny and abuses and who for nearly two years held the King a prisoner, called an irregular assemblage, but the Parliament summoned by Edward I was the beginning of the English Parliament. The Lords and higher clergy were summoned but soon claimed the right to sit without a summons. The King also summoned from the country two Knights from each Shire and two Burgesses from each of the largest towns. At first, all sat together, but very soon the Commons in one hall and the Lords and clergy in another, constituting the two houses of Parliament. From that time on a Parliament was summoned whenever the King needed money. During the reign of Edward III, the necessity for money to carry on his French wars brought a Parliament nearly every year and Edward III, who was a good politician as well as a great King, flattered his Parliament by frequently consulting with it on matters of State, which helped him greatly in getting the money he wanted.

At first the Commons were reluctant to attend. The pay was two shillings a day, the roads horrible and infested with highwaymen and the inns wretched. It was a long time before the people recognized their power and a seat in Parliament an honor to be sought. For the next 400 years the power of Parliament was in exact proportion to the poverty of the King. Thus, when Henry VII, first of the Tudors, a great miser, died, he left his son Henry VIII a full treasury. When Henry VIII broke with the Pope and confiscated the rich estates of the church he became the wealthiest monarch in Europe. This made him independent of Parliament and during his reign it became a nullity, an abject body that obeyed his every command.

Under Elizabeth it began to revive, because Elizabeth needed all the help of her protestant subjects against the Catholics. Under James I, that doddering, half-idiotic, drunken, yet tyrannical King, Parliament again began to assert its independence, and after his death, in 1628, presented the great Petition of Right, in which was boldly set forth the rights of Free-born Englishmen against the Crown. It was the day-star of the revolution and in it was used for the first time by Lord Coke, that memorable phrase, "due process of law," which is written into our Constitution.

CHAPTER XIX.

THE REVOLUTION OF 1688

This long struggle running through the Norman, Angevian, Tudor, and Stuart reigns culminated in the "Glorious Revolution of 1688." It began in 1640 with a revolt against Charles I and this again turned largely upon the question of taxation. It is well to bear this in mind and give it the proper emphasis because the question of taxation without representation was one of the main causes of the American Revolution. Charles attempted to levy taxes without the consent of the Commons. He levied a tax called the Ship Tax. It was an old tax that the coastal people had paid to maintain vessels against pirates. When it was levied upon inland people and not to build ships but to pay for the extravagance of Charles I and his Court, the English people revolted, and Charles lost his crown and his head.

The brief Protectorship of Cromwell followed. Cromwell's power was entirely unconstitutional, he left no successor, and the weak, pleasure-loving son of the beheaded Charles, Charles II, was invited back to the throne. The people were temporarily tired of Cromwell and his puritanism. Throughout the reign

of Charles II there was a constant constitutional struggle. Charles died childless and was succeeded by his
brother, James II, who attempted to revive the old
unconstitutional ideas and to impose the Catholic religion upon his Protestant subjects. William of
Orange, who had married James' daughter Mary, was
invited to England and he and Mary took the throne.
This revolution of 1688 marks the beginning of the
modern English Constitution. The English Parliament held that James had abandoned the throne, that
his son was incapable to govern, set aside the Succession, abolished forever the Divine Right of Kings and
held that the English people could choose their own
sovereign. They went back eight hundred years to
the Saxon precedent of the election of Harold. They
wiped out Feudalism, the Divine Right, hereditary
monarchy, and established the right of the English
people to self-government and to choose their own
rulers. The ordinance provided that in case of the
death of William and Mary without issue, Mary's
younger sister Anne should succeed to the throne and
if she died without issue, her younger sister Sophia,
who had married the Elector of Hanover, or her children, should succeed, as a result of which, on the death
of William and Mary, Anne and Sophia having died,
George I, Elector of Hanover, Sophia's eldest son,
succeeded to the throne of England. From thence on
the struggle between the Crown and the Commons

went on much softened, carried on within Constitutional limits, the Commons constantly growing in power and the power of the King constantly lessened until in our day the King has become almost a figurehead. While retaining nominally the power of veto over the Acts of Parliament such as our President has over the Acts of Congress, it has been more than a hundred years since that power has been exercised by an English King. The King still exercises a powerful social and diplomatic influence. He has a conservative power, and is a glorious figurehead to whom the people look up as King of Great Britain, Scotland and Ireland, Emperor of India, and the head of all the English Colonies overseas with the widest dominions that the world has ever seen. He typifies in a way the vast British Empire and his peculiar position as a Constitutional Monarch seems to fit in with the long British theory of a Constitutional King rather than a Republic.

CHAPTER XX.

THE BRITISH CONSTITUTION

With the Revolution of 1688 the British Constitution very speedily took on its present form and as it is more or less the model from which our Constitution was formed it is necessary to know just what that Constitution was. It will be understood that this British Constitution was not like ours, put into writing at one time and adopted with all its provisions by a vote of its people. It is the product of slow growth, a gradual building of one precedent on another, the result of the Constitutional struggle of the people against their King.

Generally there have been in England two parties, first the Whigs, now the Liberal Party, and the Tories, now the Conservative Party. Generally the Whigs and their successors, the Liberals, have represented the popular party, seeking to decrease the power of the King and the House of Lords, and give the people more power. The Tories and their successors, the Conservatives, have generally upheld the power of the King and the House of Lords and opposed any changes in the form of government and have opposed the extension of the franchise, that is, the right to vote, and tried to keep the government as it was, that is what the Conservative means. Broadly speaking, it may be said that the Whigs and the Liberals represent the old Saxon principles of self-government while the Tories and the Conservatives represent the Norman element seeking to keep the power in the hands of the King and the Nobles, but constantly more liberal. Out of this continuous conflict through a period of seven hundred years we have the British Constitution as it now is, growing constantly freer. But it is worth while to consider what the British Constitution was at the time our forefathers formed our Constitution.

The King was a constitutional monarch, in fact his position was much like that of Harold, the last of the Saxon Kings. The English King or Queen inherits the Crown. It descends in the royal line but it is settled that the English people may set aside this succession and take some other member of the royal family as was done in 1688. Theoretically, the King is the commander in chief of the army and navy. He makes war and peace. He selects the great ministers who carry on the business of government. He has the right of veto on the Acts of Parliament but this has become a theory. In actual practice the Ministry, as it is called, consisting of the Prime Minister and all the other Ministers who hold the various departments of government must be members of Parliament, either the House of Peers or the Commons, generally the latter. They must be able at all times to command the majority of the House of Commons. If at any time the lower house should by a majority pass a vote of "want of confidence" in the Ministry, they would immediately tender their resignation to the King, from whom they receive their commissions nominally. In such a case, the King could not choose such ministers as he would personally prefer. He must call into office the leaders of the opposition party who have succeeded in overthrowing the former Minister. So while the ministers are nominally appointed by the King, they are really appointed by a majority of the Commons, the Peers being disregarded. In fact today, and this was largely true in 1776, the House of Commons is the governing body of England. The King chooses whatever ministers the majority desire. The King upon the suggestion of the Prime Minister creates new Peers who immediately take their seats in the House of Lords. More than once by the threat to create new Peers sufficient to give him a majority in the House of Lords, the Prime Minister has been able to compel the House of Lords to adopt his measure. The King upon the suggestion of the Prime Minister appoints the heads of the army and navy, the Judges of the courts and the Bishops of the Established Church, the Episcopalean. So that in effect the Prime Minister is the real ruler of Great Britain. He is not elected to that position by the people like our Presi-

dent. He takes the position because he is the leader
of the dominant party in the House of Commons, because he has a majority of the House of Commons
back of him, but he may lose his position at any moment when he fails to command a majority of that
body.

The House of Commons is variously chosen and the
electorate that chooses it has shifted greatly in modern
times. Certain members are elected from counties,
others are elected for boroughs, small towns or districts. Others are elected from the great cities. The
two great Universities of Oxford and Cambridge are
both represented and the Inns of the Court, as they
are called, composed of lawyers, elect members. By
very recent changes all the men and women of England are voters just as they are in this country but that
was not true in the time of George III, the time of
our Revolution. At that time there were a great many
of what were called "pocket boroughs," that is, carried
in the pocket of some great Nobles who chose the
member because the voters were his tenants and voted
as he told them to. In that day there was a great deal
of corruption in the election of members of Parliament and a great deal in its deliberations. The King
still had a large number of positions he could fill and
through them he exercised a powerful influence over
Parliament. It was so that George III in spite of a
majority of the English people against him was able

to control Parliament and carry on the war with the Colonies although the most of the English people sympathized with them in their struggle for freedom.

The story of the British Constitution is the story of a long struggle of the people against the King and the Nobility, but it is fair to say that in that struggle many of the Nobility and the landed Gentry sympathized with and were leaders of the popular cause. Large numbers of the English Nobility have been men of the highest patriotism devoting their lives to the service of their country, freely exposing themselves and all their hereditary rights in opposition to despotic rule. One of the most glorious pages of English history is the leadership by many of its Nobles of the popular cause. Without their help it is doubtful if the English Constitution could ever have been liberalized to its present extent.

CHAPTER XXI.

ENGLAND AND SPAIN

Before considering the growth of the English Colonies, it will be well to trace briefly the contest between England and Spain. Toward the close of the Sixteenth Century, about the time that Shakespeare was writing his plays, Elizabeth was Queen of England, one of the great Queens of the world, called the Virgin Queen, arrogant, coarse, domineering, but with a great brain, great administrative capacity, profoundly patriotic, loving and beloved by her people.

Spain was then the greatest power of the world. Philip, its bigoted King, at the death of his father, Charles V, who was also Emperor of Germany, was King of Spain and Portugal, of the two Sicilies comprising Naples, the southern portion of Italy, and the Island of Sicily, Master of the Netherlands, what is now Holland and Belgium with their large cities and rich trade, all of Central and South America, the fertile Island of Cuba and the Philippines with other settlements. It was natural that as Columbus was in the employ of Spain, that Spain should have been first interested in the Western Hemisphere.

Early in the Sixteenth Century, Cortez conquered Mexico and Pizarro, Peru, with their enormous treas-

73

ures of gold and silver. A constant stream of wealth flowed into the Spanish treasury. The Caribbean Sea became the Spanish Main and Spain became dominant on land and sea with more ready money than all the rest of the world put together. The Spanish infantry, a standing army, was regarded as invincible in the open field. Its navigators sailed every sea. On the other hand, England was a small country when our first settlement was made at Jamestown, probably not over five million people spoke the English language, but they were blessed with the spirit of freedom derived from free institutions while Spain was slowly dying of the dry rot of despotism and bigotry, and this little England under the leadership of the great Elizabeth boldly defied the power of Spain, the mightiest in the world.

Philip, King of Spain, though a narrow minded bigot, very clearly saw that England must be crushed or his position in the New World would never be secure. The English mariners, like Drake and Hawkins, captured his towns, took and sunk his great galleons with their treasures and were fast driving the Spanish from the sea.

CHAPTER XXII.

The Spanish Armada

One of the most glorious chapters of English history is the defeat of the Spanish Armada. In the year 1588, Philip determined to end the matter and secure his American possessions by attacking England at home. He spent two years lavishing the gold drawn from America in the construction of the greatest fleet that the world has ever seen up to that time. Drake made a dash into Cadiz where the fleet was being prepared and burned or sunk a large number of the ships. Drake, who was the second man and the first Englishman to circumnavigate the globe, called it "singeing the King of Spain's beard." But a year later the great fleet was ready and sailed from Cadiz on the 19th day of September, 1588; one hundred and twenty-nine great sailing vessels with three tiers of guns, galleys propelled by oars and provision ships all manned with more than twenty thousand soldiers and eight thousand sailors. They were to proceed to Flanders where the Duke of Parma, the greatest captain of his age, was waiting with thirty-five thousand veteran soldiers to be convoyed across the English Channel for the conquest of England. To an impartial observer, it looked as though England was doomed, but the English were

75

ready. With an inferior force of small and light armed vessels but manned by the greatest sailors in the world they boldly attacked the Spanish fleet, harried it up the Channel, sinking vessel after vessel, until finally a great storm came to the aid of the English and dispersed the fleet, or what was not taken or sunk by the swift English, and the remnant not daring to return by way of the Channel in the face of the English fleet, attempted to sail northward around Scotland and Ireland. Most of the ships that remained were wrecked on the coasts of Scotland or Ireland. Only a small remnant of the great Armada returned to Spain. England was free from the fear of the Spanish and from that moment the great Spanish Monarchy began to decline into insignificance.

CHAPTER XXIII.

ENGLAND AND FRANCE

With the decline of Spain at the beginning of the Seventeenth Century, France became the great power of Europe. She had established colonies in Canada, Louisiana and outposts connecting them along the Great Lakes and down the Mississippi. France had probably four times the population of England and infinitely far greater resources, but France was a despotism while England was a Constitutional Monarchy with free institutions. Nothing shows better the value of these institutions than the contest between little feeble England and the powerful Spain and France for the control of North America. The Frenchman or Spaniard of that day, the moment he stepped from beneath the immediate shadow and control of his despotic King was a feeble being. He had no initiative and dared not take any. The home government was controlled by parasites of the King, male and female. The colonies were founded solely to make money for these parasites. The early French explorers and voyagers were great men who settled Canada, explored the Great Lakes, followed down the line of the Mississippi, founded New Orleans and hoped eventually to win and hold the North American Continent.

77

If they had been backed by the government at home the result would have been doubtful, but as England grew, Spain and France declined. Their despotic governments, rotten at the core, decreased in power while the English Commonwealth constantly grew and when in 1756, Wolff defeated Montcalm on the plains of Abraham, the French Empire in North America passed to British hands and all of Northern America east of the Mississippi with the exception of Florida and the small territory of New Orleans, became British. It was destined that North America should have a free and not a despotic government.

CHAPTER XXIV

THE ENGLISH COLONIES

Every school child knows the story of our Colonies, the settlement of Jamestown in 1608 and all the feeble struggling beginnings of the others. The essential point is that these English Colonies, few in number, brought with them English ideas of government, in most cases rather closely restricted in their political rights by the grants from the Crown or their Charter. They began from the very first the same struggle that their people at home were carrying on for popular government. Each colony has its own romantic history of struggles against the Crown. At the outset, fired by the stories of gold and silver found in enormous quantities by the Spanish in South America, the colonists were mainly adventurers looking for speedy wealth. They found no gold or silver but they found fertile and pleasant land. In Virginia they adopted from the Indians the cultivation of tobacco, who soon persuaded their English friends that the tobacco habit was a very pleasing one, and tobacco became the staple of Virginian prosperity. New York engaged in the fur trade with the Indians with great success. In the South, cotton and rice became staples. New England, unable

79

to gain a livelihood from its barren acres, turned its attention to the sea and the codfish became the emblem of Massachusetts. Every Colony in a pitifully slow way prospered and grew in numbers. There was no union between them. On the contrary there was great jealousy. There were petty wars between them, quarrels over boundaries, of rights of fisheries and trade, but at heart they were all English, proud of their English traditions and proud of the great Empire to which they belonged and which was then beginning to overshadow decadent Spain and France and was rapidly becoming the Mistress of the Seas.

CHAPTER XXV.

THE SIX NATIONS

The main struggle for the American Continent, between free institutions and despotism, was between France and England. After the founding of Quebec by Champlain and the opening of the Ottawa River and the Great Lakes by French explorers, the fur trade became enormously profitable. The French had outposts as far west as Mackinaw and south along the Mississippi to its mouth. They were on friendly terms with nearly all the Indian tribes except the Iroquois Confederacy, or the Six Nations as they were later called.

This extraordinary body of savages has played so important a part in our history that it deserves a brief description.

Originally there were five tribes all of Iroquois stock, the Mohawks, Senecas, Onandaguas, Oneidas, the Cayugas, occupying practically all of what is now the State of New York. Later they adopted a kindred tribe, the Tuscaroras, who had settled in North Carolina, and finding conditions there unsatisfactory had migrated to New York. These tribes were almost completely surrounded with the Algonquins who held

81

all of New England, Canada and a part of Ohio. Collectively the Algonquins greatly outnumbered the Iroquois but they were not united.

The great leader of the Iroquois, Hiawatha, at a date unknown but probably more than one hundred years before they came in contact with the white men, united the five tribes into a Confederation from which the Federal features of our Constitution were almost exactly copied, for the existence and nature of this savage Confederacy and the perfection with which it had worked was thoroughly known to the statesmen of the Revolution.

Each tribe continued to be an absolutely independent Republic in its own affairs. They were united in everything that affected all of the tribes exactly as our States. The "Longhouse," as it was called, the meeting place of the central body, was just south of where the city of Syracuse now stands. There the delegates from the different tribes met like our Congress under the head Chief, who was elected, usually from a certain family or families. They debated and settled their inter-tribal affairs and their relations, whether of War or Peace, with neighboring tribes. Hiawatha had given the Mohawks the name and place of "Keepers of the Eastern Gate" against the Algonquins, the

82

dangerous frontier of the Hudson, and the Senecas were "Keepers of the Western Gate," at the Niagara River. Whenever one of the Nations was attacked all united in its defense. They were the ablest and fiercest of all the Indian tribes. They practically dominated the Eastern and Northern part of the United States. They penetrated as far west as the Mississippi and exacted hostages from the Illinois tribes. The Southern Indians clear to the Gulf paid them tribute and gave hostages for their good behavior. Their name was dreaded and their commands obeyed from the Hudson to the Mississippi, and from the Great Lakes to the Gulf. They had all the savage traits in warfare of their fellows but in every other way they differed. Their relations among themselves were of the highest type. They had several brotherhoods or Clans, with members in all of the tribes, such as the Wolf and the Turtle, something like our modern secret societies. The marriage relation was strictly kept. Orphans and old people were tenderly cared for. They were not wanderers but lived in fixed dwellings, well built of wood; raised corn and vegetables and had great orchards of fruit. The women, of course, did most of the manual labor, as with all savage tribes, but were highly regarded and had an equal vote with the men in the tribal affairs, the election of chiefs, and the delegates to the "Longhouse" or Central Congress. They had an equal voice with the men in declaring war but the men alone made peace because they held that it was for the warriors to say when it was time to stop fighting. Property descended on the mother's side instead of the father's. They were undoubtedly the ablest savages that North America or perhaps the world has produced. They were tenacious to their obligations. Their word once given was never broken, and lying was the most deadly sin. By a curious chance the great French Governor, Champlain, in 1609, when he was exploring the lake that bears his name, fell in with a party of Algonquins who were attacked by the Mohawks of the Iroquois. Champlain and his soldiers sided with the Algonquins. Their firearms, which were new to the Mohawks, drove them off and killed several. The Iroquois swore undying hatred against the French and from the earliest settlements in New York and New England invariably sided with the British.

The influence of this powerful Confederacy had much to do with the final result. It probably turned the scale in our favor. During the Revolutionary War they sided with the British against the Colonies, keeping up their traditional friendship for the Redcoats until General Sullivan penetrated their country, destroyed their villages and orchards and completely pacified them.

So it was perhaps the influence of this great Confederacy that saved America for the English, and their Constitution, which had worked so admirably for three hundred years, was possibly to some extent, so Jefferson asserts, the model of our Federative System; as a historical fact it lasted longer than any other Republic yet has, largely because of its Federative principle.

CHAPTER XXVI.

THE BEGINNING OF THE REVOLUTION

It is impossible to fix any particular time as the beginning of the Revolution, whether the Boston Massacre in 1770, the Boston Tea Party in 1773, or the Battle of Lexington on April 19, 1775. As this was the first bloodshed in open battle, it is generally regarded as the beginning of the Revolutionary War.

Under the English Ministry of Lord North, who was the supple tool of the arrogant and half crazy George III, the Colonies had been bitterly oppressed by the Home Government. The Royal Governors were constantly seeking to crush colonial legislatures, subvert justice in the courts and destroy the free spirit of the Colonies. England demanded all of the foreign trade of the Colonies for its own profit. Every product of the Colonies sent abroad must be sold in England. For instance, Massachusetts could not ship its dried codfish to Jamaica in return for Jamaica's products, but must send it to London and purchase there what it wanted from the West Indies, giving the British merchants a double profit. This was true of Virginia tobacco, South Carolina rice and timber, which were the chief exports of the Colonies.

After the War of the Spanish Succession, which is generally called in this country the French and Indian War, and which ended with the conquest of Canada, the English demanded that the Colonies pay a part of this expense. The Colonies were entirely willing to do this but only upon the consent of their own legislative bodies. The old principle of "no taxation without representation," for which their English fathers had defied their Kings, was profoundly dear to them. The English Ministry in seeking to so tax the Colonies was violating its own Constitution and its own political traditions, but George III hated the English Constitution because it hampered his arrogant power.

A tax was imposed upon tea imported from England into America. A shipload of tea was thrown overboard in Boston Harbor by citizens disguised as Indians, the famous Boston Tea Party, and the Colonies generally stopped using tea because they would not pay the tax. A riot in 1770 between soldiers and citizens in Boston, which resulted in the killing and wounding of several citizens by the English soldiers, the "Boston Massacre," fanned the flame of the Revolution. The Colonists bitterly resented the presence of English troops and particularly the quartering of them in private houses. At that time the condition of public sentiment in America was peculiar. All of these Colonists, as I have said, were proud of their connection with the British Empire and if fairly treated would have been intensely loyal to it. A large minority called Tories were bitterly opposed to separating from England. A considerable minority were indifferent, but those who resented British tyranny and were prepared to go to the length of revolution, while probably not in a majority, had as their leaders the ablest men in America; that is, in the whole world at that time, because it is a fact that the chief assets of these feeble Colonies was that they had the greatest number of statesmen of the first rank that had ever been produced in one country in one generation.

Lord Bryce, who is the most acute foreign observer of America, has said of our Constitutional Convention that it was the ablest body of men that was ever gathered together in a single chamber.

These leaders were not only great statesmen but great organizers. They knew how to combine, how to arouse and guide public resentment. The Colonies were widely separated and communication between them slow and difficult, but these men formed Committees of Correspondence by which the leaders in each Colony were kept constantly informed of the state of public feeling and the events in every other Colony. In September, 1774, representatives of all the Colonies but Georgia gathered in Philadelphia in what came to be known as "The Continental Congress."

CHAPTER XXVII

THE CONTINENTAL CONGRESS

The growing discontent and exasperation of the Colonies resulted in the meeting of the first Continental Congress at Philadelphia on September 5, 1774. The delegates to this Congress had no real authority. Some of them were selected by the Committees of Correspondence and other patriotic societies and some by the Colonies. They sat until October and then adjourned, recommending the Colonies to send delegates to a new Congress which convened at Philadelphia in May, 1775.

This Congress, which continued to be the central governing body of the Colonies until the Articles of Confederation were adopted, was a curious body. Strictly speaking it had no legal authority. The delegates were really ambassadors gathered together from independent states. They had no power of legislation. They could not levy taxes; they could only make requests to each Colony for its share of the joint expense. They sat as a single body and they exercised

executive as well as legislative functions. They built
a small but very effective navy; they raised armies,
issued the Continental Currency to pay them, endeavored to collect from each Colony its share of the
expense with which to redeem this currency. The
Colonies paid when they felt like it. They were
always behind with their payments and always quar-
reling with the Congress about their respective shares.
The Colonies were extremely jealous of each other,
and particularly the small Colonies like Delaware, of
the large ones like Pennsylvania and Virginia. Each
Colony had one vote in the Congress, the members
present deciding by a majority how that vote should
be cast. It played politics all the time in the appointment of generals, thereby greatly hampering Washington's control of the army. Time and again it
ignored his recommendation for promotion in favor
of some incompetent who had curried favor with its
members. It is undoubted that if the Colonies had
had such a strong, efficient central government as we
now have, with power to tax all the people and raise
money to arm and equip the men who were willing
and eager to fight, the Revolutionary War would have
been over in two or three years.

England was fighting nearly four thousand miles from home. It was very difficult for the Mother Country to furnish its troops with military supplies. Under Washington's leadership an army properly supplied would have driven the British into the sea in a couple of years. Few of the soldiers remained long enough in the ranks to attain any discipline. Most of them were militia who came for three or six months and then returned to their homes. They were never paid, half fed, always short of ammunition and under the command of almost any other leader but Washington would have lost the war.

CHAPTER XXVIII

THE DECLARATION OF INDEPENDENCE

This Congress, however, did one great thing. It declared the Colonies free and independent of Great Britain in one of the most striking documents ever penned by human hands. It contains statements of human rights that are immortal. It contains an indictment of the British Government that even to this day keeps up a measure of ill-feeling in this country against England.

However, it should be remembered that the Revolutionary War was not a war between the American people and the English people. It was between the American people and the British Crown, backed by the Tory Party in England. The English Liberals, the Whig Party as it was then, sympathized deeply with their American brothers and did all in their power to prevent the oppression of the Colonies but the Tories, through the great nobles and their landed interests, backed by the power of King George, were able to carry through their tyrannous measures. Lord Chatham, the great Whig leader, constantly thundered in the House of Lords against every measure that the King proposed, but with no avail.

But all this changed when we concluded our alliance with France. The House of Bourbon, Kings of France, came in with Henry IV and ended with Louis XVI. Beginning with Louis XIV France had been the implacable enemy of England. Under Charles II and James I, England had been a mere vassal of Louis XIV. It was the shame of this and the fear of France that largely brought about the fall of James II. Under William and Mary and Queen Anne, England thwarted the ambitious designs of France, but at an enormous cost. For a hundred years England contended with France in Europe, America and Asia. The genius of Lord Chatham had brought the Seven Years War to a triumphant conclusion, wresting from France her American Colonies and humbling the House of Bourbon. Lord Chatham declared the House of Bourbon was his hereditary enemy. After the surrender of Burgoyne, England tired of the war and we were exhausted. North brought forward proposals of conciliation. He offered practical independence to the Colonies, nearly the same form of government that Canada now has, but we would remain a part of the British Empire and subject to the British King. Chatham was invited into the Ministry in the hope that the Colonies would accept the proposal from him, their constant friend. But for the alliance with France and her aid with money, troops and ships, we might have accepted, for we were exhausted and at the end of our resources.

The treason of Benedict Arnold was connected with this very proposal, but as a result of the battle of Saratoga, France took up our cause. The moment we allied ourselves with France, the whole face of English politics changed. We ceased to be in the eyes of the English Liberals fellow-Englishmen and became enemy allies of the House of Bourbon.

Chatham led the change and in his last and dying speech in the House of Lords denounced any conciliation with the Colonies while allied with the House of Bourbon. As a result George III was able to triumphantly declare "we have but now one people." And here let me correct a popular error. The French government did not come to our aid from any generous or disinterested motives. Vergenness, the French Minister, saw that if he could help the Colonies to win their independence, it would be the severest blow at English power. That was the motive of the French government and it succeeded. It is undoubtedly true that the success of our experiment in self-government greatly aided the English Liberals and contributed to the Liberalizing of the English government.

The Declaration of Independence was penned by Thomas Jefferson, who probably never made a speech in his life, but was one of the most accomplished writers of the English-speaking world. From the time of the battle of Lexington on, public feeling grew more and more bitter towards the Mother Country.

94

Independence, separation from Great Britain was being urged more strongly, but the Congress held back. They knew better than the people the fearful odds against such an undertaking. Three millions of people against the greatest empire in the world. They realized too that if the Revolution, or the Rebellion, as it was called in England, failed, they ran the fate of being executed as traitors to the British Crown. As Franklin expressed it, "they must hang together or they would all hang separately."

The people were ripe for Revolution long before Congress on July 4, 1776, signed the immortal Declaration. Somehow the Congress muddled through the war, or, to speak more correctly, Washington won the Revolution. Without him it would have been a failure, almost a farce.

CHAPTER XXIX.

THE CONFEDERATION

The Revolution was practically completed, although peace had not been declared, when the Confederation came into existence. It had been proposed as early as 1776, but it was not until March, 1781, that the last Colony accepted the Articles and the new Government was complete.

As we look back on it now it was a strange government. These Articles show how bitter was the jealousy between the Colonies, how strong the independence of each and how reluctant each of them was to surrender any of its powers. In fact about all of the real power that the Colonies gave up to the Confederation was the power to make peace and war, build a navy, and raise armies for the defense of the country. These things the Colonies individually were forbidden to do. The new Government could not make any effective laws or levy any sort of taxes. It decided the amount of money it needed, apportioned it among the Colonies according to the population of each, which was guessed at, and requested the Colonies to furnish the money. Not one of the Colonies ever paid its full quota. The result was that from the start the new

Government was a failure. Its currency depreciated until it was nearly worthless. The soldiers were unpaid and mutinous.

The Congress of the Confederation was held in such contempt that hardly any able men would attend its sittings. On paper it was supposed to have ninety-one members but there were hardly ever more than thirty present. Sometimes for a considerable period there would not be a quorum; that is, a majority of the Colonies represented. It took nine of the thirteen, each having one vote to do anything of importance. About all a majority could do was to adjourn from day to day. In short, as a central government it was utterly powerless. It concluded a Treaty of Peace with England but was unable to carry out the terms on its own part, so England refused to give up its forts on the Western Frontier and the Indians massacred the settlers whom the Government was unable to protect, and the Colonies continually quarreled with each other.

The Colonies levied duties against each other on their mutual commerce. The New Government was rapidly falling to pieces. The Monarchs of Europe watched its decay with undisguised pleasure and speculated on the time when they could again conquer the Colonies and subject them to foreign rule. It seemed that the world's first great experiment in democracy was about to fail, and, if it had failed, it would have

been long beyond our time before another would have
been attempted, if ever. Free men the world over
hung on this experiment, which seemed about to fail
solely for lack of a proper government; not for lack of
men or resources or patriotism but solely that the
Colonies had not yet found themselves, had not yet
come to the point where they could give up their
prejudices and independence for the sake of a strong
central government which alone could save that independence. There is but one book that fitly describes
that period, "The Critical Period of American History," by John Fiske, which has the rare merit of being
as interesting to the school child in the eighth grade
as to the most learned student of history.

CHAPTER XXX

THE CONSTITUTIONAL CONVENTION

The utter weakness of the Confederation, the prostration of trade and manufactures, the poverty of the farmer and the general contempt in which the government was held everywhere in the world had finally compelled the attention of all thoughtful men in the Colonies. Alexander Hamilton as early as 1776 had proposed a convention to adopt a strong Federal Government.

Early in 1786, commissioners from Virginia and Maryland met at Washington's home, Mount Vernon, to consider a project for extending the navigation of the upper Potomac and to settle certain differences regarding the Potomac River. The latter was easily settled. The navigation of the upper Potomac was broadened by a proposal to unite the Potomac and the Ohio by canal. This required the co-operation of Pennsylvania. Washington, who was pressing for a stronger government, saw an opening. Since Virginia and Maryland could settle their disputes, why could not the other states who were warring with each other over commercial questions do the same thing? Accordingly a convention was called for September,

1786, to meet at Annapolis that is known in history as "the Annapolis Convention," attended by delegates from New York, Pennsylvania, New Jersey, Maryland, Delaware, and Virginia for the purpose of settling commercial disputes between these states. It was agreed that nothing could be done under such an impotent government as the Confederation and the convention recommended the calling of a convention of all the states to amend the Articles of Confederation. Congress, pursuant to this recommendation, issued a call for a Constitutional Convention of all the states to meet at Philadelphia on the 14th of May. All the states responded except Rhode Island, which was bitterly opposed to any central government, and its delegates never sat in the Convention.

The Convention was not complete until June. George Washington was elected President and one William Jackson, otherwise unknown to fame and apparently not a delegate, was chosen as Secretary. The debates in this convention were held strictly secret but James Madison every night made notes of its proceedings, which were published after his death and from which alone we derive a fair picture of the measures brought forward, considered, the difficulties surrounding this union of the States and the final adoption of the various measures.

It is quite common nowadays to speak of this convention as composed of rich men and lawyers, the rich men predominating. Nothing could be farther from the truth. Of the fifty-five who at one time or another sat in the convention there were sixteen lawyers, the most eminent in the country and in fact in the world at that time. Very few lawyers in that day were rich men. The fees of the most eminent would not today pay office rent in any city in the country.

Alexander Hamilton, the leader of the Federalist Party and one of the most eminent lawyers of his time, was born in the West Indies, came to New York practically penniless and accumulated no more than a small competence although he had at one time the largest law practice in New York.

Roger Sherman of Connecticut was apprenticed to a shoemaker, studied at the cobbler's bench, became a surveyor, a merchant, later served as Chief Justice of his State and United States Senator, a poor boy who owed everything to his exertions.

James Wilson, a Scotchman, who was undoubtedly the ablest Constitutional lawyer in the convention, later a justice of the Supreme Court, died prematurely because of his worry over money troubles.

Samuel Chase, who later became a Justice of the Supreme Court, successfully defended himself against an impeachment trial, the first and only one that has ever been attempted against a member of that body.

The only banker was Robert Morris, who largely financed the Revolutionary War, bankrupted himself in his devotion to his country and died penniless.

101

There were a few great land owners in the body but very few. Among them was George Mason, who owned an estate of twelve thousand acres on the Potomac River eight miles below Washington's home, Mt. Vernon. In his personal characteristics he was perhaps the greatest aristocrat in the body; always dressed in silk with ruffles of the finest lace and was in every respect in his personal habits, an English country gentleman. His home, Gunstun Hall, was built of brick imported from Holland and was at the time one of the three or four finest houses in Virginia. He owned a thousand slaves but was opposed to slavery. He wrote the Virginia Bill of Rights and fought throughout the convention for the rights and privileges of the individual. He refused to sign the Constitution and despite his devotion to Washington bitterly opposed its ratification in the Virginia Ratification Convention because he feared what he thought was the aristocratic tendency of the Constitution and too much power in the Federal Government. Not even Washington's influence could overcome his bitter prejudice against anything that savored of aristocratic government. The two Pinckneys of South Carolina belonged also to the land-holding class but were ardently for a Democratic form of government.

Aside from Washington, Franklin was the most conspicuous figure in the Convention, then past eighty, physically feeble but with his wonderful intellect unimpaired. He was the most widely known man in the Colonies. Everyone knows his story, how he landed in Philadelphia with twopence in his pocket became a publisher in a small way, founded a newspaper, became Postmaster General of the Colonies under the British Government, and gave them the first real postal service they had ever had. He was intensely interested in scientific pursuits, corresponding on intimate terms with the greatest scientists of his day, and was known throughout the civilized world for his scientific discoveries. He was sent as our Ambassador to France during the Revolution and became the fashion in Paris. He was invited everywhere, charmed everyone with his wit and philosophy and it was undoubtedly owing to him that the French aid in money, troops, and ships was granted to the Colonies, that enabled us to win the war. At the very close of the Constitutional Convention, when the draft of the Constitution had been agreed upon and was about to be signed, he made a brief speech. On the back of the chair of the presiding officer where Washington sat as President, was carved a representation of the sun and its rays. He said that often during their deliberations he had noted this carving and wondered whether it portrayed the rising or the setting sun, that now at the conclusion of their labors, he was sure that it was the rising sun of a great country—prophetic words. When some of the members hesitated to sign because the document did not in every particular meet their views, he told of a French lady whom he had known in Paris who once said to her sister, "It is very strange that I always find everyone wrong but myself," and said he had learned in his long life that he frequently found himself mistaken in things about which he was the most sure, that he had come to believe that after all the will of the majority was nearly always right. His speech brought assent from many who had before refused to sign and throughout the deliberations of the Convention his unfailing good humor, that could always tranquilize any tumult with a witty remark, his unfailing wisdom, his common sense always exercised at the right moment, made the Constitution possible.

James Madison is called "the father of the Constitution," and probably had more to do with its framework than any other single member of the Convention. He was highly educated, with a gigantic intellect, studious, industrious and exact, simple in his manners, diffident but with a most persuasive tongue. He had made a profound study of all the governments of the world and the causes of their failure. He was more widely familiar with constitutional history than any other man of his time. He brought to the Convention a plan for a constitution that was known as "the Virginia Plan" and which formed the basis of much discussion. He was at that time a firm believer in a strong central government and had repeatedly urged the calling of a convention to form a new government. The inexplicable part of his career was that later he fell completely under the influence of Jefferson, adopted Jefferson's extreme States Rights opinion and joined with him in the preparation of the Kentucky and Virginia Resolutions, of 1798, in which the legislatures of the two states declared that whenever Congress passed a law that any state deemed unconstitutional, that state had a right to secede from the Federal Union, a doctrine that sowed the seeds of the Civil War. He was Jefferson's Secretary of State and twice President.

Of course the commanding figure was General Washington of whom no satisfactory life history has ever been written. The years that have passed since his death have changed his image and likeness into a sort of steel engraving without anything human about it. Starting with the ridiculous fable of the cherry tree, fabricated by a fiddling hard-drinking Virginia parson, myths have clustered about his memory until it is hard to find the real Washington. He, too, like nine out of ten of the members of the Convention, was self-made. The death of his father when he was twelve years old compelled him to leave school at the age of sixteen and go to work as a surveyor and after that his learning was in the rough school of active life. He excelled in all athletic sports, was the champion broad jumper of Virginia in his youth, an unexcelled horseman who knew woodcraft better than he knew books. He inherited from his brother the estate of Mt. Vernon which he increased till he owned about five thousand acres. He was the most progressive farmer in Virginia. He noted how the growing of tobacco was exhausting the fertile lands of Virginia and inaugurated what is known as the five-field system, a rotation of crops with clover to rest and fertilize the soil, raising tobacco only once in five years on each field. He was the first Virginian to send a shipload of wheat to France. He was the first man in America to recognize the value of the mule and breed them for his estate.

During all his cares as General in Chief of the American Army and later as President, he exercised the closest watchfulness over his estate, directing his overseer what should be grown on each field, how many barrels of herring should be put up and how many hogs killed for winter use on his farm. When he was elected President, he declined to receive any salary as he had declined any salary as General in Chief, accepting only his actual expenses. For that purpose during his first year as President he kept an accurate account of his living expenses, including the salary of two secretaries whom he employed, and I have in my library a photographic copy of this account showing every penny expended for living expenses, such as food and drink, wages, rent, all carried out to the last penny. At the end of the year his expenses had been about five thousand pounds English money or about twenty-five thousand dollars in our currency and it was from this that the salary of our President was fixed at twenty-five thousand dollars. By his care and thrift he accumulated what at the time of his death was the largest fortune in America, valued at $700,000.00, a sum equal, at this time, to three or four million. So far from being the cold, chilly character that we are accustomed to regard, he was intensely human, warm-blooded with a violent temper which he learned to control but whose infrequent outbursts brought abject terror to the objects of his anger. Those who knew him best felt a kind of idolatry for him that never in the least affected his natural simplicity of character. He was the only commander of an army that could lose every battle and yet win a campaign. Leading armies, never paid, half clothed, half fed, in the long run he out-generaled and defeated the best soldiers and generals that Great Britain could bring to the field. No other man but Washington could have held an equal balance between the rival factions and with the unlimited confidence of all classes carry the infant Republic through its first years and set it upon that course which it has followed with such success for one hundred and thirty-four years.

It is a matter of just pride that the greatest, wisest and most unselfish rulers in the history of the world,

Alfred the Great, Washington, and Lincoln, are of our blood. As stated before, Lord Bryce, in his "Commentaries on the American Government," declared that they were the greatest body of men that ever sat in a single chamber, and Gladstone has said that the Constitution that they wrote was the greatest instrument ever struck off by human hands at one time.

It is not the purpose here to describe the conflicts and the debates of that Convention. There were three questions upon which the delegates divided and which time and again threatened to end the Convention without any result.

The small states like Delaware and Connecticut were jealous of the numerical power of the great states like Massachusetts, Pennsylvania, and Virginia. (Strange as it may seem New York was still ranked as a small state.) If representation in the Federal Congress was based solely upon numbers, the smaller states would be overwhelmed and powerless. This was met by the provision for two bodies, the House of Representatives and the Senate. The House of Representatives was to be chosen on the basis of numbers. Each state was to have two Senators in the Senate, making the small states in that body equal to the larger ones and to further secure the small states it was provided that no state should be deprived of its equal representation in the Senate without its own consent.

The second question was that of slavery. The New

England states wished to abolish slavery and slave-trade at once, and in this Virginia joined. The cotton gin had not then been invented and the only states that desired slave labor were South Carolina and Georgia, where rice was becoming an important crop and could only be cultivated by negro labor.

The third question was commerce between states. One of the strongest reasons for a new government was the constant warfare between the states over commerce. New England insisted that commerce between the states, the Indian tribes and foreign countries should be wholly under control of the Federal Government. South Carolina and Georgia opposed this. Finally a bargain was struck. The Southern states agreed to the control of commerce by the Federal government and in return the New England states agreed that the slave trade should be abolished in 1808 and slavery left entirely to the control of the several states with which the Federal government should not interfere and these provisions were adopted by the Convention, although George Mason of Virginia, one of the largest slave-holders in the South, bitterly opposed the agreement and fought to the last for the immediate abolition of slavery.

The Convention had two great assets: in Washington, its President, whose vast reputation, practical wisdom and unruffled demeanor calmed every storm; and the wit, good humor and unvarying common sense of Franklin. At one time when passions of debate had risen very high and it seemed as though the Convention must break up and disperse, Franklin arose and called their attention to the fact that so far the help of God in the deliberations of the Convention had not been invoked and proposed that the members pause for a moment in silent prayer before they resumed their deliberations. How many of the members believed in the efficacy of prayer is not known and yet those few moments of silent communion with the Supreme Being calmed the storm and the deliberations were resumed.

At last the great instrument was agreed upon and it was turned over to Gouverneur Morris of Pennsylvania who was noted for his choice English, to correct any faults of expression. The greatest number of deputies or delegates who sat in the Convention was fifty-five and thirty-nine signed it, some of them not being present, and some, like George Mason, refusing to sign because he thought the instrument gave too much power to the Federal Government and robbed the states of their independence.

CHAPTER XXXI.

THE ADOPTION OF THE CONSTITUTION

It will be noted that this Convention far exceeded the powers contained in its call. It was called for the purpose of amending the Articles of Confederation. Instead of that it cast aside entirely the old government and proceeded to make a new one. Instead of referring the New Constitution for adoption to the Legislatures of the states, the Convention provided that it should be submitted to a convention in each state elected by the people for the sole purpose of adopting or rejecting the instrument. It was promptly adopted by a few states. There were bitter fights against it in New York by the faction opposed to Hamilton and in Virginia by a strong party led by George Mason and Patrick Henry, the orator of the Revolution. Rhode Island was the last to agree.

The chief objection to the Constitution was that it gave too much power to the Federal Government and that it did not reserve for the people certain rights that were considered a part of the birthright of the citizens of the states, and it was practically agreed that if the Constitution was adopted certain amendments to guarantee these rights should be submitted by the first Con-

111

gress, and, accordingly, the first Congress having some eighty odd proposals for amendments submitted ten, which were speedily adopted and became a part of the Constitution.

These ten Amendments adopted as they were at the very beginning, have always been treated as a part of the original instrument and are generally known as the Bill of Rights. Their adoption was necessitated by the jealousy of many of the leaders of the Revolution of any form of Central Government and a fear of its encroachments on those rights of the individual for which they had fought for nine years. They include many of the most valuable safeguards of that instrument such as the freedom of religion, of speech, of the press, and the right of petition and freedom from unreasonable search and seizure of property without a warrant supported by the affidavit of some individual; the right of trial by jury in the Federal Courts; the right to the equal protection of all citizens before the law and the right to compensation whenever private property is taken for public use. These rights under these amendments have always been jealously guarded by the courts. They were among those rights whose infringement by the British Crown had been the chief causes of the Revolution. It is not sufficiently understood nowadays that this Constitution of ours above everything else was established to safeguard the individual citizen, to protect his life and liberty, and his property; to prohibit the encroachment of any power upon those rights, whether by the President or Congress, and to place all of the citizens of the country on an equality before the law regardless of wealth, social or official positions.

CHAPTER XXXII.

WHY A WRITTEN CONSTITUTION

Those who have never studied History and Civil Government wonder why it was necessary to have a written Constitution. The Colonists were accustomed to these instruments. Their powers had been fixed by the original grants or written charters from the Crown. After they declared their independence, and by about 1781, each of the new states had adopted a new Constitution, always in writing. But there was a further and stronger reason in making the Federal Constitution written. The founders started with the proposition that all political power, the power of Government, was vested in the people and not in Kings who claimed to rule by Divine Right. These people had set up thirteen State Governments, each with a written Constitution setting forth exactly what each branch of the Government could do, the Governor, the Legislature and the Judiciary. Out of their political power they now proceeded to form a Supreme Government, National for National purposes to accomplish those things which experience had shown the State Governments could not do. They here granted certain powers to the Federal Government just as they had granted others for state purposes to the State Gov-

114

ernments and it was natural and necessary that these grants of power should be put in writing so that there could be no mistake in the future as to what Congress or the President could do. The English Constitution had been built up through the course of seven hundred years by one precedent on another. The English had never thought of having a written Constitution and so the English Parliament was omnipotent. It could do anything that the majority chose. It could and did condemn men of treason without evidence, without a trial and send them to execution and forfeit their property. This unchecked British Parliament at different times had done many vicious, cruel and unjust things. Our fathers knew that no one man and no body of men is good enough to entrust with the limitations of its own power, and so in the Constitution they limited Congress just as they limited the President. They set forth what Congress could do, and it could not do any of the things that were not set down in the Constitution. It constantly happens that men enter into written contracts, put down in black and white just what each one is to do and then they disagree as to what the contract means and they have to go to court and let the court decide. To let either party alone judge of the effect of the contract would destroy it, so here the American people were making a sort of contract with the Federal Government by which they agreed that Congress and the President could do cer-

tain things and no more. They did not intend to let
the Congress have the unlimited power that the British
parliament had but they foresaw that there would be
disputes over what this contract, the Constitution,
meant. They knew that Congress or the President
were likely to do what all other rulers had done, over-
step the limits of their powers, exceed the powers
granted to them, and so they established a Supreme
Court to be the final judge of what the Constitution
meant, what this written contract of Government
really was, just as we establish courts to hear what the
rights are under a written contract between individuals, and the Constitution, as it stands today, is largely
the outgrowth of the decisions of the Supreme Court
of the United States interpreting this great instrument.
For instance, and here is a point about which men still
quarrel vigorously, the Supreme Court has frequently
held an Act of Congress void as unconstitutional.
That is, that Congress in passing the Act has exceeded
its powers, done something that the Constitution did
not permit. It is said that Congress should be the sole
judge of its own Act, that it is wrong to permit a court
to set aside an Act of Congress, and you will hear men
frequently say: "What is the need of a Constitution?
Why cannot Congress be permitted to do just as it sees
fit? It is elected by the people and is responsible to
the people." They forget the things that the unchecked British Parliament did. They forget that the
French Convention in 1791, elected by the people,

murdered hundreds of innocent people with scarcely a form of a trial.

Thomas Jefferson, who was a great stickler for the rights of the people, said, "In questions of power, then, let no more be heard of confidence in man but bind him down from mischief by the chains of the Constitution." As a matter of fact Congress has attempted at different times to violate many of the fundamental rights of the people by legislation. It has attempted to try men twice for the same offense, which the Constitution forbids. It has tried to compel the individual citizens of the states to recognize social equality between the whites and the blacks. It has attempted to take private property for public use without compensation. It has attempted to authorize the imprisonment of persons at hard labor without a hearing before a Grand Jury. It has attempted to pass an *ex post facto* law; that is, making an act a crime that was not a crime at the time it was committed. It has attempted to impose a religious qualification for office, although the Constitution expressly forbids this. It has attempted to imprison a man without a trial by jury. It has attempted to compel a man to be a witness against himself in a criminal case. In each one of these cases the Supreme Court has interposed and held these Acts unconstitutional. Without a written Constitution and a Supreme Court to interpret it, Congress could establish a State Religion like that of England

117

and tax everyone to support one Church. It could send men to jail for some fancied contempt of its body, as has been attempted. But the real gist of the matter is this: courts are established to enforce the Constitution and the laws made under it. Every Federal Judge takes an oath to support the Constitution and laws of the United States.

A sues B, claiming some right under an Act of Congress. B answers that the Act of Congress is void because Congress had no power under the Constitution to pass such an Act. The court finds that the law made by Congress conflicts with the Constitution adopted by the people. It cannot support both; which shall it support? The temporary law made by Congress, which is the mere creature of the Constitution, a law which may be repealed next year; or the Constitution, adopted by the people themselves to stand forever, unless amended by the people themselves. Of course the Court must obey the Constitution and hold the Act invalid. Again, if Congress itself were the only judge of its Constitutional powers, it could override the Constitution at any time, change it, amend it, deform it, or destroy it utterly without the consent of the people who made it.

What has been said of the National Constitution applies with equal force to each State Constitution and each State Legislature. Time and again the Legislatures of different states, under the impulse of temporary passion, have passed laws that were clearly unconstitutional and destructive of individual rights, and it has been the duty of the State Supreme Courts to set aside these laws because they violated the State Constitution just as the Supreme Court of the United States has done with some of the Acts of Congress. Again, if we had no Federal Supreme Court to interpret the Constitution of the United States, the court of each state could place its own interpretation on it. We might have forty-nine different interpretations of the same provision of the Constitution, forty-eight by the states and another by the United States Supreme Court. The result would be utter confusion, for no one would know what the Constitution really meant, so the decisions of the Supreme Court of the United States as to the meaning of the Constitution, its laws and its treaties are binding not only upon all the state courts but upon the people. It cannot be doubted that the influence of this great Court has held the states together and been the binding force that has prevented dissolution more than once.

CHAPTER XXXIII.

THE NEW GOVERNMENT

The new Government differed from the old Confederation in many ways, but the chief difference, the great distinction, was that the Confederation was an agreement between the several states and not between the people. Article III of the Articles of Confederation says, "The said states hereby severally enter into a firm league," etc. The new Constitution starts with the preamble, "We, the people of the United States, in order to form a more perfect union, establish justice, insure domestic tranquillity, provide for the common defense, etc., do ordain and establish this Constitution for the United States of America." This difference is fundamental. The old Confederation was a mere League or Association of independent states adopted by the State Legislatures, not by the people. It operated not at all upon the people and had no direct dealings with them. It operated solely on the states. Our Constitution was adopted by all of the people of the several states in conventions selected by the people for the sole purpose of considering its adoption. Its laws operate directly upon the people. Every official in the United States takes an oath not only to support the Constitution and laws of his state but the Constitution and laws of the United States.

The effect of the new Government was immediately seen. Instead of passing the hat like a beggar to the various states for contributions to carry on the government, the new Government imposed duties on imports and quickly obtained an adequate revenue for its needs. It refunded the public debt and redeemed the old currency and completely restored the public credit. Very soon it established a bank which issued bank bills as currency that were as good as gold. It became very soon apparent to the Nations of the Old World that this Republican experiment had ceased to be experimental and was a success. Barely ten years after its start, it confronted Napoleon at the height of his power and compelled him to make peace and cease his depredations on American commerce. Five years later and before any European Nation had dared to, it sent its fleet to the Mediterranean, overawed the Algerian Pirates and rendered American Commerce in the Mediterranean safe from their piracy without tribute, and at the end of twenty-five years had met Great Britain on sea and land and inflicted such losses on her commerce that the Mother Country from then on abandoned her bullying tactics and treated the United States as a Great Power. It is not my intention to enter into the technical details of the Constitution. I have rather sought to show how our Constitution grew from the free spirit of our ancestors, the struggle of eighteen hundred years with which our freedom was bought and won.

CHAPTER XXXIV.

THE NEW CONSTITUTIONAL STRUGGLE

From the beginning of the new Government, there was a determined continuous Constitutional struggle on peaceful lines. The old struggle of the people against the Crown had ended with a victory for the people. While the people of England were slowly but surely binding their Kings in the chains of law, constantly reducing their powers, we had abolished Kingships entirely and substituted in their place a citizen President, an officer who, while exercising most of the functions of the King of England, was still a mere citizen on an equality before the law with every other citizen. His position is lofty but in the eye of the law he is no more than a common citizen. But the combination of these individual states into a Federal Government brought on a new struggle that lasted for more than seventy years, the struggle between State and National power.

The old jealousies of the Colonies against any Central Government persisted and it was not until the close of the Civil war, which it largely caused, that this struggle was finally ended. However, it was for seventy years fought out not on the field of battle but

122

in the Supreme Court of the United States, where, by succeeding decisions of that court, it was finally established that our Federal Government is a true National Government, supreme within the limits fixed by the Constitution; that the state governments cannot directly or indirectly interfere or check these powers, or in any way hinder the operations of the National Government. The Story of the Constitution and this long struggle would be incomplete without some reference to John Marshall.

CHAPTER XXXV.

JOHN MARSHALL

John Marshall was the fourth Chief Justice of the United States, taking office in February, 1801. He filled the position until the day of his death in October, 1835, almost thirty-five years. When Marshall became Chief Justice the Supreme Court of the United States was very little respected. Jay had resigned as Chief Justice to become Governor of the State of New York, because he thought the Court powerless to accomplish anything and refused a renomination for the same reason.

Marshall was born on the Western frontier of Virginia, receiving but a meager education; was a soldier in the Revolutionary War, serving as a captain, and underwent the privations of Valley Forge. He studied law but six months, but that under Chancellor Wythe of Virginia, a member of the Constitutional Convention and probably the greatest lawyer of his time. Marshall was a Federalist in politics; that is, he believed in a strong Central Government, supreme within its sphere. Marshall was a member of Congress when he was sent as one of the Ministers to France to negotiate a treaty with the Government of Napoleon and won great distinction by his firmness and wisdom in these

124

negotiations. Adams later made him Secretary of State and then in February, 1801, Chief Justice. He was not in any sense a learned lawyer. Storey, who was his associate for more than twenty years, far surpassed him in learning, but Marshall had a mind so profoundly original in character that it needed no assistance from others. He was perhaps more of a statesman than a lawyer. He had been a close observer of the utter weakness of the old Continental Congress and the chaos into which the country was drifting under the Articles of Confederation. He was firmly determined that the new National Government should be a real government with all the powers necessary to carry out what he believed to be the purpose and inspiration of its founders. It might be said that his text in every case where the rights of the State and Nation conflicted was that provision of Section 8 of Article 22 which provides that Congress shall have power "to make all laws which shall be necessary and proper for carrying into execution the foregoing powers and all other powers vested by this Constitution in the Government of the United States or in any department or officer thereof." In other words, he held that the government was not confined to the powers set down in black and white in the Constitution, but that the Constitution intended also to give to the General Government all powers that might be necessary to fully carry out the powers expressly granted. This was the

125

controversy that was raised between the Federalists and their successors, the Whigs, and the Democrats for more than seventy years. The Democrats insisted that the states had only parted with certain definite rights which could not be added to by implication. It was this doctrine of implied power that Marshall brought into his decisions. Naturally, no other court decisions could be looked to for a guide in determining these questions. There had never been a government like this or a Constitution like this. No other court had claimed the power to render a decision that would set aside a law of its Congress or Parliament. The profoundly original mind of Marshall sought no precedent, asked no one's advice, but reasoned from original principles of government. Storey, who was perhaps the most learned lawyer of his time, if not of any time, once said, "When I start to write an opinion in a case, I creep from one headline to another of decided cases, precedents that I can plainly see. Marshall sets his compass and puts straight out to sea." Nothing could better express the difference between the two men. There are four great decisions of Marshall that must be noted to understand the growth of the Constitution.

The first was Marbury vs. Madison,[1] decided in 1804, in which for the first time the court held that it was not bound by an unconstitutional law of Congress and that any officer of the Government, no matter how lofty his position, could be compelled by the court to

---

1. 5 U. S. (1 Cr.) 137,2 L. ed. 60. Discusses post Part III, Chapter I.

perform his legal duty. That no one in this Republic, not even the President of the United States, is above the law.

In Cohen vs. Virginia,[2] the court held that the decision of the Supreme Court of the United States in any matter concerning the Constitution, laws or treaties of the United States was supreme and overruled any judgment of a state court. Undoubtedly it was this decision that saved this country from the same chaos into which the Confederacy had fallen. If each state, as I have said before, could interpret a law of Congress or a provision of the Constitution in its own way we might have had forty-eight different meanings applied to such a law or such a provision. The law of the United States would have meant one thing in Massachusetts and another in Kansas.

In McCulloch vs. Maryland,[3] when the State of Maryland attempted to tax the bills of the United States Bank, he held that the instruments by which the Federal Government carried out and exercised its powers could not be taxed or controlled in any way by the states; that while each state government was supreme within its own territory and as to its own local affairs, that the National Government was supreme in everything that concerned the Nation, or of the people of

2. 19 U. S. (6 Wheat.) 264, 5 L. ed. 257. Discusses post Part III, Chapter II.
3. 17 U. S. (4 Wheat.) 316, 4 L. ed 579. Discussed post Part III, Chapter III.

the United States. And he there pointed out with great clearness the distinction between the old Confederacy, which was formed by the states and operated only on the states, and the New Government, which was formed by "We, the people of the United States," and operated in its laws and measures not upon the states but directly upon all of the citizens of the whole country.

In Gibbons vs. Ogden[4] the court held that the Federal Government alone had absolute and exclusive control of Commerce not only between this country and foreign countries, but between the states. This was perhaps the most important decision of his long career. One of the things against which the states which had no harbors complained was the restrictions placed upon their commerce which was compelled to pass through seaports like New York and Boston. Marshall held that one of the main purposes of the Constitution was to do away with this divided conflicting control of commerce by the separate states which wrought the greatest injustices against the Colonies that had no seaports. In this case New York had attempted to grant a monopoly of steam navigation in the waters of New York to Livingston and Fulton who had invented the steamboat and was attempting to exclude Connecticut, New

---

4. 22 U. S. (9 Wheat.) 1, 6 L. ed. 23, reversing 17 Johns. (N. Y.) 488.

Jersey and all the other states from navigating these public waters without a license from Livingston and Fulton. Connecticut was attempting to do the same thing with its waters; South Carolina with the harbor of Charleston. As a result of this decision, interstate commerce is wholly under the control of the Federal Government. No state can interfere with it, tax or hinder it in any way. These four great decisions may fairly be said to be the cornerstones of the Constitutional structure.

Washington made the Union; Marshall consolidated it; Lincoln saved it.

CHAPTER XXXVI

The Federative Principle

The United States is a Federative Union, a Federal government composed of independent states, each controlling its own domestic affairs, but united in everything that concerns all the states. As Webster phrased it, "an indissoluble union of indestructible states." Those who made the Constitution relied for its perpetuation as much upon the independence of the states as upon the strength of the Union. They know that all the Republics of the world theretofore had perished by too much centralization of power, which enabled one man, or a group of men, to seize it. So fell the Greek Republic, Rome, Venice, and all the others. As a practical matter, it should be impossible for one legislative body, like Congress, to legislate for a country so vast and varied as ours. Laws suited to a mining state would be unsuitable for an agricultural state; laws for a state with ample rainfall, like Ohio, would not do for an arid state like Arizona—where there must be careful control of the water for irrigation; laws necessary for a manufacturing state, like Massachusetts, would be unnecessary for a pastoral state, like Nebraska. From every consideration of the future of the

130

Republic, those rights of the state fixed by the Constitution must be preserved. One of the greatest dangers to our country today is the increasing centralization of power in Washington, creating a vast horde of office-holders, and the slow destruction of the dignity and independence of the state. I do not mean by this the old States Rights doctrine, that perished in 1865, but the true rights of the states set forth in the Constitution, and settled by the decisions of Marshall and his associates.

I do not think that I exaggerate the immeasurable importance of the Federative principle and the independence of the States.

I quote from the greatest American historian of our time, John Fiske, in The Critical Period of American History.

"If the day should ever arrive (which God forbid!) when the people of the different parts of our country shall allow their local affairs to be administered by prefects sent from Washington, and when the self-government of the states shall have been so far lost as that of the departments of France, or even so far as that of the counties of England,—on that day the progressive political career of the American people will have come to an end, and the hopes that have been built upon it for the future happiness and prosperity of mankind will be wrecked forever."

CHAPTER XXXVII.

Conclusion

It would seem now, when we look back one hundred and thirty-four years, as though no argument for our Constitution should be necessary; no other government in the world so completely and carefully protects the rights of the individual; no other country in the world has ever so prospered under any government; no other country has ever enjoyed such a long period of comparative peace, of prosperity and liberty within the law as we have under this great instrument. Under its protection, the United States is today the richest, most intelligent, the most powerful and I venture to say the happiest Nation the world has ever seen; and yet there are fanatics, idealists, cranks, and foolish dreamers who would destroy this great fabric for some experiment like the Soviet Government in Russia.

The trouble is, we have come to take this government of ours as we take the air and the sunshine, as a matter of course. It was a free gift to us. It has cost us nothing. We forget that with our own race it is the result of a struggle that lasted for more than seven hundred years from the Norman Conquest to the surrender at Yorktown. We forget that this freedom of

132

ours was not peacefully won; that our fathers bought it with a bitter price; bought it with their blood shed on a hundred battle fields; bought it with wounds and stripes; with banishment and confiscation of their property; with confinement in foul dungeons; subjection to the rack and thumbscrew and every cruel punishment that wicked and despotic kings could inflict; we forget that every line of that great instrument was bought with the blood of your fathers and mine. They gave it to us. Is it too much to ask that we cherish, guard, and preserve it?

For interesting and informing correspondence regarding the origin of the United States Constitution, see post Part V.

PART III.

PART III.

DECISIVE BATTLES OF THE CONSTITUTION

CHAPTER I.

MARBURY VS. MADISON[1]

The case of Marbury vs. Madison, perhaps the most important in the judicial history of this country or any other, involved so small a matter as the right to the office of justice of the peace for the District of Columbia. Marbury had been appointed by President Adams for a term of five years, an office not revocable at the will of the President. The appointment was duly confirmed, the commission signed and attested with the great seal of the United States by Marshall, who was then Secretary of State, but for some reason, probably carelessness, had not been delivered when Jefferson became President.

Jefferson, conceiving that a commission, like a deed, took effect at the time of its delivery, revoked the appointment and gave it to another. At the December term, 1801, Charles Lee, Attorney-General of the

---

1. 5 U. S. (1. Cr.) 147, 2 L. ed. 60.

137

United States under Adams, appeared before the court at its first sitting in the city of Washington and the first session at which Marshall presided as Chief Justice, and asked for a rule to James Madison, Jefferson's Secretary of State, to show cause why a writ of mandamus should not issue, commanding him to deliver this commission to Marbury. Lee made a brief statement to the court and presented affidavits to prove the facts above stated. The rule was granted requiring Madison to show cause why the mandamus should not issue.

The case was unique in several respects. Madison did not appear and no argument was made for him or brief filed on his behalf. No written brief was filed by Lee. The case in effect was *ex parte*. The court was not aided, as it was in its later constitutional decisions, by the genius and eloquence of such lawyers as Webster, Pinckney and Wirt. The case was not finally heard until February, 1803. This delay was caused by political maneuvers on the part of the Republican majority in Congress. The triumph of Jefferson had carried with it a Republican majority in both branches of the national legislature.

Just before the expiration of Adams' term the Federalists, seeking to reform the old Judiciary Act of 1789, had provided for sixteen new circuit judges to relieve the Justices of the Supreme Court from the onerous labor of riding circuit, a labor which was deemed by the Federalists and most of the Justices themselves

138

unconstitutional. Adams had promptly filled these positions with staunch Federalists, almost in the last moments of his term. "The midnight judges," they were termed by the Republicans. The new Judiciary Act was repealed by the Republicans, the new judges ousted, and in order to prevent Marshall and his associates from interfering in any way judicially with the operation of the repeal, the August term, 1802, was discontinued, so there was an interval of fourteen months after Marbury vs. Madison was filed before the court again met.

In the meanwhile the case had been much bruited and had become political in its aspect. The Republicans were determined to purge the Supreme Court of its Federalist majority. Judge Pickering, district judge of New Hampshire, had been impeached for "high crimes and misdemeanors," although it was clearly proven that he was insane. Chase, an associate of Marshall, was then under impeachment, although he was later acquitted by a narrow margin.

In the discussion during the winter of 1801 and 1802 over the repeal of the Judiciary Act, the question of the power of the Supreme Court to declare invalid an act of Congress or to issue a writ of mandamus to a member of the President's cabinet was warmly debated. It was a cardinal doctrine of the Republican faith that Congress was the sole judge of the constitutionality of its own acts. The Republicans openly declared that if Marshall issued a writ of mandamus to Madison, it would be ignored and Marshall would be impeached.

This was the political situation when Marshall pronounced this decision, a decision which he knew would be rejected and its force denied by the President and his cabinet, by a majority of both houses of Congress and by at least two-thirds of the citizens of the United States. If I shall speak here of the decision as Marshall's decision, I do no injustice to the other Justices. Marshall conceived the idea of pinning this great judgment upon the trifling case before the court, and he persuaded the other judges to concur with him. The judgment is Marshall's; the opinion is Marshall's. Nearly seventy years were to elapse before the court was again called upon to declare unconstitutional an act of Congress. If Marshall had not seized this occasion, it is highly probable that long acquiescence in the assertion of the right of Congress to judge of its own acts would have foreclosed the court from ever uttering such a judgment.

Deprived of advice of counsel for the defendant, the court itself acted as counsel for Madison and suggested every possible objection that might be urged to the issuance of the writ, and then answered them. Marshall propounded three questions to be answered. First, "Has the applicant a right to the commission he demands?" Second, "If he has a right, and that right has been violated, do the laws of his country afford him a remedy?" Third, "If they do afford him a remedy, is it a mandamus issuing from this court?"

Upon the first proposition Marshall held that a commission is unlike a deed; that there are three things that constitute a lawful appointment; first, the appointment by the President; second, the confirmation by the Senate; third, the signing of the commission by the President. These three are all voluntary acts, with the exercise of which the court could not interfere, but when the commission is signed all of those things necessary to the appointment which are done in the exercise of a discretion have spent their force. Nothing remains but to attest it with the Great Seal of the United States by the Secretary of State, and the law makes this his duty. Marshall held that the appointment was complete when the President had signed the commission; that it would be complete without the affixing of the seal, which was simply incontestable proof of the fact that the commission had lawfully issued; that the duty of affixing the seal and delivering the commission were administrative acts, which added nothing to the validity of the commission. He showed that universally the tenure of an office dates from the date of the commission and not its delivery; the salary begins at the date of the commission. If the appointee refuses the office after the commission has issued, the new appointee succeeds him and not the prior incumbent. He held that to make the validity of the commission dependent upon

141

the actual delivery of the commission, through the mails for instance, was to expose the tenure of office to all the accidents, of theft, fire, etc.

Upon the second branch, whether a mandamus would issue to Madison, Marshall admitted the court was treading upon delicate ground, but he drew that clear distinction, novel then, which has been followed as a conclusive precedent from that date, that the court could not and would not interfere with the political powers of the Executive; that whenever the Secretary of State acted under the orders of the President in the exercise of his political duties, the court could not interfere, but when the act is administrative, no officer is too highly placed to be beyond the writ of a court when his failure to perform his administrative act violates the right of a citizen; that no citizen is too humble or his right too minute to deny the relief. So the court held that Marbury was entitled to the office and entitled to a writ of mandamus to the Secretary of State to compel the delivery of his commission.

In closing this branch of the case Marshall said:

"It is not by the office of the person to whom the writ is directed, but the nature of the thing to be done that the propriety or impropriety of issuing a mandamus is to be determined. Where the head of a department acts in a case, in which executive discretion is to be exercised; in which he is the mere organ of executive will; it is again repeated, that any application to a court to control, in any respect, his conduct would be rejected without hesitation.

"But where he is directed by law to do a certain act affecting the absolute rights of individuals, in the performance of which he is not placed under the particular direction of the President, and the performance of which the President cannot lawfully forbid, and therefore is never presumed to have forbidden; as for example, to record a commission, or a patent for land, which has received all the legal solemnities; or to give a copy of such record; in such cases, it is not perceived on what ground the courts of the country are further excused from the duty of giving judgment that right be done to an injured individual, than if the same services were to be performed by a person not the head of a department."

Proceeding to the third branch of the case, the question involved was whether the Judiciary Act of 1789, which attempted to confer original jurisdiction in mandamus upon the Supreme Court, was valid, or whether the grant in the Constitution of the subjects of original jurisdiction, although in affirmative words, was a limitation and a restriction to the particular jurisdiction there described. It is impossible to abstract or digest Marshall's opinion on this point. I prefer to quote:

"The question, whether an act, repugnant to the constitution, can become the law of the land, is a question deeply interesting to the United States; but, happily,

143

not of an intricacy proportioned to its interest. It seems only necessary to recognize certain principles, supposed to have been long and well established, to decide it.

"That the people have an original right to establish, for their future government, such principles, as, in their opinion, shall most conduce to their own happiness is the basis on which the whole American fabric has been erected. The exercise of this original right is a very great exertion; nor can it, nor ought it, to be frequently repeated. The principles, therefore, so established, are deemed fundamental. And as the authority from which they proceed is supreme, and can seldom act, they are designed to be permanent.

"This original and supreme will organizes the government, and assigns to different departments their respective powers. It may either stop here, or establish certain limits not to be transcended by those departments.

"The government of the United States is of the latter description. The powers of the legislature are defined and limited; and that those limits may not be mistaken, or forgotten, the constitution is written. To what purpose are powers limited, and to what purpose is that limitation committed to writing, if these limits may, at any time, be passed by those intended to be restrained? The distinction between a government with limited and unlimited powers is abolished, if those limits do not confine the persons on whom they are imposed, and if acts prohibited and acts allowed, are of equal obligation. It is a proposition too plain to be contested, that the constitution controls any legislative act repugnant to it; or, that the legislature may alter the constitution by an ordinary act.

"Between these alternatives there is no middle ground. The constitution is either a superior paramount law, unchangeable by ordinary means, or it is on a level with ordinary legislative acts, and, like other acts, is alterable when the legislature shall please to alter it.

"If the former part of the alternative be true, then a legislative act contrary to the constitution is not law; if the latter part be true, then written constitutions are absurd attempts, on the part of the people, to limit a power in its own nature illimitable.

"Certainly all those who have framed written constitutions contemplate them as forming the fundamental and paramount law of the nation and, consequently, the theory of every such government must be, that an act of the legislature, repugnant to the constitution, is void.

"This theory is essentially attached to a written constitution, and, is consequently, to be considered, by this court, as one of the fundamental principles of our society. It is not therefore to be lost sight of in the further consideration of this subject.

"If an act of the legislature, repugnant to the constitution, is void, does it, notwithstanding its invalidity, bind the courts, and oblige them to give it effect? Or, in other words, though it be not law, does it constitute a rule as operative as if it was a law? This would be to overthrow in fact what was established in theory; and would seem, at first view, an absurdity too gross to be insisted on. It shall, however, receive a more attentive consideration.

"It is emphatically the province and duty of the judicial department to say what the law is. Those who apply the rule to particular cases, must of necessity expound and interpret that rule. If two laws conflict with each other, the courts must decide on the operation of each.

"So if the law be in opposition to the constitution; if both the law and the constitution apply to a particular case, so that the court must either decide that case conformably to the law, disregarding the constitution; or conformably to the constitution, disregarding the law; the court must determine which of these conflicting rules governs the case. This is of the very essence of judicial duty.

"If, then, the courts are to regard the constitution, and the constitution is superior to any ordinary act of the legislature, the constitution, and not such ordinary act, must govern the case to which they both apply.

"Those, then, who controvert the principle that the

constitution is to be considered, in court, as a paramount law, are reduced to the necessity of maintaining that courts must close their eyes on the constitution, and see only the law.

"This doctrine would subvert the very foundation of all written constitutions. It would declare that an act which, according to the principles and theory of our government, is entirely void, is yet, in practice, completely obligatory. It would declare that if the legislature shall do what is expressly forbidden, such act, notwithstanding the express prohibition, is in reality effectual. It would be giving to the legislature a practical and real omnipotence, with the same breath which professes to restrict their powers with narrow limits. It is prescribing limits, and declaring that those limits may be passed at pleasure.

"That it thus reduces to nothing what we have deemed the greatest improvement on political institutions, a written constitution, would of itself be sufficient, in America, where written constitutions have been viewed with so much reverence, for rejecting the construction. But the peculiar expressions of the constitution of the United States furnish additional arguments in favor of its rejection.

"The judicial power of the United States is extended to all cases arising under the constitution.

"Could it be the intention of those who gave this power, to say that in using it the constitution should not be looked into? That a case arising under the constitution should be decided without examining the instrument under which it arises?

"This is too extravagant to be maintained.

"In some cases, then, the constitution must be looked into by the judges. And if they can open it at all, what part of it are they forbidden to read or to obey?

"Why otherwise does it direct the judges to take an oath to support it? This oath certainly applies in an especial manner, to their conduct in their official character. How immoral to impose it on them, if they were to be used as the instruments, and the knowing instruments, for violating what they swear to support!

"The oath of office, too, imposed by the legislature, is completely demonstrative of the legislative opinion on this subject. It is in these words:

" 'I do solemnly swear that I will administer justice without respect to persons, and do equal right to the poor and to the rich; and that I will faithfully and impartially discharge all the duties incumbent on me as ————, according to the best of my ability and understanding, agreeably to the constitution and laws of the United States.'

"Why does a judge swear to discharge his duties agreeably to the constitution of the United States, if that constitution forms no rule for his government? if it is closed upon him, and cannot be inspected by him?"

And he closes with this blow from the hammer of Thor:

"If such be the real state of things, this is worse than solemn mockery. To prescribe, or to take this oath, becomes equally a crime."

Thousands of pages have been written in support or defense of this decision. Other thousands have been written in criticism or condemnation, not a line of which has added to or detracted from this great opinion. At the time it was rendered the country was tremendously excited over the acquisition of Louisiana, and for a time it was little noted except by the bar. Jefferson denied its validity, declared it was extrajudicial, and anathematized it to the day of his death and his fellow Republicans followed suit, but it remained the law of the land.

Magna Charta, that great achievement of the Anglo-Saxon race, was a limitation upon the power of the Crown only. The power of Parliament remains omnipotent, despotic, with no check or restriction. For hundreds of years after Magna Charta Parliament condemned men without trial, sent them to the block, forfeited their goods, punished the guilty and innocent alike. The peculiar distinction of the American constitution was that it for the first time protected the individual against the aggression, not only of the executive, but of the legislative. But this constitution would have failed in that particular but for the decision in Marbury vs. Madison. This feature of the constitution, interpreted by the great Chief Justice is

America's contribution to the democracy of the world. It remains today the cornerstone of American liberty.

Thirty years later, Rufus Choate, speaking of the effect and conclusiveness of this decision, declared that no one "but a demagogue in the last stages of intoxication would now question it." We have demagogues today, apparently not in any state of intoxication, who do question it and some of them are in Congress.

The assertion that the power of the Supreme Court to declare an Act of Congress unconstitutional is an usurpation, certainly springs from ignorance. During Colonial times an appeal lay from an act of the Colonial Assembly to the Privy Council of England, which was and still is the High Court of Justice of the English Colonies. Four hundred sixty-nine Colonial Acts were disapproved, of which over two hundred were on the ground that the Colonies had exceeded their power under their charter, which constituted their written constitution. Some of these decisions excited bitter resentment in the Colonies, but they accustomed the people of America to the idea of the limitation of legislative power and the right of an independent tribunal to declare invalid, acts of the legislature. Invalid because they were beyond its granted powers. Between the beginning of the Revolution and the adoption of the Federal Constitution, all of the Colonies except Connecticut and Rhode Island adopted new Constitutions befitting their new status as independent sovereign states, establishing in each a Republican form of government with a written Constitution, limiting the powers of the executive and legislative departments.

There are several precedents in the state courts under those constitutions before the decision in Marbury vs. Madison. In New Jersey, in the case of Holmes vs. Walton, decided in 1780, the question turned on a war measure providing for a trial, by a jury of six, without appeal of persons found with goods of the enemy in their possession. The Act was held void as violative of the state constitution. In the Virginia case of Commonwealth vs. Gaton, Judge Wythe and Chancellor Blair, both members of the Constitutional Convention, expressed their opinions in 1782 that the state courts had power to declare unconstitutional, acts of the legislature which infringed the organic law. In Travett vs. Weeden, decided in 1786, the court held that the Rhode Island statute in aid of paper currency, denying a trial by jury was unconstitutional. In May, 1787, the North Carolina court held in Bayard vs. Singleton that an act of the state legislature abolishing the common law right of a trial by jury in certain instances was unconstitutional. James Iredell, one of the first justices of the United States Supreme Court, was Chief Counsel for the plaintiff, and had associated with him William R. Davie, who as a delegate from North Carolina was a member of the Constitutional Conven-

151

tion when the decision was returned and was thoroughly familiar with it.

It has been asserted that the question of the right of the Supreme Court to declare an Act of Congress unconstitutional was proposed in the convention and rejected. This is untrue. It was proposed that the President and the members of the Supreme Court as a Council of Revision should have the power to veto any Act of Congress, a provision similar to that of New York. It was objected that this would give the members of the Supreme Court a double veto because they would have anyway the power to declare an act unconstitutional.

George Mason, of Virginia, pointed out the distinction that as Justices of the Supreme Court they would veto an act because it was unconstitutional, but as members of the proposed Council of Revision, they would veto the act on general principles, because it was unwise or vicious. Over and over again in the Convention the great lawyers like Luther Martin, of Maryland, James Wilson, of Pennsylvania, Ellsworth, of Connecticut, and Alexander Hamilton and Gouverneur Morris stated that the Supreme Court, wholly independent of Congress and the Executive would have the power to limit these two branches within their Constitutional grants. This was thoroughly understood by every member of the Convention. Hamilton in the Federalist asserted this power with arguments that

152

were closely followed by Marshall in this case. In the Virginia Convention considering the adoption of the Constitution, Patrick Henry, who opposed the adoption because he feared the centralization of power, in the Federal government, commented on this right of the Supreme Court and praised it in the highest terms as the very best feature of the proposed Constitution. Every member of the convention, and nearly every leading man in the Colonies understood that the Supreme Court should have this power. Jefferson, who bitterly condemned the decision in Marbury vs. Madison, never denied the power of the court to hold an Act of Congress unconstitutional. His objection was that part of the decision was extra-judicial, not necessary to a decision of the case and that it interfered unduly with the operation of the Executive department.

As a matter of history, political parties have objected to this power, not on principle but because at one time or another it checked their party policies. Thus, it has from time to time been condemned for this reason by Federalists, Republicans, Whigs, Democrats, and by the new Republican Party.

CHAPTER II.

COHEN VS. VIRGINIA[1]

From the time Jefferson became President, his power in Virginia was supreme. Together with Spencer Roane, Chief Justice of Virginia, a very able man, and John Taylor of Roanoke, he controlled Virginia politics. In Massachusetts, the political unit was the township and the New England "town meeting," where the voters met and voted *viva voce,* established a democracy. In Virginia, the county was the unit. The county judges, who administered the financial affairs of the county, also selected the members of the legislature, and the judicial officers. Under the control of this triumvirate, for a quarter of a century, the political principles of Jefferson: "States Rights," "opposition to a strong central government," and "the United States Bank,"—were the watch-words of the Republican party in Virginia.

It was under these conditions that the case of Cohen vs. Virginia, appealed from the highest court of the state, came up for decision. I indulge here in a speculation. I firmly believe that Marshall contemplated, continuously for many years, the establishment of certain Federal principles which he believed to be essential to the central government. I think this because in

---

1. 19 U. S. (6 Wheat.) 264, 5 L. ed. 257.

both Marbury vs. Madison, and Cohen vs. Virginia, he went out of his way to seize an opportunity to declare, first, the supremacy of the Constitution as interpreted by his court upon Congressional legislation; and second, in the case we are considering, the overruling power of the Federal Supreme Court in everything that related to the Federal Constitution, its laws and treaties.

The case of Cohen vs. Virginia, decided in 1821, is not next in point of time to Marbury vs. Madison, in Marshall's great constitutional decisions; but it is next in point of interest. The former proclaimed the interpretive power of the Supreme Court over Congress. The latter established the appellate power of the Supreme Court over the courts of the various states, in every case involving the Constitution, laws, or treaties of the United States.

Congress, in the act providing for the government of the District of Columbia, had authorized that government to establish a lottery for the purpose of making internal improvements in the city of Washington. The lottery was established. The Cohens were convicted under a Virginia statute of selling, in the city of Norfolk, two half tickets and four quarter tickets in this lottery. They appealed to the Supreme Court of the United States. So slight was the cause. The case was tried upon an agreed statement of facts, which set forth in full the act of Congress, the Virginia statute and the fact of the sale, and this record was before the court.

Barbour, for the State of Virginia, filed a motion to dismiss on three grounds: First, because of the subject-matter of the controversy (that the act establishing a lottery was purely local in its application and gave no right to sell tickets outside of the District of Columbia); second, that the state was a party; and third, that the Supreme Court had neither original nor appellate jurisdiction in such a case; and the cause came on to be heard first upon the motion to dismiss.

In 1813, in the case of Martin vs. Hunter[2], the Supreme Court of the United States had upheld its appellate jurisdiction in a case between private parties. The case involved the title to a portion of the Lord Fairfax land. Virginia attempted to forfeit these lands during the Revolutionary War, and Hunter claimed under a grant from the state. Martin, who was a nephew of and devisee under the will of Lord Fairfax, claimed that the Treaty of Peace of 1783, and the Jay Treaty with England of 1794, protected his rights. The Supreme Court held that this raised a question under a treaty of the United States and reversed the judgment of the Court of Appeals of Virginia in Hunter's favor and held that Martin was the owner. Spencer Roane was then president of the Vir-

2. 14 U. S. (1 Wheat.) 304, 4 L. ed. 97, revers'g 4 Munf. (Va.) 1.

ginia Court of Appeals, an able lawyer, and one of
the most bitter anti-nationalists in the country. He
was one of the Republican triumvirate that for years
controlled Virginia, with a political machine more
perfect than the Albany Regency or Tammany Hall.

The Virginia Court of Appeals unanimously refused to obey the judgment of the Supreme Court and
spread their reasons at large on the record. They
denied the right of appeal from their final judgment
in any case to the Supreme Court of the United States,
declaring they were separate sovereignties, in matters
of judicature, unrelated.

A second writ of error was taken to the Supreme
Court in the case just above cited. Marshall did not
sit, as he and his brother had bought large tracts of the
Fairfax lands. Story wrote the opinion, a very able
one, reiterating the former judgment. So the matter
rested until the case of Cohen vs. Virginia.

The motion was very ably argued on behalf of the
state by Barbour and Snaith. Pinckney and Ogden of
New York appeared for the Cohens. Eighteen years
had elapsed since the decision in the Marbury case.
Marshall had been twenty years on the bench. His
great constitutional decisions had established his reputation. The court, under his guidance, had established
its power. It was universally respected by the bar, and
profoundly feared by the Republican party. In any
other court, and probably at any other time, the motion

to dismiss would have been sustained on the grounds advanced in the opening of their arguments by both of the counsel for the state, that the act of Congress in question was a mere municipal ordinance for the city of Washington, having no extra-territorial force; as Barbour expressed it, no more force beyond the limits of the District of Columbia than an act providing for the paving of a street in the city of Washington. This was the first ground presented in the motion, and the first ground argued. Snaith suggested further that even though the act were general, the state of Virginia might, under its reserve police power, prohibit the sale of lottery tickets within its territory, for the protection of the morals of its citizens. This ground, today, would be sustained almost without examination.

The second ground was, that the state being a party, under the Eleventh Amendment, the Court had neither appellate nor original jurisdiction; that it was a suit against the state; and third, that no appeal lay to the Supreme Court in any case. Marshall seized upon this ground, ignoring the others, as a hook upon which to hang his decision affirming the appellate jurisdiction of his court. If Barbour had paused in his motion to dismiss, with the first ground, and confined his argument to that, it is difficult to see how the court could have refrained from sustaining the motion to dismiss without considering the other grounds. By accident or design,—and it was alleged by the Republicans that Barbour framed the issue to give Marshall his opportunity,—it included the whole question of the appellate jurisdiction of the Supreme Court. The Chief Justice, somewhat disingenuously, reversed the order of the objections set forth in the motion and plunged immediately into the consideration of the appellate power of his court, and overruled the motion to dismiss.

The case then came up on its merits, Webster appearing for the state, and in a very brief opinion the Court held that the act was local and affirmed the decision of the lower court. This was done upon the face of the record, which was fully before the Court upon the motion to dismiss, and that ground strongly urged. But Marshall was determined to go to the root of the whole controversy and settle it on the motion. Because the state was a party, because Marshall wrote the opinion, Cohen vs. Virginia is generally considered as the decisive case on the appellate power of the Supreme Court of the United States. Whatever may be said of Marshall's opinions in ordinary cases, like equity or maritime law, when he proceeds to examine a constitutional question where there are no precedents to guide, no judge, living or dead, has ever equalled him. There is an Olympian power, a Jovian force, about his utterances that are irresistible. It is as though a god stooped to instruct a mortal. It is as Whistler said once, "I am not arguing with you; I am telling you." He will announce that a certain contention "is absurd and extravagant, but we will give it careful attention"; an attention that devastates the argument and withers its proponent. Nowhere, except perhaps in McCulloch vs. Maryland,[3] has he appeared to better advantage than in this great case.

At the very opening of his opinion Marshall settled the case, and destroyed every argument of the defendants in error, by this simple statement of their claim:

"They maintain that the nation does not possess a department capable of restraining peaceably, and by authority of law, any attempts which may be made, by a part, against the legitimate powers of the whole; and that the government is reduced to the alternative of submitting to such attempts, or of resisting them by force. They. maintain that the constitution of the United States has provided no tribunal for the final construction of itself, or of the laws or treaties of the nation; but that this power may be exercised in the last resort by the courts of every state of the Union. That the constitution, laws, and treaties, may receive as many constructions as there are states; and that this is not a mischief, or, if a mischief, is irremediable. These abstract propositions are to be determined; for he who demands decision without permitting inquiry, affirms that the decision he asks does not depend on inquiry."

3. See, post, Part III, Chapter III.

160

He shows that this is not a case against a state, although the state is a party. He defines a suit against a state as a suit in law or equity in which the plaintiff demands something from the state, seeks to recover something of value. In the case at bar the Cohens demanded nothing from Virginia, could secure nothing except the right to sell these tickets, a right denied by the state. He gives an interesting historical survey of the reasons for the adoption of the Eleventh Amendment, and dismisses that contention which had already been settled by McCulloch vs. Maryland. He comes then to the general appellate power of the Supreme Court over decisions of state courts where the Constitution, laws, or treaties of the United States are drawn in question:

"The American States, as well as the American people, have believed a close and firm Union to be essential to their liberty and their happiness. They have been taught by experience, that this Union cannot exist without a government for the whole; and they have been taught by the same experience that this government would be a mere shadow, that must disappoint all their hopes, unless invested with large portions of that sovereignty which belongs to independent states. Under the influence of this opinion, and thus instructed by experience, the American people, in the conventions of their respective states, adopted the present constitution.

"If it could be doubted, whether from its nature, it were not supreme in all cases where it is empowered to act, that doubt would be removed by the declaration, that 'this constitution, and the laws of the United States, which shall be made in pursuance thereof, and all treaties made, or which shall be made, under the authority of the United States, shall be the supreme law of the land; and the judges in every state shall be bound thereby; anything in the constitution or laws of any state to the contrary notwithstanding.'

"This is the authoritative language of the American people; and, if gentlemen please, of the American States. It marks, with lines too strong to be mistaken, the characteristic distinction between the government of the Union and those of the states. The general government, though limited as to its objects, is supreme with respect to those objects. This principle is a part of the constitution; and if there be any who deny its necessity, none can deny its authority.

"To this supreme government ample powers are confided; and if it were possible to doubt the great purposes for which they were so confided, the people of the United States have declared, that they are given 'in order to form a more perfect union, establish justice, insure domestic tranquillity, provide for the common defense, promote the general welfare, and secure the blessings of liberty to themselves and their posterity.'"

He then plunges into his favorite theme, nationalism:

"That the United States form, for many, and for most important purposes, a single nation, has not yet been denied. In war, we are one people. In making peace, we are one people. In all commercial regulations, we are one and the same people. In many other respects, the American people are one; and the government which is alone capable of controlling and managing their interests in all these respects, is the government of the Union. It is their government, and in that character they have no other. America has chosen to be, in many respects, and to many purposes, a nation; and for all these purposes, her government is complete; to all these objects, it is competent. The people have declared, that in the exercise of all powers given for these objects it is supreme. It can, then, in effecting these objects, legitimately control all individuals or governments within the American territory. The constitution and laws of a state, so far as they are repugnant to the constitution and laws of the United States, are absolutely void. These states are constituent parts of the United States. They are members of one great empire—for some purposes sovereign, for some purposes subordinate.

"In a government so constituted, is it unreasonable that the judicial power should be competent to give efficacy to the constitutional laws of the legislature? That department can decide on the validity of the constitution or law of a state, if it be repugnant to the constitution or to a law of the United States. Is it unreasonable that it should also be empowered to decide on the judgment of a state tribunal enforcing such unconstitutional law? Is it so very unreasonable as to furnish a justification for controlling the words of the constitution?

"We think it is not. We think that in a government acknowledgedly supreme, with respect to objects of vital interest to the nation, there is nothing inconsistent with sound reason, nothing incompatible with the nature of government in making all its departments supreme, so far as respects those objects, and so far as is necessary to their attainment. The exercise of the appellate power over those judgments of the state tribunals which may contravene the constitution or laws of the United States, is, we believe, essential to the attainment of those objects."

He quotes from "a very celebrated statesman" (unnamed) :

"Thirteen independent courts [and we now have 48], of final jurisdiction over the same causes, arising upon the same laws, is a hydra in government, from which nothing but contradiction and confusion can proceed."

In the argument on behalf of Virginia, it was suggested that not every constitutional question could be appealable, and hence none were. For instance, suppose a state should grant a title of nobility. Could the Supreme Court act on this? Marshall answered:

"If the question cannot be brought into a court, then there is no case in law or equity, and no jurisdiction is given by the words of the article. But if, in any controversy depending in a court, the cause should depend on the validity of such a law, that would be a case arising under the constitution, to which the judicial power of the United States would extend."

It was suggested again that the various states could destroy the Constitution by simply failing to elect senators. He says:

"It is very true that, whenever hostility to the existing system shall become universal, it will be also irresistible. The people made the constitution, and the people can unmake it. It is the creature of their own will, and lives only by their will. But this supreme and irresistible power to make or to unmake, resides only in the whole body of the people; not in any subdivision of them. The attempt of any of the parts to exercise it is usurpation, and ought to be repelled by those to whom the people have delegated their power of repelling it.

"The acknowledged inability of the government, then, to sustain itself against the public will, and, by force or otherwise, to control the whole nation, is no sound argument in support of its constitutional inability to preserve itself against a section of the nation acting in opposition to the general will."

He points out, as conclusive of the whole matter, that the Constitution of the United States was not adopted by the states, and is not the creature of the state governments. "We, the people of the United States," framed and adopted the Constitution. It was not ratified by the states as such, but by conventions called in each state springing directly from the people, speaking the voice of the people of the United States. True, the conventions were called in each separate state, but that was because the only machinery that existed for calling the convention was found in the separate states. So they, the people of each state, had formed the government of that state, and helped to form a government of all the states, supreme in all that concerns national affairs. There is no answer to that argument.

Of course, the decision was bitterly denounced. It was asserted that it prostrated every state government, and made every decision of the state courts appealable to Washington. These apprehensions, if they really existed, were allayed and these statements answered in the case of Bank vs. Dudley, Lessee,[4] in which the Supreme Court held that the interpretation of the Constitution, or a law of any state, by the highest court of that state, is binding upon the Supreme Court of the

4. Bank of Hamilton v. Dudley, 27 U. S. (2 Pet.) 492.7 L. ed. 496.

United States. From that time on the two jurisdictions have proceeded side by side without friction, although many cases of conflicting jurisdiction, surrounded with much doubt, have since arisen. Marshall, the soldier of the Revolution, who had suffered at Valley Forge, who knew the utter incapacity of the old federative system, had devoted himself to the cause of nationalism. That was his religion. That was the altar at which he worshipped. Despite the strongest opposition, the fiercest criticism; despite the settled opinions and convictions of a great majority of his countrymen, step by step he was building up a national government.

The importance of this case cannot be exaggerated. If each state had the power to determine for itself its own interpretation of the Constitution, laws, and treaties of the United States, chaos would result. This case has been the centripetal force that has held the Union together. Without it, this country would have long since dissolved into "dissevered, discordant and belligerent fragments."

CHAPTER III.

McCulloch vs. Maryland[1]

Throughout the first seventy years of our national life, there was one issue that overshadowed all others, —the States Rights issue. Upon that depended, or around it were grouped, nearly all the political controversies of those years. Political parties were formed, rose to power, dissolved and disappeared; but this issue remained, and was more or less responsible for the existence of each of these parties. The slavery question divided the North and the South, yet, fundamentally, the issue was whether the States were independent and had a right to secede when displeased with certain tendencies of the Federal government; or whether the Federal Union was indissoluble, and the slavery question to be determined peacefully within the limits of the Constitution,—by Constitutional amendment or otherwise. It was slavery that precipitated the final determination of this issue of States Rights upon the field of battle, which had once before almost brought on a civil war on a question wholly disconnected with slavery,—the Nullification Act of 1831. So the question presented in the case we are considering, grew out

1 17 U.S. (4 Wheat.) 316, 4 L. ed. 579.

168

of this very issue. The question was whether the government, under its implied powers, could establish a National Bank for its fiscal purpose; and this opened the whole controversy as to implied powers.

The advocates of States Rights opposed this view, and held that the States alone could create corporations for banking or other purposes. The fatal consequences of state banks, with unlimited and unsupported issues of paper money, had been fully shown after the charter of the first United States Bank had expired. If the issue could have been separated from States Rights, and presented purely as an economic and financial measure, as it finally was in the '60's, when the present national banking system was established,—since immensely broadened and strengthened by the Federal Reserve Bank Act,—there could have been little doubt of the result.

But, unfortunately for the Democratic Party, always committed to the doctrine of States Rights, it has always been compelled, until recently, to oppose the only sound banking and currency system,—a Federal system. So it has been continually yoked with all the mistakes, failures, and miseries of state bank issues, paper money and inflation. By it the country, too, has paid dearly for this alliance of financial policy with States Rights,—and it is only within recent years that the long contest between sound and unsound money has ceased to be a political issue. The decision we are

169

now considering, established for all time the right of the Federal government to charter and regulate banks of issue, whose bills should be as good as gold, whenever the Federal idea should finally prevail.

This case, generally known as Bank vs. Maryland, was the most important case, financially, that, up to that time, had ever engaged the attention of any court in this country. It involved the whole doctrine of implied powers, and the very existence of the Bank of the United States, with its capital of $35,000,000.00, twenty-five branches, and innumerable ramifications, financial and political.

This bank had been the football of politics since the beginning of the government, and the center of a continuous conflict. It was Hamilton's pet measure for the stabilization of the finances of the new country. In Washington's cabinet, Jefferson bitterly opposed it as unconstitutional. Hamilton's argument prevailed with Washington, and the bank was established in 1791, with a charter to run twenty years. It was profitable from the start, but its stock largely fell into British hands, and that, and the growing conviction of the Republicans that it was unconstitutional, made it unpopular, and its charter was not renewed.

An orgy of private banking followed which, coupled with the War of 1812, left our finances in chaos. Specie payments had been suspended, and the country, financially, was in a bad way when, in 1816, the

Bank was re-incorporated and began business on the first day of January, 1817. It had a capital of $35,000,000.00,—an enormous sum in those days,—of which $7,000,000.00 was held by the government, and five of the directors were appointed by the President. It acted as the fiscal agency of the government, collecting the revenue, disbursing it, and transferring funds from one point to another without expense to the government. It issued bills redeemable in specie, and it was so profitable that its stock was worth fifty per cent above par.

The State of Maryland passed a statute that all bills issued by banks not chartered by the state of Maryland must be printed on stamped paper furnished by the state, with a tax of twenty cents on five-dollar bills, and graduated upward. McCulloch, the treasurer of the Maryland branch, refused to pay, and suit was brought. The lower court, of course, decided in favor of the state, and an appeal was taken to the Supreme Court.

For the Government appeared Webster, Wirt and Pinckney; for the State, Hopkinson of Pennsylvania,— who, by the way, wrote "Hail, Columbia,"—Luther Martin of Maryland, and Jones of Washington; the greatest array of legal talent that ever sat at one counsel table, except possibly at the trial of Warren Hastings. The argument occupied nine days. Pinckney alone talked for three days; outdid himself, and far

171

surpassed **Webster**. It was this speech that caused Marshall to declare that Pinckney was the greatest lawyer who ever entered a court room.

Beveridge thinks Jones was a great lawyer, and his name appears in the reports of that time as frequently as any other; but he made an unfortunate argument in this case, contending that the federal government was formed by the states, that the old confederation was a true sovereignty, when in fact it was only a collection of ambassadors from independent states,—errors which Marshall was swift to seize upon.

Martin was then in his seventieth year; had been more or less continuously intoxicated for fifty years, but was in his day the ablest all-around lawyer in America, and still a formidable opponent.

Marshall's opinion was handed down in three days after the argument was closed. Undoubtedly much of it must have been conceived during the year the case had been pending. It was inevitable that great constitutional lawyers, like Webster, Pinckney and Marshall, earnest believers in nationalism, should think together, that their minds should run in the same channel. Marshall borrowed Webster's famous expression that "the power to tax carries with it the power to destroy," but, in the main, his opinion gains little from the argument.

The first proposition was the constitutionality of the Bank. The constitution does not empower congress to charter a corporation nor to use it as one of the instrumentalities of government. If found at all, it must be found by implication. Marshall said:

"The counsel for the state of Maryland have deemed it of some importance, in the construction of the constitution, to consider that instrument not as emanating from the people, but as the act of sovereign and independent states. The powers of the general government, it has been said, are delegated by the states, who alone are truly sovereign; and must be exercised in subordination to the states, who alone possess supreme dominion.

"It would be difficult to sustain this proposition. The convention which framed the constitution was indeed elected by the state legislatures. But the instrument, when it came from their hands, was a mere proposal, without obligation, or pretensions to it. It was reported to the then existing Congress of the United States, with a request that it might 'be submitted to a convention of delegates, chosen in each state by the people thereof, under the recommendation of its legislature, for their assent and ratification.' This mode of proceeding was adopted; and by the convention, by Congress, and by the state legislatures, the instrument was submitted to the people. They acted upon it in the only manner in which they can act safely, effectively, and wisely, on such a subject, by assembling in convention. It is true, they assembled in their several

173

states,—and where else should they have assembled?
No political dreamer was ever wild enough to think of
breaking down the lines which separate the states, and
of compounding the American people into one common mass. Of consequence, when they act, they act in
their states. But the measures they adopt do not,
on that account, cease to be the measures of the people themselves, or become the measures of the state
governments."

On the question of the reserved power of the states
he said:

"It has been said that the people had already surrendered all their powers to the state sovereignties, and
had nothing more to give. But, surely, the question
whether they may resume and modify the powers
granted to government does not remain to be settled
in this country. Much more might the legitimacy of
the general government be doubted, had it been created
by the states. The powers delegated to the state
sovereignties were to be exercised by themselves, not
by a distinct and independent sovereignty, created by
themselves. To the formation of a league, such as was
the confederation, the state sovereignties were certainly competent. But when, 'in order to form a more
perfect union,' it was deemed necessary to change this
alliance into an effective government, possessing great
and sovereign powers, and acting directly on the people, the necessity of referring it to the people, and of

deriving its powers directly from them, was felt and acknowledged by all.

"The government of the Union, then (whatever may be the influence of this fact on the case), is, emphatically, and truly, a government of the people. In form and in substance it emanates from them. Its powers are granted by them, and are to be exercised directly on them, and for their benefit."

In developing his theory of nationalism, this was a favorite argument of Marshall's, and is repeated many times in different forms. The suggestion here repelled, and his answer, disclosed the true nature of the controversy with which Marshall dealt in all of his great constitutional decisions,—the conflict between **State Rights and Nationalism.** The burden of all this long dispute, running through sixty years, until it was settled by the Civil War, is the argument of the Jeffersonian school, that the states established the federal government, delegated to it certain powers, reserving all others to the several states "or the people thereof." The nationalist doctrine was that the people, who had created the state governments for certain local purposes, had then created the national government for another, a general national purpose; that the people had intended the federal government to be a full sovereignty within the scope of the powers granted for national purposes, with all the attributes of sovereignty.

He goes on to assert that, under the confederation, nothing could be taken by implication, wherein it differs from the present government, which was formed to repair the weaknesses of the former.

"Although, among the enumerated powers of government, we do not find the word 'bank' or 'incorporation,' we find the great powers to lay and collect taxes; to borrow money; to regulate commerce; to declare and conduct a war; and to raise and support armies and navies. The sword and the purse, all the external relations, and no inconsiderable portion of the industry of the nation, are entrusted to its government. It can never be pretended that these vast powers draw after them others of inferior importance, merely because they are inferior. Such an idea can never be advanced. But it may with great reason be contended, that a government, entrusted with such ample powers, on the due execution of which the happiness and prosperity of the nation so vitally depend, must also be entrusted with ample means for their execution. The power being given, it is the interest of the nation to facilitate its execution. It can never be their interest, and cannot be presumed to have been their intention, to clog and embarrass its execution by withholding the most appropriate means. Throughout this vast Republic, from the St. Croix to the Gulf of Mexico, from the Atlantic to the Pacific, revenue is to be collected and expended, armies are to be marched and sup-

176

ported. The exigencies of the nation may require that the treasure raised in the north should be transported to the south, that raised in the east conveyed to the west, or that this order should be reversed. Is that construction of the constitution to be preferred which would render these operations difficult, hazardous, and expensive? Can we adopt that construction (unless the words imperiously require it) which would impute to the framers of that instrument, when granting these powers for the public good, the intention of impeding their exercise by withholding a choice of means? If, indeed, such be the mandate of the constitution, we have only to obey; but that instrument does not profess to enumerate the means by which the powers it confers may be executed; nor does it prohibit the creation of a corporation, if the existence of such a being be essential to the beneficial exercise of those powers. It is, then, the subject of fair inquiry, how far such means may be employed."

He comes then to the consideration of the word "necessary," and notes that, in other parts of the constitution, "necessary" is qualified by "absolutely"; that only in this one section, which gives to congress "all necessary and proper" powers, the word "absolutely" is omitted. In that he finds the strongest evidence that the word "necessary," as there used, does not mean indispensable, but rather, expedient, convenient or appropriate, and he sums up the rule in the sentence so often quoted, as follows:

"Let the end be legitimate, let it be within the scope of the constitution, and all means which are appropriate, which are plainly adapted to that end, which are not prohibited, but consist with the letter and spirit of the constitution, are constitutional."

This granted, it followed that the choice of "necessary" means lay with congress, and not with the judiciary. Unless congress employed means clearly unconstitutional, the court would not interfere.

Having thus established the constitutionality of the Bank, Marshall addressed himself to the power of the state to tax it. It was strenuously contended that the government was a mere stockholder in the Bank, owning one-fifth of the stock; that its holdings were merged in the general mass; that it was, therefore, not a governmental institution, but a private corporation for profit, like any other bank; that it could be taxed wherever it had a branch that created a situs for taxation. To this Marshall replied that it was a corporation chartered by the federal government for its financial necessity; that it was the fiscal agency of the government; that its bills circulating as currency, were necessary to the bank's existence, as well as furnishing stable currency for all the people of the United States. In fact, at that time the Bank's bills were the only bills that could be carried from one state to another without discount. The bills of every state bank were under a cloud, and varied from par to nothing. He

178

announced the axiom that Webster had coined, that the power to tax carried with it the power to destroy, and adopted it as the view of the court.

Speaking of the right of taxation he says:

"It is obvious that it is an incident of sovereignty, and is co-extensive with that to which it is an incident. All subjects over which the sovereign power of a state extends, are objects of taxation; but those over which it does not extend, are, upon the soundest principles, exempt from taxation. This proposition may almost be pronounced self-evident.

"The sovereignty of a state extends to everything which exists by its own authority, or is introduced by its permission; but does it extend to those means which are employed by Congress to carry into execution— powers conferred on that body by the people of the United States? We think it demonstrable that it does not. Those powers are not given by the people of a single state. They are given by the people of the United States, to a government whose laws, made in pursuance of the constitution, are declared to be supreme. Consequently, the people of a single state cannot confer a sovereignty which will extend over them.

"If we measure the power of taxation residing in a state, by the extent of sovereignty which the people of a single state possess, and can confer on its government, we have an intelligible standard, applicable to every case to which the power may be applied. We

179

have a principle which leaves the power of taxing the people and property of a state unimpaired; which leaves to a state the command of all its resources, and which places beyond its reach, all those powers which are conferred by the people of the United States on the government of the Union, and all those means which are given for the purpose of carrying those powers into execution. We have a principle which is safe for the states, and safe for the Union. We are relieved, as we ought to be, from clashing sovereignty; from interfering powers; from a repugnancy between a right in one government to pull down what there is an acknowledged right in another to build up, from the incompatibility of a right in one government to destroy what there is a right in another to preserve. We are not driven to the perplexing inquiry, so unfit for the judicial department, what degree of taxation is the legitimate use, and what degree may amount to the abuse of the power. The attempt to use it on the means employed by the government of the Union, in pursuance of the constitution, is itself an abuse, because it is the usurpation of a power which the people of a single state cannot give.

"We find, then, on just theory, a total failure of this original right to tax the means employed by the government of the Union, for the execution of its powers. The right never existed, and the question whether it has been surrendered, cannot arise.

"But, waiving this theory for the present, let us resume the inquiry, whether this power can be exercised by the respective states, consistently with a fair construction of the constitution.

"That the power to tax involves the power to destroy; that the power to destroy may defeat and render useless the power to create; that there is a plain repugnance, in conferring on one government a power to control the constitutional measures of another, which other, with respect to those very measures, is declared to be supreme over that which exerts the control, are propositions not to be denied. But all inconsistencies are to be reconciled by the magic of the word CONFIDENCE. Taxation, it is said, does not necessarily and unavoidably destroy. To carry it to the excess of destruction would be an abuse, to presume which, would banish that confidence which is essential to all government.

"But is this a case of confidence? Would the people of any state trust those of another with a power to control the most insignificant operations of their state government? We know they would not. Why, then, should we suppose that the people of any one state should be willing to trust those of another with a power to control the operations of a government to which they have confided the most important and most valuable interests? In the legislature of the Union alone, are all represented. The legislature of the Union alone, therefore, can be trusted by the people with the power of controlling measures which concern all, in the confidence that it will not be abused. This, then, is not a case of confidence, and we must consider it as it really is.

"If we apply the principle for which the state of Maryland contends, to the constitution generally, we shall find it capable of changing totally the character of that instrument. We shall find it capable of arresting all the measures of the government, and of prostrating it at the foot of the states. The American people have declared their constitution, and the laws made in pursuance thereof, to be supreme; but this principle would transfer the supremacy, in fact, to the states.

"If the states may tax one instrument, employed by the government in the execution of its powers, they may tax any and every other instrument. They may tax the mail; they may tax the mint; they may tax patent-rights; they may tax the papers of the custom house; they may tax judicial process; they may tax all the means employed by the government, to an excess which would defeat all the ends of government. This was not intended by the American people. They did not design to make their government dependent on the states."

Of course, the decision was bitterly criticized by the Republicans, and particularly by their press. To those who are interested in this phase of the controversy, I recommend the Fourth Volume of Beveridge's incomparable "Life of Marshall."

But there is here a new note in the criticism. Marshall had established his reputation as a judge beyond any power of derogation. The very articles that criticize his decision, speak of him with the profoundest respect. They admire, they praise him, while they hate and criticize him. They see their favorite doctrine of the independent sovereignty of the states crumbling under Marshall's powerful blows. And the curious thing is that, however much they may criticize his decisions, no critic attempts to answer his logic.

CHAPTER IV.

GIBBONS VS. OGDEN[1]

From the beginning of history, commerce has been the handmaiden of civilization. The great commercial cities, Tyre, and Sidon, Carthage, Venice, Genoa, the Hanse Towns, and London, exploring the earth for new commodities, exchanging the products of every clime, brought to the warrior-shepherds and husbandmen of a ruder age the arts of civilization and a knowledge of the world. It was the impulse of commercial gain that rounded the Cape of Good Hope, circumnavigated the globe, discovered the new world, and peopled it. In 1786 commercial rivalries were about to destroy the new Confederation. The swiftly growing settlements beyond the Alleghenies, barred by distance from selling their products to the eastward, had but one outlet, the Mississippi, and this was in effect closed to them by the Spanish at New Orleans. New England and New York were utterly regardless of, if not openly hostile to, these new settlements. When Jay, of New York, proposed a treaty with Spain that might close the mouth of the Mississippi for twenty-five years, the Southwest was in a flame. It was pro-

---

1. 19 U. S. (6 Wheat.) 448, 5 L. ed. 302, dissm'g appeal from 17 Johns (N. Y.) 488.

posed to secede from the Confederation, raise an armed force, seize New Orleans, open the Mississippi, and seek the protection of England. New York, with its noble harbor and imperial situation, was discussing secession, as were the New England colonies, who believed that their maritime supremacy made them independent of the rest of the country.

Only the South, led by Washington, was sympathetic with the people beyond the mountains. Washington, with his colossal mind, far-seeing, was the first of his time to conceive the stupendous grandeur that might come to us through western development. He approved strongly of Pitt's plan to crush the western march of the French, and joined Braddock's ill-fated expedition, which his courage and skill alone saved from annihilation. He early surveyed and bought large tracts of land beyond the mountains which, before his death, made him a very rich man. He saw that, to hold these vast possessions together, the States must have easier communication between the East and the West. In 1783, before he had resigned as Commander-in-Chief, he explored the route from the Hudson to Lake Erie—which later became the Erie Canal —and predicted its future development. He sought and explored a waterway westward from the Potomac, which later became the Cumberland Canal. But his project was even more ambitious. He proposed to unite, by water, the Potomac and the Ohio, and the

Baltimore and Ohio Railroad today follows the route he then surveyed.

In 1785 he had become president of a corporation for extending the navigation of the Potomac and James Rivers; and early in that year a joint commission from Virginia and Maryland met at Washington's home, at Mount Vernon, for consultation. But as Washington's scheme involved the head-waters of the Ohio, it was necessary to invite Pennsylvania to join. Washington took the occasion, as an entering wedge, to suggest that Virginia and Maryland should agree upon a uniform system of duties and other commercial regulations, and upon a uniform currency. Nothing could better exhibit the chaos of the Confederation than the fact that these two neighboring States were hampering mutual intercourse by duties and regulations, and by two forms of currency, each of which was at a discount with the other. These suggestions, together with the project for the waterway, were sent to the legislatures of Virginia and Maryland, and promptly adopted. Maryland then suggested that Delaware as well as Pennsylvania ought to be consulted, since the scheme should rightly include a canal between the Delaware River and Chesapeake Bay—which was constructed many years later—and why not join them in the compact for uniform duties, and why not invite commissioners from all the thirteen states to attend such a conference. This very sensible proposal,

186

as it now seems to us, was put forward in the most hesitating, the most deprecating manner. It was suggested that an informal discussion could hurt nobody. It was with such halting steps that the Colonies approached the great conclusion. James Madison, who was known as an ardent nationalist, procured John Tyler, father of the future President, a strong States Rights man, to present the resolution, and it was adopted. Commissioners from all the States were invited to meet at Annapolis on the first Monday in September, 1786. (There has been much confusion among historians as to the origin of the Annapolis Convention. I take the above from "The Critical Period of American History", by John Fiske, which I believe to be the most authentic.) When the convention met at Annapolis, on the 11th of September, 1786, commissioners were present from Virginia, Delaware, Pennsylvania, New Jersey, and New York. Commissioners had been appointed by Massachusetts, New Hampshire, Rhode Island, and North Carolina, who failed to attend. Maryland, which had first moved the matter, sent no commissioner, and no action was taken by Georgia, South Carolina, or Connecticut. With only five States represented, the commissioners contented themselves with adopting an address, written by Alexander Hamilton. It was sent to all the States, urging that commissioners be appointed to meet in convention at Philadelphia on the second Monday of the following May, to strengthen the Federal government. Congress at first rejected Hamilton's address, but before the close of the winter of 1786-1787 it became apparent, even to that moribund body of little intelligence, that the Confederation was in the throes of dissolution, and so, at last, the Congress proposed a convention at Philadelphia identical in every way, including the time, with the one suggested by Hamilton. Such was the origin of the Great Constitutional Convention, which met in Philadelphia in May, 1787.

In the Constitutional Convention, the control of commerce by the new Federal government was one of the bitterly contested questions. Some of the southern States feared that Congress might lay an export duty on their rice and indigo, which were becoming valuable products. They feared that the New England States, with their maritime supremacy, would control ocean carriage, and perhaps monopolize it to their detriment. After the great compromise gave equal representation to every State in the Senate, and brought in the allegiance of the smaller States, this question became paramount. New England desired the immediate abolition of both the slave trade and slavery. Virginia was strongly for abolition, although at that time, she had nearly one-half of all the slaves of the country, 293,000 out of about 600,000. George Mason, then the largest slave owner and the bitterest opponent of slavery, was willing to compromise on the imme-

diate suppression of the slave trade and the total abolition of slavery in 1808.   In one of the most notable
speeches delivered in the convention, in denouncing
slavery, he predicted every evil it would bring to the
nation at large, and to the South particularly.   On the
other hand, it was known that South Carolina and
Georgia would never enter the Union without slavery,
and the overwhelming influence of Rutledge and the
two Pinckneys was felt to be necessary to the adoption
of the Constitution. The Middle States were generally
opposed to slavery.   South Carolina and Georgia made
a "swap" with New England.   By this compromise
Congress was given control over commerce with foreign countries, between the States, and with the Indians, but was forbidden to lay an export-tax, or discriminate between the States and the ports thereof.
The slave trade was to cease in 1808, and slavery was
to be left wholly to the control of the several States.
Possibly this ignoble compromise was necessary, but it
sowed the dragon's teeth of Civil War, created an artificial sectional division that still exists, and left the
South for a hundred years far behind the rest of the
world.   In spite of this very clear provision in the Constitution, its exact meaning and effect remained in
doubt for thirty-five years, until Marshall's decision in
this case.

This case might well have been docketed as the State
of New York vs. the United States.   The interest of

Gibbons and Ogden was contemptible in amount, compared with the vast results that have flowed from this decision. Beveridge thinks it the most important of all Marshall's decisions. Measured by commercial results, it is, but the decision could not have been rendered nor enforced had it not been for Cohen vs. Virginia,[2] giving the Supreme Court appellate jurisdiction over decisions of State Courts where the constitution, laws, or treaties of the United States are involved.

In 1803, Robert Livingston, of New York, then Minister to France who had just negotiated the purchase of the Louisiana territory, witnessed Fulton's first experiment with the steamboat on the Seine. The experiment was made for the French government; but the scientists designated by Napoleon to watch the experiment were not impressed, and the French dropped it. Livingston and Fulton became friends and returned to America together and entered into a partnership, which resulted in the building of the North River (afterwards named the Clermont), which made the first successful steamboat voyage on the Hudson from New York to Albany in August, 1807. As early as 1798 Livingston had procured a 20-year monopoly to navigate the waters of New York by steam vessels. The grant was then considered a huge joke. Livingston had connected with himself, as his agent, one Nicholas J. Roosevelt, a keen, active and capable man, who, in

2. See, ante, Part III, Chapter II.

190

1803, procured an extension of Livingston's monopoly for 20 years. This grant, like the one of 1798, became forfeit and in 1807 it was extended for two years. In 1808 a new monopoly was granted which provided that for each new boat established on New York waters by Livingston and Fulton and their associates, they should be entitled to five years' extension of their grant, the whole term not to exceed 30 years. All other persons were forbidden to navigate New York waters without a license from these grantees, and an unlicensed vessel was forfeit to them.

From the beginning the business was a great success, and highly profitable. The fare from New York to Albany was $7.00, and the Monopoly began immediately operating boats between New York and New Jersey. Roosevelt was dispatched to Pittsburgh, where he built a flat boat and floated down the Ohio and Mississippi to New Orleans, investigating the possibilities of steamboat traffic on that great waterway, interesting the citizens, and, with prudent foresight, purchasing en route a large tract of coal land in Ohio. On his return, the steamboat New Orleans was built at Pittsburgh, and the Mississippi was opened to steam navigation. Roosevelt immediately secured from the legislature of Orleans Territory a monopoly of steam navigation for the lower waters of the Mississippi, which, by force of the situation of the city of New Orleans—the entrepot for the Mississippi and its tributaries—made a practical monopoly on the whole river; a monopoly that was later assured by the legislature of the State. The Monopoly in New York did not go unquestioned. Citizens of New Jersey attempted to operate a ferry between Hoboken and New York, which was forbidden by the New York Monopoly.

In 1811 the New Jersey legislature passed an act of retortion, which authorized the owner of any New Jersey boat seized under the New York law, to capture and hold any steam craft belonging in whole, or in part, to a citizen of New York, which should be forfeited to the New Jersey owner of the boat seized. New York countered with a still more stringent law in favor of the Monopoly. Connecticut forbade any vessel licensed by Livingston and Fulton from entering Connecticut waters. Georgia granted a monopoly for steam navigation on the Savannah River. Massachusetts did the same for her waters. Vermont followed with a monopoly on Lake Champlain, and this commercial warfare between the States was in full swing when Gibbons vs. Ogden came before the Supreme Court of the United States on an appeal from the New York Court of Errors, granting Ogden an injunction against Gibbons. Gibbons was operating a boat between New Jersey landings and Elizabeth Town, in the same State, without securing permission from the New York Monopoly. At the last named point he exchanged passengers with Ogden, who continued the traffic to New York City. Upon an application of the Monopoly, Chancellor Kent exonerated Ogden because he held a license from the Monopoly, but enjoined Gibbons from navigating the waters in the Bay of New York or Hudson River between Staten Island and Powlas Hook. Gibbons immediately began to run his boat between New York and New Jersey in direct competition with Ogden, claiming the right under a Federal coasting license, and the latter applied to Chancellor Kent for an injunction which was granted and upheld by the New York Court of Errors. Appeal was taken by Gibbons to the Supreme Court of the United States, claiming that the New York Monopoly was void, under the commerce clause of the constitution. Gibbons was represented by Wirt and Webster; Ogden, by Oakley, then Attorney General of New York, and Emmet, that great Irish expatriate who made the leading argument for Ogden.

Undoubtedly the argument of Webster in this case was his greatest. Marshall borrows more freely from it, follows more closely his logic than that of any other lawyer in any other case. Emmet argued at great length that the power over commerce was concurrent in the Federal government and the States. That Congress, not having specifically legislated as to the waters of New York, the State had a right to grant the monopoly. Webster declared that the original object sought by the new government was control of commerce. That the Annapolis convention which opened the way for the constitutional convention was called solely to consider the confusion and chaos existing, because of conflicting regulations of commerce in the different colonies. That was the primary object; that concurrent jurisdiction was impossible and was clearly forbidden by the commerce clause of the Federal Constitution.

Marshall states the two questions before the court. First, whether the monopoly is repugnant to that clause in the constitution which authorizes Congress to regulate commerce, or second, to that which authorizes Congress to promote the progress of science and useful arts. The second question while strongly urged in the argument, was rejected and the decision based wholly on the commerce clause. The opinion of the court below had been written by Chancellor Kent, then at the height of his fame, and Marshall at the outset paid this tribute to him.

"It (the decision) is supported by great names—by names which all the titles to consideration that virtue, intelligence, and office can bestow. No tribunal can approach the decision of this question without feeling a just and real respect for that opinion which is sustained by such authority, but it is the province of this Court, while it respects not to bow to it implicitly; and the judges must exercise, in the examination of the subject, that understanding which Providence has bestowed upon them, with that independence which the people of the United States expect from this department of government."

He then once more connotes the distinction between the old confederacy and the new government.

"As preliminary to the very able discussions of the constitution, which we have heard from the bar and as having some influence on its construction, reference has been made to the political situation of these states, anterior to its formation. It has been said that they were sovereign, were completely independent, and were connected with each other only by a league. This is true. But when these allied sovereigns converted their league into a government, when they converted their Congress of Ambassadors, deputed to deliberate on their common concerns, and to recommend measures of general utility, into a legislature, empowered to enact laws on the most interesting subjects, the whole character in which the states appear, underwent a change, the extent of which must be determined by a fair consideration of the instrument by which that change was effected."

He then produced his favorite argument for a liberal construction of the new constitution, in one of those profound and impressive paragraphs that leaves nothing to be added to the argument and nothing to be said by way of answer.

195

"This instrument contains an enumeration of powers expressly granted by the people to their government. It has been said that these powers ought to be construed strictly. But why ought they be so construed? Is there one sentence in the constitution which gives countenance to this rule? In the last of the enumerated powers, that which grants, expressly, the means of carrying all others into existence, Congress is authorized 'to make all laws which shall be necessary and proper' for the purpose. But this limitation on the means which may be used is not extended to powers which are conferred, nor is there one sentence in the constitution which has been pointed out by the gentlemen of the bar, or which we have been able to discern, that prescribes this rule. We do not, therefore, think ourselves justified in adopting it. What do gentlemen mean by a strict construction? If they contend only against that enlarged construction which would extend words beyond their natural and obvious import, we might question the application of the term, but should not controvert the principle. If they contend for that narrow construction which, in support of some theory not to be found in the constitution, would deny to the government those powers which the words of the grant, as usually understood, import, and which are consistent with the general views and objects of the instrument; for that narrow construction which would cripple the government and render it unequal to the objects for which it is declared to be instituted, and to which the powers given, as fairly understood, render it competent; then we cannot perceive the propriety of this strict construction, nor adopt it as the rule by which the constitution is to be expounded. As men, whose intentions require no concealment, generally employ the words which most directly and aptly express the ideas they intend to convey, the enlightened patriots who framed the constitution and the people who adopted it, must be understood to have employed words in their natural sense, and to have intended what they have said. If, from the imperfection of human language, there should be serious doubts respecting the extent of any given power, it is a well-settled rule that the objects for which it was given, especially when those objects are expressed in the instrument itself, should have great influence in the construction. We know of no reason for excluding this rule from the present case. The grant does not convey power which might be beneficial to the grantor, if retained by himself, or which can enure solely to the benefit of the grantee, but is an investment of power for the general advantage, in the hands of agents selected for that purpose; which power can never be exercised by the people themselves, but must be placed in the hands of agents, or lie dormant. We know of no rule for construing the extent of such powers, other than is given by the language of the instrument which confers them, taken in connection with the purpose for which they were conferred."

Quoting the clause of the constitution, "Congress shall have power to regulate commerce with foreign nations and among the several states, and among the Indian tribes," he says: "Our constitution being, as was aptly said at the bar, one of enumeration and not of definition." Webster voiced this at length. Marshall, in these seven words compressed Webster's argument and so briefly sets forth the whole doctrine of the liberal constructionists. The keynote of Marshall's theory of the constitution was that the constitution enumerated the powers granted, but did not define, limit, or constrict them. Nor was it intended to deny to Congress such powers as were necessary or expedient, or proper to carry out, the granted powers, because the constitution expressly granted to Congress whatever is necessary and proper to carry out the enumerated powers.

This argument has been so fully developed in the article on McCulloch vs. The Bank,[3] that I shall not repeat it here.

Considering the meaning of the word "commerce," which, counsel for Ogden had claimed, meant solely the exchange and carriage of goods between the states, Marshall coins his celebrated phrase, "commerce is intercourse." Under this definition commerce has come

---

3. See, ante, Chapter III.

to include not only travel of persons and the carriage of goods, but also the transmission of intelligence. He argued at length that from the fact that the power of Congress to regulate navigation under this clause, has never been denied, that a narrow meaning was not intended to be given to it. That it had been universally admitted that this clause comprehends every species of commercial intercourse between the United States and foreign nations.

"To what commerce does this power extend? The constitution informs us, to commerce 'with foreign nations, and among the several states and with the Indian tribes.'

"It has, we believe, been universally admitted that these words comprehend every species of commercial intercourse between the United States and foreign nations. No sort of trade can be carried on between this country and any other, to which this power does not extend. It has been truly said that commerce as the word used in the constitution is a unit, every part of which is indicated by the term.

"If this be the admitted meaning of the word, in its application to foreign nations, it must carry the same meaning throughout the sentence, and remain a unit, unless there be some plain, intelligible clause which alters it.

"The subject to which the power is next applied is to commerce 'among the several states.' The word 'among' means intermingled with. A thing which is among others is intermingled with. Commerce among the states cannot stop at the external boundary line of each state, but may be introduced into the interior.

"It is not intended to say that these words comprehend that commerce which is completely internal, which is carried on between man and man in a state, or between different parts of the same state, and which does not extend to or affect other states. Such a power would be inconvenient, and is certainly unnecessary.

"Comprehensive as the word 'among' is, it may very properly be restricted to that commerce which concerns more states than one. The phrase is not one which would probably have been selected to indicate the completely interior traffic of a state, because it is not an apt phrase for that purpose; and the enumeration of the particular classes of commerce to which the power was to be extended, would not have been made had the intention been to extend the power to every description. The enumeration presupposes something not enumerated; and that something, if we regard the language or the subject of the sentence, must be the exclusively internal commerce of a state. The genius and character of the whole government seem to be that its action is to be applied to all the external concerns of the nation, and to those internal concerns which affect the states generally; but not to those which are completely within a particular state, which do not affect other states, and with which it is not necessary to interfere, for the purpose of executing some of the general powers of the government. The completely internal commerce of a state, then, may be considered as reserved for the state itself.

"But in regulating commerce with foreign nations, the power of Congress does not stop at the jurisdiction lines of the several states. It would be a very useless power if it could not pass those lines. The commerce of the United States with foreign nations is that of the whole United States. Every district has a right to participate in it. The deep streams which penetrate our country in every direction pass through the interior of almost every state in the Union, and furnish the means of exercising this right. If Congress has the power to regulate it, that power must be exercised whenever the subject exists. If it exists within the state, if a foreign voyage may commence or terminate at a port within a state, then the power of Congress may be exercised within a state."

One of the chief arguments for Odgen upholding concurrent power was the concurrent power of the nation and state to levy taxes, and this was strongly urged by Emmet. Marshall says:

"In imposing taxes for state purposes, they are not doing what Congress is empowered to do. Congress is not empowered to tax for those purposes which are within the exclusive province of the states. When, then, each government exercises the power of taxation, neither is exercising the power of the other. But, when a state proceeds to regulate commerce with foreign nations, or among the several states, it is exercising the very power that is granted to Congress, and is doing the very thing which Congress is authorized to do. There is no analogy, then, between the power of taxation and the power of regulating commerce."

He holds that the state government, in levying taxes, is exercising merely the prerogative of the state. That the levy is no part of the Federal tax, and such levy in nowise interferes with the levy of taxes which support the general government. He concedes that the state may pass inspection laws, laws governing pilotage, and similar local regulations which are within the reserve police power of the state, and when not so unreasonable as to interfere with commerce with foreign nations, or among the states, will be upheld.

The vast and beneficent results of this decision, the uniform regulation of all intercourse with foreign nations, among the states and with the Indians, could not have been imagined, when this decision was handed down in 1824. The steamboat was then supposed to be the last word in transportation. Railroads, telegraphs and telephones were undreamed of. If the New York

Monopoly had been upheld the union would have reverted to the same chaotic, conflicting and even belligerent local regulations, which made commerce between the states enormously difficult, and at times impossible. The unvexed interstate commerce which we have enjoyed under this decision, vastly greater than the foreign commerce of any other nation, owes its growth, its security and its prosperity, to Gibbons vs. Ogden.

CHAPTER V.

The Dartmouth College Case[1]

I have not followed the strict chronology of Marshall's decisions. Gibbons vs. Ogden was later than the Dartmouth College case. I preferred to group together the four great cases, Marbury vs. Madison, Cohen vs. Virginia, Bank vs. Maryland, and Gibbons vs. Ogden, because these four decisions established the power of the Federal government, and are the cornerstones upon which the whole edifice rests.

I turn back now to 1819, to consider the Dartmouth College case. This is the most famous of all Marshall's decisions. It is more widely known among laymen than perhaps any other case in the Supreme Court reports. It has been more praised and more criticized, more blessed and more banned, than any other of his great cases.

Dartmouth College was founded by the Reverend Eleazer Wheelock, who had established on his own estate a school for Indians, that was highly successful. In 1765 he sent Nathaniel Whitaker to England to secure donations. Whitaker secured over eleven thou-

---

1. The Trustees of Dartmouth College v. Woodward, 17 U. S. (4 Wheat.) 518, 4 L. ed. 629, revs'g 1 N. H. 111.

sand pounds, and shortly thereafter the Crown granted to the College a perpetual charter, naming it after the Earl of Dartmouth, who was one of the principal donors. Twelve trustees suggested by Wheelock were named in the charter who had complete and autocratic control of the affairs of the College, with power in a majority to select the successors of any who died or resigned. Wheelock became president and the charter gave him power, at his death, to appoint his successor. He died in 1779, and by his will appointed his son John, who was then but 25 years of age, and had been a colonel of the Revolutionary Army. The College was established on the Connecticut River in Western New Hampshire, and, as the charter provided, open to whites as well as Indians. Large donations of land were given to it, and it speedily became one of the chief seats of learning in New England.

War broke out between the Congregationalists and Presbyterians. Wheelock, the president, and Bellamy, one of the trustees, became bitter enemies. Very shortly the issue became political. The Federalists on one side, the Republicans on the other. A war of pamphlets was waged between the two factions, and the whole state of New Hampshire engaged on one side or the other. Undoubtedly this state of affairs was very injurious to the College.

In 1816, the Republicans being then in power in New Hampshire, a bill was passed for the management of Dartmouth College, which changed the name of Dartmouth College to "Dartmouth University," increased the number of trustees from 12 to 21, nine to be appointed by the governor; established a board of overseers of 21 members, of which the governor and other state officials were ex officio members. The practical effect was to annul the old charter, completely deny the intentions and wishes of Wheelock and the original donors, and make the control of the University completely political. A majority of the old trustees refused to recognize the new government and, when forced to leave the College buildings, kept up their tuition in town, most of the students following them. A suit was brought by the trustees of the College against Woodward, the secretary of the University, in trover, to recover the seal of the College, the original charter and other papers. The Supreme Court of New Hampshire decided in favor of the University. The case was appealed to the Supreme Court of the United States. Holmes, a member of Congress, but a very inferior lawyer, and Wirt, then Attorney General, appeared for the University. Webster and Hopkinson of Pennsylvania, for the College. Webster never appeared in a case where his whole heart and soul were so deeply engaged as this. He loved his College. He was a Federalist and the Republicans were, as he believed, seeking to destroy his Alma Mater.

Although conceding that the court could only consider the question whether the Act of the New Hampshire legislature was invalid under the contract clause of the constitution, Webster devoted the most of his argument to general consideration, arguing that the Act was against abstract justice, against the law of the land, and a denial of a property right, elaborating the early history of the College. His argument on the constitutional phase is brief but masterly. Holmes made a stump speech. Wirt acquitted himself poorly, while Hopkinson, for the College, made one of the best of his great arguments. It developed, in consultation, that the judges were divided. The case was taken under advisement, and was not decided until February, 1819.

Beveridge's story of the case from here on is curious and interesting. Marshall, Story and Washington were for the College. Duvall and Todd were against it, believing the Act valid. Livingston and Johnson were in doubt. Webster, himself, had little confidence in winning the case. This seems strange when we remember that in Terrett vs. Taylor,[2] the court had held that a state could not revoke a private charter, and in Fletcher vs. Peck,[3] it had held that the state could not revoke a grant of land, even though procured by the open corruption of the legislature that passed the Act,

2. 13 U. S. (9 Cr.) 43, 3 L. ed. 650.
3. 10 U. S. (6 Cr.) 87, 3 L. ed. 162.

and in New Jersey vs. Wilson,[4] a contract between New Jersey and certain Delaware Indians, a grant before the Revolution, was held sacred.

Apparently the case hinged on whether the College was a public or private corporation. The whole controversy, in effect, settled on that. If it was a public corporation exercising political power, the legislature could amend or revoke its charter. If it was a private corporation, the court was bound, by its previous decisions, to hold the charter intact.

Webster's argument was printed in pamphlet form, widely circulated and generally approved. Livingston and Johnson apparently consulted Chancellor Kent sometime during that summer, and he endorsed Webster's logic.

The officers of the University, who had expected an easy victory, became alarmed and employed Pinckney, then at the height of his fame. Pinckney let it be known that he intended to ask for a reargument after it had leaked out that the court was divided, some of the judges doubtful. On the first day of the February 1819 term, Pinckney, having spent a week in preparation, appeared to ask that the case be reopened. Marshall aparently not knowing that Pinckney was on his feet and about to address the court, although Beveridge says that his purpose was well known to the chief justice, much to the disgust of Pinckney, calmly proceeded

---

4. 11 U. S. (7 Cr.) 164, 166, 3 L. ed. 303, revs'g 2 W. J. L. (1 Pen.) 300.

to read the judgment in favor of the College, five judges agreeing. After reciting the history of the College and describing its charter, Marshall considers one of the contentions of counsel for the University, that not every contract is covered by the clause of the constitution. He admits this and says: "The provision of the constitution never has been understood to embrace other contracts than those which respect property or some object of value, and confer rights which may be asserted in a court of justice." He holds that the College is possessed of such a right; that the trustees, although serving as such without pay, and without interest save as trustees, could assert this right.

Coming to the nature of the contract he thus states the question:

"If the act of incorporation be a grant of political power, if it create a civil institution to be employed in the administration of the government, or if the funds of the college be public property, or if the state of New Hampshire as a government, be alone interested in its transactions, the subject is one in which the legislature of the state may act according to its own judgment, unrestrained by any limitation of its power imposed by the constitution of the United States.

"But if this be a private eleemosynary institution, endowed with a capacity to take property for objects unconnected with government, whose funds are bestowed by individuals on the faith of the charter; if the donors have stipulated for the future disposition and management of those funds in the manner prescribed by themselves, there may be more difficulty in the case, although neither the persons who have made these stipulations nor those for whose benefit they were made, should be parties to the cause. Those who are no longer interested in the property, may yet retain such an interest in the preservation of their own arrangements as to have a right to insist that those arrangements shall be held sacred. Or, if they have themselves disappeared, it becomes a subject of serious and anxious inquiry, whether those whom they have legally empowered to represent them forever may not assert all the rights which they possessed, while in being; whether, if they be without personal representatives who may feel injured by a violation of the compact, the trustees be not so completely their representatives, in the eye of the law, as to stand in their place, not only as respects the government of the college, but also as respects the maintenance of the college charter.

"It becomes, then, the duty of the court most seriously to examine this charter, and to ascertain its true character."

He then discusses the question of education, the public interest in it; but denies that it is altogether in the hands of the government, or that donations for the purpose necessarily become public property, subject to the will of the legislature. Then comes his famous description of a corporation and its effects.

"Among the most important are immortality, and if the expression may be allowed, individuality; properties by which a perpetual succession of many persons are considered as the same, and may act as a single individual. They enable a corporation to manage its own affairs, and to hold property without the perplexing intricacies, the hazardous and endless necessity, of perpetual conveyances for the purpose of transmitting it from hand to hand. It is chiefly for the purpose of clothing bodies of men, in succession, with these qualities and capacities, that corporations were invented, and are in use. By these means, a perpetual succession of individuals are capable of acting for the promotion of the particular object, like one immortal being. But this being does not share in the civil government of the country, unless that be the purpose for which it was created. Its immortality no more confers on it political power or a political character, than immortality would confer such power or character on a natural person. It is no more a state instrument than a natural person exercising the same powers would be. If, then, a natural person, employed by individuals in the education of youth, or for the government of a seminary in which youth is educated, would not become a public officer, or be considered as a member of the civil government, how is it that this artificial being, created by law, for the purpose of being employed by the same individuals for the same purposes, should become a part of the civil government of the country? Is it because its existence, its capacities, its powers, are given by law? Because the government has given it the power to take and to hold property in a particular form, and for particular purposes, has the government a consequent right substantially to change that form, or to vary the purposes to which the property is to be applied? This principle has never been asserted or recognized, and is supported by no authority. Can it derive aid from reason?"

He then distinguishes between public and private corporations. He defines the former as those, and those only, which exercise political power, and he makes the assertion, somewhat startling to modern ears, that a corporation, not exercising political power, can no more be controlled by the legislature than a private individual, carrying on the same business. The modern assertion of the police power of the state over corporations, has rendered all this portion of the decision entirely obsolete. He then considers the question whether this charter is a contract.

"This is plainly a contract to which the donors, the trustees, and the crown (to whose rights and obligations New Hampshire succeeds), were the original parties. It is a contract made on a valuable consideration. It is a contract for the security and disposition of property. It is a contract, on the faith of which real and personal estate has been conveyed to the corporation. It is then a contract within the letter of the constitution, and within its spirit also, unless the fact that the property is invested by the donors in trustees for the promotion of religion and education, for the benefit of persons who are perpetually changing, though the objects remain the same, shall create a particular exception, taking this case out of the prohibition contained in the constitution.

"It is more than possible that the preservation of rights of this description was not particularly in the view of the framers of the constitution when the clause under consideration was introduced into that instrument. It is probable that interference of more frequent recurrence, to which the temptation was stronger, and of which the mischief was more extensive, constituted the great motive for imposing this restriction on the state legislatures. But although a particular and a rare case may not, in itself, be of sufficient magnitude to induce a rule, yet it must be governed by the rule, when established, unless some plain and strong reason for excluding it can be given. It is not enough to say that this particular case was not in the mind of the convention when the article was framed, nor of the American people when it was adopted. It is necessary to go farther, and to say that, had this particular case been suggested, the language

213

would have been so varied as to exclude it, or it would have been made a special exception. The case being within the words of the rule, must be within its operation likewise, unless there be something in the literal construction so obviously absurd, or mischievous, or repugnant to the general spirit of the instrument as to justify those who expound the constitution in making it an exception."

Story assented, and wrote one of the best of his many opinions. Marshall, as usual, cited no authority. Story's opinion bristles with them, and he uses one illustration, that, unlike most illustrations, is as conclusive as an argument. He says:

"If a grant of land or franchises be made to A, in trust for special purposes, can the grant be revoked and a new grant thereof be made to A, B and C in trust for the same purposes, without violating the obligation of the first grant? If property be vested by grant in A and B, for the use of a college, or a hospital, of private foundation, is not the obligation of that grant impaired when the estate is taken from their exclusive management, and vested in them in common with ten other persons? If a power of appointment be given to A and B is it no violation of their right to annul the appointment, unless it is assented to by five other persons, and then confirmed by a distinct body?

If a bank, or insurance company, by the terms of its charter be under the management of directors, elected by the stockholders, would not the rights acquired by the charter be impaired if the legislature should take the right of election from the stockholders, and appoint directors unconnected with the corporation? These questions carry their own answers along with them."

To measure the effect of this case one must consider the conditions of it. Public and private credit were at a low ebb. Times were hard. Debts loomed large and many were the schemes for their direct or indirect repudiation. Legislatures were passing Stay Laws, Insolvent Acts and depreciating bank notes were destroying the obligation of pecuniary contracts. Marshall was a fanatic on the subject of plighted faith, whether public or private. To him a contract was a sacred thing, and throughout his long career he sternly held to these views, going, in many cases, to extremes, from which the court later retired.

Immediately following this decision, the states began either by their constitutions or legislative enactments, attaching conditions to the charters of every corporation, so that now almost universally a corporation charter may be amended or repealed. So the sacredness of a corporation charter has almost entirely disappeared. The growing police power of the states now regulates, over-regulates, every corporation, public or private, but the decision was of overwhelming importance to capital in protecting its investment, its security and freedom from political control of chartered companies. Much of the extraordinary financial development of the country, for the ensuing half century, is due to this great decision.

CHAPTER VI.

THE CHARLES RIVER BRIDGE CASE[1]

Before Marshall's death, in 1835, the oppressive force of the Dartmouth College case, carried as it was to extravagant lengths by the inferior Federal courts and by some State courts, was severely felt. Improvident grants of exclusive privileges by the Crown, before the Revolution, and by the new states after it, were cramping growing communities and stifling new enterprise. The old turnpike companies, whose roads were falling into decay, but who claimed a monopoly in the territory which they traveled, hung as a threat over the investment of capital in new railroad and canal enterprises. The decision in the Charles River Bridge Case was therefore awaited with the utmost anxiety.

Of the "old court," as it was called, there remained only Thompson and Story. McLean was appointed in 1829, Baldwin in 1830, Wayne in 1834, Barber and Taney in 1836,—all by Jackson. At Marshall's death the Charles River Bridge Case, Briscoe vs. Commonwealth Bank of Kentucky,[2] involving the right of the

---

1. The Charles River Bridge Company v. The Warren Bridge, 36 U. S. (11 Pet.) 420, 9 L. ed. 773, aff'g 24 Mass. (7 Pick.) 344.

2. 34 U. S. (9 Pet.) 85, 9 P. ed. 60.

217

State to permit a state bank to issue bank notes, and the case of New York vs. Miln,[3] involving the right of a state to impose certain restriction on foreign commerce, were left undecided. Of these the Charles River Bridge Case was the most important. It was argued first in 1831. Owing to the absence or disability of two of the judges, and the inability of the remainder to agree upon an opinion by a majority of the court, it was continued.

The case of Green vs. Biddle,[4] which had been decided by a minority of the court, and deprived hundreds of the pioneers of Kentucky, not only of their lands, but of the improvements which they had placed upon them, had subjected the court to the bitterest criticism. Marshall was determined that thereafter there should be no decision in an important case by a divided court, unless the majority agreed. The case was again continued, in 1832 and 1834, and was reargued in January, 1837, Webster and Dutton appearing for the plaintiff in error. The Charles River Bridge Company, and Simon Greenleaf and John Davis, all of Massachusetts, appearing for the defendant in error, the Warren Bridge Company.

The facts in the case were, that in 1650 the legislature of Massachusetts granted to the President of Harvard College, for its benefit, the right to operate a

3. 39 U. S. (11 Pet.) 102, 9 L. ed. 648.
4. 21 U. S. (8 Wheat.) 1, 5 L. ed. 547.

ferry between Charlestown and Boston, by lease or otherwise; and the ferry was so operated. In 1785 a company was incorporated by the name of "The Proprietors of the Charles River Bridge," with a charter giving the corporation power to build and operate a bridge between the two towns, with certain tolls, the company to pay two hundred pounds annually to Harvard College, and at the expiration of forty years the bridge was to be the property of the commonwealth. The bridge was built and operated. In 1792 the charter was extended to seventy years, making its final period 1856. In 1828 the legislature incorporated another company by the name of "The Proprietors of the Warren Bridge," for the purpose of erecting another bridge over the Charles River, sixteen rods from the old bridge where it commenced on the Charlestown side, and about fifty rods from its termination on the Boston side, both bridges deriving their traffic from the public square in Charlestown, in which centered all the roads leading into that village.

The Warren Bridge Company, by the terms of its charter, was to revert to the state, as soon as the expense of building and operating should be reimbursed, the term in any event not to exceed six years. It was admitted during the argument, though not plead, that the proprietors of the Warren Bridge had been reimbursed, that the bridge had become the property of the state, was therefore, a free bridge, and naturally had

219

destroyed the value of the charter and franchise of the old bridge. Here was the clearest-cut kind of a case for the application or refusal to apply the principle of the Dartmouth College Case, the act of the legislature in chartering the new bridge, which subsequently became free of tolls, clearly destroying the value of the old charter and the investment in the bridge. Not only was the charter of the old company in effect annulled and its investment destroyed, but Harvard College was deprived of a considerable income, which had nearly thirty years yet to run.

The opinion is by Taney, the first that he delivered, and it is well to mark the singular clearness and lucidity of his statement of the contentions of the plaintiff in error, as well as the manner in which he grounds the decision upon prior decisions of the old court; he says:

"The plaintiffs in error insist, mainly, upon two grounds: 1st. That by virtue of the grant of 1650 Harvard College was entitled, in perpetuity, to the right of keeping a ferry between Charlestown and Boston; that this right was exclusive, and that the Legislature had not the power to establish another ferry on the same line of travel, because it would infringe the rights of the college; and that these rights upon the erection of the bridge in the place of the ferry, under the charter of 1785, were transferred to, and became vested in 'the proprietors of the Charles

River Bridge'; and that under and by virtue of this transfer of the ferry right, the rights of the bridge company were as exclusive in that line of travel, as the rights of the ferry. 2nd. That independently of the ferry right, the acts of the Legislature of Massachusetts of 1785 and 1792, by their true construction, necessarily implied that the Legislature would not authorize another bridge; and especially a free one, by the side of this, and placed in the same line of travel, whereby the franchise granted to the 'proprietors of the Charles River Bridge' should be rendered of no value; and the plaintiffs in error contend that the grant of the ferry to the college, and of the charter to the proprietors of the bridge, are both contracts on the part of the State; and that the law authorizing the erection of the Warren Bridge in 1828 impairs the obligation of one or both of these contracts."

Having thus stated the contentions of the plaintiff in error, he discusses the result upon the old ferry charter of the granting of the bridge charter, which, with the consent of Harvard College, destroyed the ferry rights, created a new means of travel and a new obligation to the college, and holds that this annulled forever all rights under the old ferry grant, and ends the discussion upon that point.

He then discusses earlier decisions of the court, opinions both by Marshall and Story.

221

"But we are not now left to determine, for the first time, the rules by which public grants are to be construed in this country. The subject has already been considered in this court, and the rule of construction above stated, fully established. In the case of The United States v. Arredondo,[5] the leading cases upon this subject are collected together by the learned judge who delivered the opinion of the court, and the principle recognized, that in grants by the public nothing passes by implication.

"The rule is still more clearly and plainly stated in the case of Jackson v. Lamphire.[6] That was a grant of land by the State; and in speaking of this doctrine of implied covenants in grants by the State, the court use the following language, which is strikingly applicable to the case at bar: 'The only contract made by the State is the grant to John Cornelius, his heirs and assigns, of the land in question. The patent contains no covenant to do, or not to do any further act in relation to the land; and we do not feel ourselves at liberty, in this case, to create one by implication. The State has not by this act, impaired the force of the grant; it does not profess or attempt to take the land from the assigns of Cornelius and give it to one not claiming under him; neither does the award produce that effect; the grant remains in full force; the prop-

5. (8 Pet.) 738.
6. 28 U. S. (3 Pet.) 280, 299, 7 L. ed. 679.

222

erty conveyed is held by the grantee, and the State assents no claim to it.'

"The same rule of construction is also stated in the case of Beaty v. Knowler[7] decided in this court in 1830. In delivering their opinion in that case, the the court say: 'That a corporation is strictly limited to the exercise of those powers which are specifically conferred on it, will not be denied. The exercise of the corporate franchise being restrictive of individual rights, cannot be extended beyond the letter and spirit of the act of incorporation.'

"But the case most analogous to this, and in which the question came more directly before the court is the case The Providence Bank v. Billings & Pittman,[8] and which was decided in 1830."

He quotes the late Chief Justice in the Providence Bank case:

"As the whole community is interested in retaining it undiminished, that community has a right to insist that its abandonment ought not to be presumed, in a case in which the deliberate purpose of the State to abandon it does not appear."

Then comes a striking note, indicative of Taney's future policy on the bench. For the first time "happiness and prosperity of the community," is put to the

7. 29 U. S. (4 Pet.) 152, 168, 7 L. ed. 813.

8. 29 U. S. (4 Pet.) 514, 7 L. ed. 939.

fore, as against vested rights, which had so strong a hold on the old court.

"It may perhaps be said that in the case of The Providence Bank, this court were speaking of the taxing power; which is of vital importance to the very existence of every government. But the object and end of all government is to promote the happiness and prosperity of the community by which it is established, and it can never be assumed that the government intended to diminish its power of accomplishing the end for which it was created. And in a country like ours, free, active and enterprising, continually advancing in numbers and wealth, new channels of communication are daily found necessary, both for travel and trade, and are essential to the comfort, convenience and prosperity of the people. A State ought never to be presumed to surrender this power, because, like the taxing power, the whole community have an interest in preserving it undiminished. And when a corporation alleges that a State has surrendered for seventy years, its power of improvement and public accommodation, in a great and important line of travel, along which a vast number of its citizens must daily pass, the community have a right to insist, in the language of this court above quoted, 'that its abandonment ought not to be presumed in a case in which the deliberate purpose of the State to abandon it does not appear.' "

He comes then to consider the most potent argument against these special privileges, so strongly and firmly insisted upon, under the claimed doctrine of the Dartmouth College Case:

"Indeed, the practice and usage of almost every State in the Union old enough to have commenced the work of internal improvement, is opposed to the doctrine contended for on the part of the plaintiffs in error. Turnpike roads have been made in succession, on the same line of travel; the latter ones interfering materially with the profits of the first. These corporations have, in some instances, been utterly ruined by the introduction of newer and better modes of transportation and traveling. In some cases railroads have rendered the turnpike roads on the same line of travel so entirely useless, that the franchise of the turnpike corporation is not worth preserving. Yet in none of these cases have the corporations supposed that their privileges were invaded, or any contract violated on the part of the State."

He concludes, with what seems to be an irresistible argument against the contention of the old bridge company. Not merely the impolicy and improvidence of such grants, but the practical impossibility of limiting them when once recognized:

"We can not deal thus with the rights reserved to the States; and by legal intendments and mere technical reasoning, take away from them any portion of that power over their own internal police and improvement, which is so necessary to their well-being and prosperity.

"And what would be the fruits of this doctrine of implied contracts on the part of the States, and of property in a line of travel by a corporation, if it should now be sanctioned by this court? To what results would it lead us? If it is to be found in the charter to this bridge, the same process of reasoning must discover it in the various acts which have been passed within the last forty years, for turnpike companies. And what is to be the extent of the privileges of exclusion on the different sides of the road? The counsel who have so ably argued this case, have not attempted to define it by any certain boundaries. How far must the new improvements be distant from the old one? How near may you approach without invading its rights in the privileged line? If this court should establish the principles now contended for, what is to become of the numerous railroads established on the same line of travel with turnpike companies; and which have rendered the franchises of the turnpike corporations of no value? Let it be once understood that such charters carry with them these implied contracts, and give this unknown and undefined property in a line of traveling, and you will soon find the old turnpike corporations awakening from their sleep, and calling upon this court to put down

226

the improvements which have taken their place. The millions of property which have been invested in railroads and canals, upon lines of travel which have been before occupied by turnpike corporations will be put in jeopardy. We shall be thrown back to the improvements of the last century, and obliged to stand still until the claims of the old turnpike corporations shall be satisfied, and they shall consent to permit these States to avail themselves of the lights of modern science, and to partake of the benefit of those improvements which are now adding to the wealth and prosperity, and the convenience and comfort, of every other part of the civilized world. Nor is this all. This court will find itself compelled to fix, by some arbitrary rule, the width of this new kind of property in a line of travel; for if such a right of property exists, we shall have no lights to guide us in marking out its extent, unless, indeed, we resort to the old feudal grants, and to the exclusive rights of ferries, by prescription, between towns; and are prepared to decide that when a turnpike road from one town to another had been made, no railroad or canal between these two points, could afterwards be established. This court is not prepared to sanction principles which must lead to such results."

The opinion is a long one, worthy of the study of every lawyer. I have given the claim of the plaintiff in error, the gist of the argument of the court against

227

it. As Taney's first opinion, as the first decision of the new bench, reconstituted (as his enemies said, "packed") by Jackson, the decision was looked for with the profoundest interest. Of course it provoked the severest criticism on the part of vested interests, and the highest praise from more liberal quarters. It has never been reversed, criticized, or its force in the slightest degree impaired by that court in more than eighty years. It is the foundation of the modern doctrine that a state may not abdicate its police power, which it holds in trust for the happiness and general welfare of all the people. Few decisions have had a more lasting or broader effect than this, the first opinion of Taney.

CHAPTER VII.

THE GENESEE CHIEF[1]

The case of the Genesee Chief, a libel in admiralty, decided in 1851, presents the extraordinary spectacle of the court headed by Taney, expanding the Federal jurisdiction and power, restricted by the old court in The Thomas Jefferson,[2] where it was held that the jurisdiction of the courts of admiralty was limited to the ebb and flow of the tide.

The Cuba, a sailing vessel, was rammed by the Genesee Chief, a steam propeller, on Lake Ontario, and sunk. The owner of the Cuba libeled the Genesee Chief in the District Court of the United States, a proceeding in rem, under the Act of February 26, 1845, extending the jurisdiction of the District Courts in admiralty, to the lakes and navigable waters connecting the same, none of which are tidal waters. Strenuous objection was made to this admiralty jurisdiction of the court, because of the authority of The Thomas Jefferson, and the case carried to the Supreme Court upon that point. The court was confronted at the outset with the authority of The Thomas Jefferson, which follows slavishly the English rule that the ad-

1. The Genesee Chief v. Fitzhughe, 53 U. S. (12 How.) 443, 13 L. ed. 1058.
2. 23 U. S. (10 Wheat.) 428, 6 L. ed. 358.

229

miralty jurisdiction is confined to the ebb and flow of the tide; that only tidal waters are public waters and, under the English law, within the control of the crown. This doctrine has grown up in England with all its concurrences of riparian rights; rights of fisheries, flotsam, jetsam, and the concomitants of public waters. The doctrine was a natural one in England, where in effect there are no navigable streams except tidal waters.

On all the great rivers of England, like the Thames, the Severn, and the Humber, navigation ceases with the tide. Nor at the time the decision was rendered in The Thomas Jefferson, in the days of sail, was any stream with a steady current navigable. On the navigable tidewater rivers vessels generally were compelled to go up with the flood and out with the ebb. The opening of navigation of the great rivers of America, like the Mississippi and Ohio. by the use of steam, had entirely changed conditions. The English law was no longer applicable, but it required courage and foresight to reverse the case of The Thomas Jefferson, which had been the law for almost forty years, and been recognized as such by at least one other decision. But the court held there were no property rights involved in that decision, that it had not become a rule of property and that, therefore, *stare decisis* was not compelling.

There was but one question before the court, whether the Act of 1845, extending the admiralty jurisdiction to waters not tidal in their character was constitutional. The court held that the jurisdiction of the court could not be made to depend upon the commerce clause; that it could only be sustained on the ground that the great lakes and the great rivers of the country, navigable in fact, were navigable in law, as such, public waters under the jurisdiction of the Federal government, and subject to the jurisdiction of the constitutional Federal courts. The court says:

"If this law, therefore, is constitutional, it must be supported on the ground that the lakes and navigable waters connecting them are within the scope of admirality and maritime jurisdiction, as known and understood in the United States when the Constitution was adopted.

"If the meaning of these terms was now for the first time brought before this court for consideration, there could, we think, be no hesitation in saying that the lakes and their connecting waters were embraced in them. These lakes are in truth inland seas. Different states border on them on one side, and a foreign nation on the other. A great and growing commerce is carried on upon them between different states and a foreign nation, which is subject to all the incidents and hazards that attend commerce on the ocean. Hostile fleets have encountered on them, and prizes been

231

made; and every reason which existed for the grant of admiralty jurisdiction to the general government on the Atlantic seas, applies with equal force to the lakes. There is an equal necessity for the instance and for the prize power of the Admirality Court to administer international law, and if the one cannot be established, neither can the other.

"Again the union is formed upon the basis of equal rights among all the States. Courts of admiralty have been found necessary in all commercial countries, not only for the safety and convenience of commerce, and the speedy decision of controversies, where delay would often be the ruin, but also to administer the laws of nations in a season of war, and to determine the validity of captures and questions of prize or no prize in a judicial proceeding. And it would be contrary to the first principles on which the Union was formed to confine these rights to the States bordering on the Atlantic, and to the tidewater rivers connected with it, and to deny them to the citizens who border on the lakes, and the great navigable streams which flow through the western States. Certainly such was not the intention of the framers of the Constitution; and if such be the construction finally given to it by this court, it must necessarily produce great public inconvenience, and at the same time fail to accomplish one of the great objects of the framers of the Constitution; that is, a perfect equality in the rights and the privileges of the citizens of the different states; not only in the laws of the general government but in the mode of administering them. That equality does not exist, if the commerce on the lakes and on the navigable waters of the West are denied the benefits of the same courts and the same jurisdiction for its protection which the Constitution secures to the States bordering on the Atlantic.

"The only objection made to this jurisdiction is that there is no tide in the lakes or the waters connecting them; and it is said that the admiralty and maritime jurisdiction, as known and understood in England and in this country at the time the Constitution was adopted, was confined to the ebb and flow of the tide.

"Now, there is certainly nothing in the ebb and flow of the tide that makes the waters peculiarly suitable for admiralty jurisdiction, nor anything in the absence of a tide that renders it unfit. If it is a public navigable water, on which commerce is carried on between different states or nations, the reason for the jurisdiction is precisely the same. And if a distinction is made on that account, it is merely arbitrary, without any foundation in reason and, indeed, would seem to be inconsistent with it.

"In England, undoubtedly, the writers upon the subject, and the decisions in its courts of admiralty, always speak of the jurisdiction as is confined to tide water. And this definition in England was a sound

233

and reasonable one, because there was no navigable stream in the country beyond the ebb and flow of the tide; nor any place where a port could be established to carry on trade with a foreign nation, and where vessels could enter and depart with cargoes. In England, therefore, tide water and navigable water are synonymous terms, and tide water, with a few small and unimportant exceptions, meant nothing more than public rivers, as contradistinguished from private ones; and they took the ebb and flow of the tide as the test, because it was a convenient one, and more easily determined the character of the river. Hence the established doctrine in England, that the admiralty jurisdiction is confined to the ebb and flow of the tide. In other words it is confined to public navigable waters.

"At the same time the Constitution of the United States was adopted, and our courts of admiralty went into operation, the definition which had been adopted in England was equally proper here. In the old thirteen States the far and greater part of the navigable waters are tide waters. And in the states which were at that period in any degree commercial, and where courts of admiralty were called on to exercise their jurisdiction, every public river was tide water to the head of navigation. And indeed, until the discovery of steam boats, there could be nothing like foreign commerce upon waters with an unchanging current

234

resisting the upward passage. The courts of the
United States, therefore, naturally adopted the English mode of defining a public river, and consequently
the boundary of admiralty jurisdiction. It measured
it by tide water. And that definition having found its
way into our courts, became, after a time, the familiar
mode of describing a public river, and was repeated
as the cases occurred, without particularly examining
whether it was as universally applicable in this country as it was in England. If there were no waters in
the United States which are public, as contradistinguished from private, except where there is tide, then
unquestionably here as well as in England, tide water
must be the limit of admiralty power. And as the English definition was adopted in our courts, and constantly
used in judicial proceedings and forms of pleading borrowed from England, the public character of the river
was in process of time lost sight of, and the jurisdiction
of the admiralty treated as if it was limited by the tide.
The description of a public navigable river was substituted in the place of the thing intended to be described. And under the natural influence of precedents
and established forms, a definition originally correct
was adhered to and acted on, after it had ceased, from
a change in circumstances, to be the true description
of public waters. It was under the influence of these
precedents and this usage, that the case of The Thomas

Jefferson, was decided in this court; and the jurisdiction of the courts of admiralty of the United States declared to be limited to the ebb and flow of the tide. The Steamboat Orleans v. Phoebus,[3] afterwards followed this case, merely as a point decided."

In the case of Waring vs. Clarke,[4] the court had shown a disposition to depart from the doctrine of The Thomas Jefferson, but it was finally decided that the collision there considered was within the limit of tidal waters. The court, as further evidence of contemporary opinion on this point, cited an early Act of Congress:

"It is evident that a definition that would at this day limit public rivers in this country to tide-water rivers is utterly inadmissible. We have thousands of miles of public navigable water, including lakes and rivers in which there is no tide. And certainly there can be no reason for admiralty power over a public tide water, which does not apply with equal force to any other public water used for commercial purposes and foreign trade. The lakes and the waters connecting them are undoubtedly public waters; and we think are within the grant of admiralty and maritime jurisdiction in the Constitution of the United States.

"We are the more convinced of the correctness of the rule we have now laid down, because it is obviously the

3. 36 U. S. (11 Pet.) 175, 9 L. ed. 677.
4. 46 U. S. (5 How.) 141, 12 L. ed. 226.

one adopted by Congress in 1789 when the government went into operation. For the 9th section of the Judiciary Act of 1789, by which the first courts of admiralty were established, declares that the district courts 'shall have exclusive cognizance of all civil causes of admiralty and maritime jurisdiction, including all seizures under the laws of impost, navigation, or trade of the United States, where the seizures are made on waters which are navigable from the sea by vessels of ten or more tons burden, within their respective districts, as well as upon the high seas.'

"The jurisdiction is here made to depend upon the navigable character of the water, and not upon the ebb and flow of the tide. If the water was navigable it was deemed to be public and if public, was regarded as within the legitimate scope of the admiralty jurisdiction conferred by the Constitution."

From that time on, under many circumstances, in many cases, the Supreme Court has consistently approved the case of the Genesee Chief, and held steadfast to the doctrine that navigable in fact is navigable in law; that the true test of navigability and the settlement of rights in connection therewith, depends wholly upon the question whether commerce, as generally understood, is borne upon the waters in question. As corollary to this definition of "public waters" is the inclusion of all rights pertaining to such waters, as for instance, upon a navigable water, the riparian owner owns to the ordinary low-water mark, upon non-navigable streams which are private waters, to the center of the main channel or thread of the stream.

If the stream be navigable, the bed of it belongs to the State, and may not be encroached upon by private parties. The State of Kansas has held that the Arkansas River is navigable in law and that the bed of that stream belongs to the State, and derives a considerable revenue from sand and gravel taken from the stream. This is, however, contrary to the very recent decision of the Supreme Court of the United States, as to the same stream in Oklahoma.

If the rule of The Thomas Jefferson had prevailed, there would have been endless confusion as to all rights upon the great rivers, in the operation of interstate ferries, and the construction of interstate bridges; conflicting jurisdiction in cases of collision, and the like. Under this decision under review all of the navigable waters of the United States are public waters, subject to Federal control, and under the jursidiction of the Federal courts in admiralty. Few decisions have been of greater importance than this.

CHAPTER VIII.

DRED SCOTT VS. STANFORD.[1]

Few men have suffered so bitterly, for a single mistake, as Taney, for the fatal decision in this case. He was a great judge, exalted in character, pure, upright, and learned. His character has been so much misunderstood, his reputation overloaded with calumny, that I pause to give a few little known facts of his life.

He began the practice of law at Fredericktown, Maryland, and immediately took high rank. He was in the Senate of Maryland from 1816 to 1818 and attorney-general of his state from 1827 to 1831, when Jackson appointed him attorney-general of the United States. Jackson had determined upon the removal of the government deposits from the United States Bank, a policy in which Taney heartily concurred. Duane, the secretary of the treasury, refused to remove the deposits, refused to resign his office, was summarily removed, and Taney was invited to take his place. Although reluctant to exchange his professional position for one purely political, he felt called upon to accept what he deemed to be the post of duty, and issued the famous order direct-

1. 60 U. S. (19 How.) 393, 15 L. ed. 691.

ing the collectors of revenue to cease making deposits in the Bank, leaving the amount actually on deposit to be drawn out at intervals.

At that time the Whigs were in the majority in the Senate, and refused to confirm his appointment as secretary of the treasury. Taney retired to private life, returning to his practice in Baltimore. In the following January, Justice Duvall of the Supreme Court, resigned his office in consequence of extreme deafness, and the name of Taney was sent to the Senate to supply the vacancy. It is known that Chief Justice Marshall favored his appointment, but the Senatorial opposition was so strong that it failed of confirmation.

Marshall died in the summer of 1835. Jackson appointed Taney Chief Justice. Clay again labored to defeat the nomination, but was unsuccessful, and the commissions of Taney and Barbour were dated March 15, 1836. Clay, many years later, frankly apologized for his bitter assault on Taney, and sincerely regretted it. He went even further, and declared him a fit successor of Marshall. Taney was in his fifty-ninth year when he was appointed to succeed Marshall, who had served almost thirty-five years.

Probably no chief justice has brought to the position such varied experience, ripe learning, and general knowledge of the law, as Taney had at the time of his appointment. In 1816 he had removed to Baltimore, and thereafter was almost continuously employed in the Supreme Court of the United States, where he contended on equal terms with such lawyers as Webster and Pinckney, and, after Pinckney's death, became the unquestioned leader of the Maryland bar, then, as now, one of the most distinguished in the United States.

In person he was tall and spare of frame, never robust in health, of strong passions and, sometimes, of vehement speech, both of which he learned to control in later years. His style was extraordinarily lucid. Wirt dreaded his "apostolic simplicity," and on one occasion spoke of his "Moonlight mind—the moonlight of the Arctic, with all the light of day without its glare." He was a strong Union man, but a strict constructionist of the Constitution, in opposition to Marshall's view. He was opposed to slavery, and emancipated his own slaves. He was the only lawyer in Maryland who would defend a Northern Methodist Minister, charged with inciting the slaves of Maryland to insurrection, and was for a time extremely unpopular. In the course of his argument in that case he said:

"Hard necessity compels us to endure the evil of slavery for a time, but while it continues, it is a blot on our national character."

In many ways he was the antithesis of his predecessor, and something of this was due to their difference in education. Marshall was a soldier of the Revolution, a man grown when it broke out. He saw the chaos in government that followed the Revolution, and the utter futility of the Congress of the Confederation. He passed through the "crisis of American history." A Federalist in politics, he naturally believed in a strong central government. He was determined that the United States should be a nation and not a loose confederacy, as its predecessor had been. To that end Marshall bent his extraordinary genius for statesmanship, as well as the law. He brought little legal learning to the bench. He relied largely upon Story for that, but his profound and original mind attacked the new problems that were presented to the infant government and the infant court with absolute certainty. Story said of himself that when he wrote an opinion he proceeded from headland to headland of decided cases, but that Marshall set his compass and put straight out to sea.

Marshall was a man of robust constitution, a natural farmer, a great land speculator, of convivial habits, with hosts of friends. He enjoyed the rough work of riding on his circuits; the long journeys, the stay at rude taverns, the converse with the common man. Taney was dignified; abstemious in his habits, reserved, making few friends. He was scholarly, thoughtful; a profound and diligent student. During much of his life he was in feeble health. His eyesight was never good, and towards the last, very bad. By nature and training he was a strict constructionist, but he was never a pro-slavery man. Some of the strongest

242

opinions in the Supreme Court Reports against disunion and for the Constitution were written by Taney.

Marshall occupied the bench for almost thirty-five years; Taney for more than twenty-eight years. The terms of the two comprise almost one-half the life of the court. Nor can it be doubted, upon an examination of the whole of this record, that this country was extremely fortunate in having Marshall first and Taney succeeding. Marshall laid broad and deep the foundation of the Union, but he had established principles that, if carried too far, would have tended to centralization of government and monopolistic control of all public utilities. In Taney, and his brethren on the bench, a majority of whom had been appointed by Jackson, the pendulum swung the other way towards more freedom from government, less centralization, and greater power to the States.

In Ableman vs. Booth,[2] there is a striking opinion by the Chief Justice upon the supremacy of the Federal Constitution and its laws, which has never been surpassed by any of Marshall's decisions. He said:

"Nor is there anything in this supremacy of the General Government or the jurisdiction of its judicial tribunals to awaken the jealousy or offend the natural and just pride of State sovereignty. Neither this government nor the powers of which we are speaking, were forced upon the States. The Constitution of the

---

2. 59 U. S. (18 How.) 479, 15 L. ed. 465.

243

United States, with all the powers conferred by it on the General Government, and surrendered by the States, was the voluntary act of the people of the several States, deliberately done for their own protection and safety against injustice from one another; and their anxiety to preserve it in full force in all its powers, and to guard against resistance to, or evasion of its authority on the part of a State, is proved by the clause which required that the members of the State Legislatures, and all Executive and Judicial officers of the several States (as well as those of the General Government), shall be bound by oath or affirmation to support this Constitution. . . . Now it certainly can be no humiliation to a citizen of a Republic to yield a ready obedience to the laws as administered by the constituted authorities. On the contrary, it is among his first and highest duties as a citizen, because free government cannot exist without it; nor can it be inconsistent with the dignity of a sovereign State to observe faithfully, and in the spirit of sincerity and truth, the compact into which it voluntarily entered when it became a State of this Union. On the contrary, the highest honor of sovereignty is untarnished faith, and certainly no faith could be more deliberately and solemnly pledged than that which every State has plighted to the other States, to support the Constitution as it is, in all its provisions, until they shall be altered in the manner which the Constitution itself prescribes."

In 1856, when the Dred Scott Case came before the court, Taney had been on the bench twenty years. He was then in his seventy-ninth year, his faculties unimpaired, his reputation at its height. He had conquered all prejudices that existed against him; he was universally admired and trusted by the Bar, and time had mellowed the asperities of his character. Instead of growing more aloof on the Bench, as many judges do, he had grown more human. There is a little anecdote that illustrates that fact.

In 1855 Jeremiah Black, then at the height of his fame, was arguing a case for the plaintiff in error before the court. He made a very extended argument, copiously illustrated with decisions. When he sat down, it lacked fifteen minutes of the recess. Judah P. Benjamin, then of New Orleans and later of London, was on the opposing side. Chief Justice Taney suggested that as the time was limited his argument might be deferred until after lunch. Benjamin said fifteen minutes was all the time he needed, and he would conclude his argument before the court rose. He talked ten minutes. He cited no authorities, read from no law books. He merely stated the facts and the law of the case, with that marvelous lucidity which gave him the unique distinction of being one of the leaders of the American Bar, and later of the English Bar. When the court rose, Taney and Black walked out together. Taney put his arm around Black's shoulder and said

245

to him: "Jerry, that little Jew has stated you out of court."[3]

If Taney had died or retired from the Bench in 1856, his fame would have been second only to that of Marshall. The current of life ran smoothly between its banks with no premonition of the dread abyss into which it was about to plunge.

Dred Scott was a slave in Missouri, the property of Dr. Emerson, a surgeon and officer of the army, a servant of the United States. In 1834 Emerson was ordered to the military post of Rock Island, in the free state of Illinois, and took Scott with him. He remained on duty there two years, and was then ordered to Fort Snelling, Minnesota, then in the territory of Wisconsin, but on the west bank of the Mississippi River in the upper portion of the Louisiana Purchase, and there remained two years more. While at Rock Island he purchased a negro woman, Harriet, from a brother officer, and with his consent Scott and Harriet were married. In 1838 Emerson returned to Missouri, taking Scott and his wife with him. On the steamboat,

---

3. This anecdote is attributed to Judge Field by Pearce Butler, in his life of Field. Of course this is a mistake. Field was not appointed until 1863, at which time Benjamin was Secretary of War in the Confederate Cabinet. Upon Lee's surrender, he fled to London, where he became a Queen's counsellor and a leader of the English Bar. The anecdote was related to me by one who overheard it as he walked out of the court room behind Taney and Black, my old preceptor, Judge Claughton of Alexandria, Virginia, who knew both men well.

246

Gypsy Queen, a child was born to the Scotts at a time when the boat was north of the parallel of thirty-six degrees and thirty minutes, and north of the State of Missouri. A second child was born to them in Missouri. Scott brought suit for his freedom in the Supreme Court of Missouri and failed.[4] After Emerson's death Mrs. Emerson married Dr. Chaffee, an abolition congressman, and transferred Scott and his family to her brother Sandford, a resident of New York, apparently for the purpose of giving jurisdiction to the Federal court, and in 1853 Scott began suit in the Circuit Court of the United States for the District of Missouri against the defendant Sandford, in trespass, claiming that Sandford had unlawfully restrained him and his wife and two children of their liberty, whereby they had suffered great damage in their persons and in their earnings. Counsel for defendant filed a plea in abatement to the jurisdiction, in which it was alleged that the plaintiff was "a Negro of African descent, whose ancestors were of pure African blood, and were brought into this country and sold as Negro slaves." Observe, it is not stated that the plaintiff was a slave, but that he was of African descent and descended from slaves, that he was a "free man of color," as the expression was then, and it was around this proposition that much of the controversy, both in the case itself and in the public discussion of it, raged. To this plea in abate-

4. Dred Scott v. Emerson, 15 Mo. 576.

ment the plaintiff filed a demurrer, which was sustained by the lower court. The defendant then answered over and set up the fact that the plaintiff and his wife and two children were slaves. Upon the trial the facts were agreed substantially as I have set them forth above; the court thereupon found for the defendant and the plaintiff appealed.

The case was argued in the early spring of 1856. Taney, Wayne, Daniel and Campbell thought that the plea in abatement was good, that a free man of color could not maintain an action in the Federal court. Catron agreed but held that because the plaintiff's demurrer to the plea in abatement was sustained that the plaintiff could not allege error upon this; but he agreed with the preceding four, and with Grier and Nelson, making seven, that Scott, as a slave, could not maintain the action, and that his removal to Rock Island and later to Fort Snelling, whatever its effect, was nullified by his return to the slave state of Missouri, which left him in his former status.

In the course of the discussion among the justices, it developed that six of the justices believed that the Missouri compromise was unconstitutional, and that Congress had no power to exclude slavery from the Louisiana Territory. Wayne conceived the brilliant idea that here was a chance to settle the whole Kansas-Nebraska question, whose fierce animosities were driving the country into civil war; that a judgment of the

Supreme Court of the United States, in which six of the justices should agree, would be received by the people of the United States as conclusive, and the legal matter being thus settled, there would be nothing left for the politicians to fight over. Taney in a fatal hour agreed.

This is Carson's account of it. Warren claims that Wayne had discovered that McLean and Curtis had injected the Missouri Compromise into their dissenting opinions, and that it was necessary for the majority to meet it. It was agreed that Taney should write the opinion of the court, as Nelson did not agree with the other six on the invalidity of the Missouri Compromise. The case was set down for reargument and was submitted in the fall of 1856 upon all of the questions involved in the record. The final decision was handed down on March 6, 1857, two days after Buchanan's inauguration, which of itself gave rise to much criticism.

I proceed now to an examination of these various opinions, as briefly as possible. The Chief Justice considered that there were three questions to be decided in the case: First, the status of the plaintiff as a free man of color; second, on the whole record, it appearing that he was a slave, the effect upon his status as a slave by his removal with his master to Rock Island, in the free state of Illinois; third, the effect of his removal to Fort Snelling, in the Louisiana Territory, which involved the right of Congress to enact the Missouri Compromise, forbidding slavery north of the line of 36°30'.

Upon the first question Taney's opinion is elaborate. He discusses the condition of the colored race throughout the world at the time the Constitution was adopted; that they were everywhere considered an inferior people, subject to be seized and sold as slaves, a practice carried on by the citizens of all the European nations, and particularly those of Great Britain. It was in the course of this discussion that he used the phrase that a Negro "had no rights that a white man was bound to respect." This was not Taney's opinion. He was simply describing accurately the view held by the white men of the world as to the Negro in 1776. That it was not his view is shown by his entire life, by his opinion of slavery, and the emancipation of his own slaves. But this phrase was torn from its context and published as the opinion of a majority of the Supreme Court of the United States; and one can imagine with what fury the free soil men of the north seized upon it as an argumentative weapon. He admitted that in five of the colonies at that time the free Negroes were permitted to vote, but he held that did not make them citizens of the United States; that the white men who formed the Constitution, many of them large slave holders, never intended to receive as political equals

250

this servile race, inferior in intelligence and incapable of self-government.

But the fact that the Negro might not have been a citizen of the United States is not all of the question. His right to sue depends upon another question.[5] One need not necessarily be a citizen to have access to state and federal courts. In many states aliens are permitted to own property, and wherever they are they have access to all the courts to protect that property; and an alien not a citizen may sue in the Federal court.[6] It seems to me the acid test is whether the free Negro was empowered to own property. If he was, he must be given access to the courts; otherwise, his property rights are a mockery. Anyone might trespass upon his property or deprive him of his personal rights, and he would have no remedy. This was Madison's view; that the free negro, while not a citizen of the United States in a political sense, was entitled to access to the courts whenever he had a right to own property under the state law.

Curtis' argument was that inasmuch as in five States at the beginning of our government the Negroes were voters, they were citizens and entitled to all the privileges and immunities of all the other citizens in other States, that, therefore, a free Negro could sue in a

5. Hepburn v. Ellzey, 6 U. S. (2 Cr.) 445, 2 L. ed. 332; Brown v. Strode, 9 U. S. (5 Cr.) 303, 3 L. ed. 108.

6. Mossman v. Higginson, 4 U. S. (4 Dall.) 12, 1 L. ed. 720.

federal court upon his property rights; but here is another curious thing about this amazing case; conceding that a free Negro in New York was a citizen of that state, entitled to own property and have access to its courts, that, therefore he was entitled by the privileges and immunities clause to have access to the courts of every other state, or to the federal courts, for the protection of his property rights, that had nothing to do with Dred Scott, who alleged he was a citizen of Missouri. Conceding that the federal constitution established no citizenship, as Curtis claimed, and that it depended upon state law, the natural inquiry was, what was the status of the plaintiff in the state in which he was a citizen, Missouri? The astonishing thing is that neither side inquired as to that, or referred to it in the remotest way. Missouri had been a slave-holding state for thirty-six years. It is unquestionable that there must have been something in its constitution or statutes fixing the status of the free Negro. Either he was entitled to hold property in Missouri, with access to the courts to protect it, or he was not; but we are left ignorant as to that status. It was conceded that if Dred Scott was a slave at the time of bringing the suit, he had no standing in court. The question then recurred upon the effect of his removal with his master to and stay in the free state of Illinois, and two years in the Louisiana Purchase territory, north of the Missouri Compromise.

Upon this point Curtis, one of the ablest lawyers of his time, a very great judge, who quit the court in a huff after this decision, is hardly fair. The law of Ilinois provided that a slave owner who came to Illinois and became a resident, bringing his slaves with him, thereby emancipated them; but the constitution used the word "resident," and an Illinois court had distinctly held that this did not apply to a sojourner, or a person passing through with his slaves.[7] Curtis ignored this decision. Again—Curtis was unfair in this. It was conceded that Emerson, the then owner of the plaintiff, was an officer of the United States Army, a servant of the government; that he was sent to the military post at Rock Island, and remained there two years, simply in the course of his duty; that he was then sent to Fort Snelling, still in the service of his government, temporarily, and acquired no home. Curtis said that residence was to be presumed from personal presence. There is no such decision in the world. Residence is determined by two things; personal presence and intention to establish a residence. One is not presumed from the other. Both are questions of fact, arising frequently in the question of registration, wills, rights of dower, taxation, etc., and the burden is upon him who asserts the residence; but all courts, without exception, except from this principle army officers, who are birds of passage, residing on the

7. Willard v. People, 5 Ill. (3 Scam.) 461.

soil owned by the United States, with no fixed residence.

Coupled with this question was the other of the effect of the return of the plaintiff to Missouri. Assuming that he might have asserted his right to freedom in the free state of Illinois, or while at Fort Snelling, in the territorial court of Wisconsin, which had the same law that Illinois had, what was the effect of his return to Missouri? Curtis argued he could not have returned voluntarily because he was a slave. He cites a number of cases where slaves were held to be freed by their master becoming a resident of a free state. He cites a Maryland case, but the Maryland statute simply provided that when a resident of another state comes to Maryland, bringing his slaves with him, that his slaves become free. Maryland, in effect, prohibited slave trade within its borders without prohibiting it locally. Upon that point Chief Justice Shaw, of Massachusetts, one of the greatest judges America has produced, who certainly cannot be accused of any prejudice toward slavery, in Commonwealth vs. Ames,[8] held that where the slave did not raise the point on free soil, but returned to the slave state, he had waived his right.

Assuming that Scott and his wife were slaves, were compelled to return from Fort Snelling to Missouri,

_____
8. 35 Mass. (18 Pick.) 193.

the state of their servitude, there was never an hour for four years that he might not by habeas corpus have asserted his claim, either in Illinois or the territory of Wisconsin. Much stress was laid by Curtis and Mc-Lean upon the Somerset case,[9] decided by Lord Mansfield in England, in 1775, where a slave was brought to England by his master, and by the decision of Lord Mansfield given his freedom. Sheridan flamboyantly paraphrased this decision: "That the air of England was such that no man could breathe it and remain a slave." Mansfield held that freedom was the natural state of mankind; that slavery could only exist by virtue of positive municipal law, and as there was no such law in England, Somerset was free while on English soil.

In the later case of the slave Grace[10] who was held a while in England and later returned to Antigua, a slave territory, Lord Stowell, while upholding the decision in Somerset case, held that the plaintiff, by returning to Antigua, had waived her right.

Curtis failed to cite a single case where temporary residence freed the slave, or where it was held that the slave might maintain his status as a free man after he had returned to the slave state.

I speak of Curtis' opinion particularly, because it was the only dissenting opinion worthy of notice.

9. 20 Howell's State Trials 79.
10. 2 Hazard Admiralty Reports 94.

McLean was a very old man; had been on the bench for twenty-seven years, and his opinion is purely free soil propaganda. There is a tone of incoherent passion running all through that deprives it of any judicial value. He denounces slavery with the utmost vehemence, which, of course, has nothing to do with the case.

Upon this point, then, seven of the judges agreed in the opinion that the temporary sojourn of the plaintiff's master, either in Illinois or Fort Snelling, did not free him, because the sojourn was temporary. Second, that having returned to Missouri, a slave state, he had waived his right, could not there assert it, and that as a slave he could not sue in any court upon a property right. The case was at an end. There was nothing more except to affirm the final decision of the lower court, that there was no difference between his being held at Fort Snelling in the Louisiana purchase, and in Illinois, a free state. So far as the rights of the plaintiff were concerned, the Missouri Compromise had no more to do with his status and standing in court, and his rights in the case, than the rule in Shelley's case. Taney makes a long argument to show that in the Federal court, the rule is not the same as in the State court, and that they were compelled to explore the whole record. He cites no authority, while Curtis cites some very conclusive authority against that view.

The question then recurred upon the validity of the Missouri Compromise, which had already been repealed, upon the field that apparently both parties were anxious to accept as the scene of the sham battle,—the status of slavery in the territory of the United States.

The Chief Justice attempted to establish some shadowy distinction between the territory owned by the United States at the adoption of the Constitution, and territory acquired later,—a distinction too tenuous for me to grasp. Curtis argued that because of the Ordinance of 1787, passed by the Congress of the Confederation, which declared all of the Northwest territory forever free, an Ordinance afterwards acted upon by Congressional legislation under the new Constitution, that therefore Congress had plenary power as to slavery over the territory of the United States. The argument utterly lacked foundation. When Virginia, in 1784, conveyed to the Continental Congress the Northwest territory, the Congress attempted to pass this Ordinance, which failed by a few votes. In 1787 it was passed and referred back to Virginia. Virginia promptly accepted this condition as part of the cession, and the Congress accepted it in trust for the new government, which was soon to be formed. In effect, this condition was attached to the grant. It was a covenant that ran with the land, and the new Congress, by appropriate legislation, merely effectuated the covenant, exercising no legislative power. This was so thoroughly understood that when, in 1802, Georgia ceded the territory that afterwards became Alabama and Mississippi, the cession was silent on the question of slavery, because all public men at that time believed that Congress had no power to prohibit slavery in the territory.

Lincoln, in his Cooper Union speech, derived no such argument from the Ordinance of 1787. He cited it to show how the Fathers felt on the question of slavery.

Of all the arguments upon this subject, there is only part of one that stands out, and that is the last ten pages of Taney's opinion, holding that Congress had no power to forbid slavery in the Louisiana purchase. It is in his best styled, brief, lucid and convincing. The tone is lofty, free from partisan bias, a clear-cut legal argument that will carry conviction to any lawyer who reads it. His argument is simply this:

The Constitution recognized slavery. True, by an euphuism. It spoke of "persons held to service," but everybody knew that meant slavery, and the fugitive slave law flatly spoke of them as slaves. If a slave fled from his master he could be reclaimed on free soil. If he was abducted and taken to a free state, he could be reclaimed. His title in court was the same as a horse or ox. He was a chattel the same as a mule or a cow; nothing more, nothing less. Curtis argued that the fugitive slave law constituted an exception; that slavery could only exist by municipal law, and where there was no municipal law there could be no slavery, but time and again slaves who fled to the United States men-of-war were returned to their masters, because the men-of-war were federal soil for the time being, and the federal constitution recognized slavery.

This argument broadened itself into Taney's supreme conclusion, which was this:

The Constitution recognized slavery, recognized the right and title of the slave owner, just as it recognized the right and title of a northern owner of a horse or mill. The Louisiana Purchase was bought with the common treasure of all the people of the United States, north and south. It was paid for by general taxation of all the people of the United States. It was policed by the general government at the expense of all the people. It was surveyed at the expense of all the people; its lands were opened to settlement and purchase by all the people. In short, it was bought and held in trust until it reached the status of statehood, for the benefit of all the people of the United States equally. Congress, therefore, had no right to discriminate and distinguish between the classes of citizens, between those whose property was in slaves and those whose property was in cattle or machinery in a mill; that when Congress undertook to forbid slavery in the Louisiana Purchase north of 36° 30', and north of the

Missouri line, it practically forbade those whose property was in slaves to settle there. It deprived them of their interest and heirship in this great territory. It discriminated between them and those whose property was in other forms; that the right to such distinction could not be found in the Constitution; that to say to the slave owner that when he crossed the line of 36° 30′ he must leave his slaves behind or have them emancipated was to deny him equal protection with a northern man who owned cattle. In effect, it opened the country for settlement to the north and closed it for settlement to the south.

The decision was received with execration by a large portion of the people of the North. Its extra-judicial character, its apparent intended political effect, and the time at which it was delivered, combined to reduce the respect for the court to its lowest point before or since. It was no more extra-judicial than the mandamus part of Marbury vs. Madison, or the main part of Cohen vs. Virginia. It was the time and the occasion that denounced the decision. "It was worse than a crime; it was a blunder."

Lincoln, the fairest partisan of his time, did not hesitate to charge a conspiracy between Roger Taney, Stephen Douglas and James Buchanan. The North saw in it the entering wedge for the further extension of slavery. The South realized that the North would never consent to the extension of slavery beyond its then boundaries; that the growing wealth and power of the North would inevitably be reflected in Congress, in the White House and on the Supreme Bench, and it drew the sword. From the hour of the decision, the Court declined in repute and influence. Before Taney's death he saw the entire personnel of the Bench change. The appointment of Clifford in 1858, who became a Republican, and the appointment by Lincoln of Swayne, Davis, Miller, and Field, made the court Republican.

In 1861 Taney rendered his last decision, sitting in circuit, in the case of Ex Parte Merriman,[11] in which he issued a writ of habeas corpus for the delivery of Merriman, who was held by the military arm. The writ was refused. Bates, Lincoln's Republican attorney-general, rendered an opinion that the executive was not bound by the decision of the Supreme Court in constitutional questions, but must interpret the constitution for himself,—a doctrine that Jackson had announced in 1831, when Taney was his attorney-general. It is astonishing now that a Republican attorney-general should have ever uttered such a doctrine, but it will be found in Opinions of the Attorneys-General.

From that time on Taney never sat on the Bench, nor participated in the work of the court. He refused

11. See 3 Warren's Supreme Court in United States History 90-96. Taney's doctrine in Merriman Case upheld in Milligan's Case. See, post, Chapter IX.

to resign, and held tenaciously to his seat, hoping, no doubt, that he might out-live Lincoln's term, and his successor be appointed by a Democrat, as seemed probable in the summer of 1864. In fact, this was so well known that in the spring of 1864, when defeats of the Union Armies, and general dissatisfaction with the burdens of the war, made it probable that Lincoln would be defeated and McClellan, if nominated, elected, rough old Ben Wade, of Ohio, said to some of his associates: "No man ever prayed to the Almighty as hard as I did that Taney might outlive Jeemes Buchanan; and now I guess, by God, I have overdone it."

Taney died after the October elections of that year had demonstrated that Lincoln would be re-elected. He was a great and good man, who made one fatal mistake. He lived too long.

CHAPTER IX.

IN RE MILLIGAN[1]

The situation of the Federal Government during the Civil War was unique in one respect. Throughout the North, and particularly in the Border States, there was strong sympathy with the South. Many upheld slavery. Many believed that the South had a right to secede, and that the North had no right to prevent secession by force of arms. In the Border States sentiment was almost equally divided between the two hostile camps. It resulted that no nation in time of war was ever so permeated with open and secret hostility, with treason and espionage, as was the Federal territory. Powerful secret organizations were formed that enrolled men, procured arms, and threatened open insurrection. There was a constant stream of spies crossing the lines with important information. It was apparent that even the departments in Washington, charged with the conduct of the war, were honeycombed with disloyalty. Plans of campaigns were known to the battle leaders of the South almost as soon as formed. Many of the tragic incidents of battles, like Fredericksburg, with its terrible slaughter, were

---

1. 71 U. S. (4 Wall.) 2, 18 L. ed. 281.

due to advance information of the Federal plans. Foes within were almost as numerous as those without.

Great numbers of the disloyal were arrested by the Military Arm, incarcerated in military prisons, and denied a trial in court. Military Tribunals were constituted to try the accused by drum-head court-martial, without deference to the right of a trial by jury. President Lincoln, very early, in effect suspended the writ of habeas corpus, not by a general or open proclamation, but by refusing to surrender the prisoners under the writ.

There was a notable instance in 1861, when Chief Justice Taney, sitting at Circuit at Baltimore, issued a writ of habeas corpus to the commander of Fort McHenry, for the production of one Milligan, held there by the Military Arm. The officer, acting under the instructions of the President, refused to produce his prisoner or make return on the writ. Again a storm of obloquy overwhelmed the aged Chief Justice. Northern papers denounced him as a traitor who deserved to be hung. Five years later, in the above case, the Supreme Court of the United States approved his action by declaring that in all cases it was the duty of the court, upon proper application, to issue the writ; that neither the President's action nor the Act of March 3, 1863, suspended the issuance of the Writ, but merely excused obedience to it, and Taney was fully justified by this decision.

Of all the rights that the English-speaking people have cherished, none is dearer than this great Writ of Right. That, and trial by jury, are the two sacred bulwarks of Anglo-Saxon freedom. At a time when the other nations of Europe were prostrate at the foot of thrones stained with every crime, when personal liberty was a phrase unknown to either the Lay or Ecclesiastical power, our ancestors had wrested from their monarchs, at the sword's point, these two guaranties of human freedom.

No act of Lincoln's was so bitterly condemned by his opponents in the North, so fiercely denounced as the virtual suspension and denial of this great Writ. It required all of that iron firmness that inhered beneath the great President's kindliness, to lay a violating hand upon this sacred ideal. He believed that the time demanded it, that he had a constitutional right, for the protection of the very life of the Republic, to deal with these offenses with the swiftness that only the Military Arm could employ.

In many localities, like Baltimore and Louisville, it would have been impossible to secure a jury that would render an unanimous verdict of guilty in such cases, such was the division of public sentiment. Nevertheless, many of Lincoln's warmest supporters doubted his constitutional power to suspend the Writ. They believed that it could only be done by Congress, and that congressional action was necessary to the validity of these Military arrests and trials. Accordingly the act of March 3, 1863, authorized the President to suspend the Writ anywhere in the United States, but required that lists of all persons arrested should be delivered to the United States Circuit Courts of the district before the next term, in order that indictments might be found against them and trials had in the ordinary course if the courts were open. It provided further, upon the failure of the Grand Jury to indict, that twenty days after the Grand Jury had been discharged, the accused might sue out a Writ of habeas corpus and procure his discharge.

The President, in September, 1863, issued a proclamation suspending the Writ generally throughout the United States, but the law was silent as to the Military Tribunals, which had been constituted and were trying offenders summarily.

Such was the condition when a Military Tribunal of the district of Indiana, under General Hovey, the commander, in November, 1864, arrested Milligan, charged him with treason, with giving aid and comfort to the enemy, with inciting insurrection in Indiana, and other crimes. He was summarily tried and sentenced to be hung on May 19, 1865. On the 10th day of May he sued out a Writ of habeas corpus, and upon a hearing, the circuit judges being divided, they certified the questions involved to the Supreme Court of the United States.

The case was very ably argued by Attorney-General Speed, Stanberry of Ohio, whom Johnson appointed to the Supreme bench, but who was not confirmed, and Benjamin F. Butler for the Government; by former Attorney-General Jeremiah S. Black, James A. Garfield, later President, and David Dudley Field for the Petitioner.

One of the curious things in the case was the suggestion gravely made by the counsel for the government, that the case had become moot. As Milligan was sentenced to be hung on May 19, 1865, (the case was argued in April, 1866), it was to be presumed that the officers charged with his execution had performed their duty, and that the Petitioner was very, very dead. The court, with equal gravity, said that it had no judicial information as to whether Milligan was dead or alive, but it would not presume that the eminent counsel who appeared for the Petitioner would be there representing a dead man. As a matter of fact, President Johnson had postponed the execution on May 10, 1865, the day the Writ issued, and in June commuted his sentence to imprisonment for life. He was discharged, under the order of the Supreme Court in April, 1866, immediately brought suit against General Hovey in the State Court, and upon removal to the Federal Court, recovered nominal damages, and disappears from history.

267

Although the judgment of the Court discharging the Petitioner was rendered in April, the opinion of the court was not delievered until December, 1866, by Judge David Davis. Judge Davis had been a Democrat before the war, and was serving on the circuit bench in Illinois when appointed to the Supreme Court by Lincoln, in 1862. He was a close personal friend of Lincoln, the administrator of his estate and an ardent Union man. He was considerably afflicted by the political bee. He was much opposed to the radical policies of the Republican leaders, and very open in expressing his opinion. He was nominated for President in 1872 by the Union Labor party on a Greenback platform, because of his strong support of the Legal Tender Acts. He accepted the nomination formally, but failing to receive the endorsement of the Liberal Republican party, declined to run. In 1877 he was elected to the Senate from Illinois by a combination of Greenbackers and Democrats, defeating John A. Logan, and resigned from the bench. He acted in the Senate generally with the Democrats where, upon the death of Garfield and the accession of Arthur, as President of the Senate, he became the acting Vice-President. He was not particularly distinguished for ability or learning. His opinions lacked finish. The best of all of them is his opinion in this case.

The court was unanimously agreed that Milligan should be discharged, because he had not been presented or indicted by the Federal Grand Jury under the act of 1863. Davis, Field, Nelson, Grier and Clifford, further held that Congress was incompetent, under the Constitution to establish Military Tribunals, and try persons by Military law except where an actual state of war existed and the courts were closed. To this part of the opinion the Chief Justice Chase, joined by Miller, Swayne and Wayne, dissented. The crux of this dissent was in the then political situation. The radical Republican leaders were fighting President Johnson. While the courts in the South were open and functioning, and the state governments were being restored, there was much lawlessness and acts of violence all over the South, against the negroes lately emancipated. It was claimed that the operations of the Federal Government were impeded and its authority defied. That the local courts were either powerless to suppress this lawlessness, or were in sympathy with it; that in effect in many parts of the South this lawlessness amounted to an insurrection against the authority of the Federal government, which justified Martial Law.

The radical leaders were planning to establish government by Military Commissions throughout the South, to suppress these acts of violence, this general lawlessness. The effect would have been the rule of a large part of our country by Martial Law. The decision of these five judges, while practically dictum, because it was not necessary to the decision of the case, produced the 15th Amendment. Unable to protect the negro with Federal bayonets, the radicals gave him the ballot for self-protection. The effect of this dictum was as profound, as far-reaching in its results, as any decision the Supreme Court has ever rendered.

Judge Davis said:

"No graver question was ever considered by this court nor one which more nearly concerns all the rights of the whole people, for it is the birthright of every American citizen when charged with crime to be tried and punished according to law. . . . . . The Constitution of the United States is a law for rulers and people equally, in war and in peace and covers with the shield of its protection all classes of men at all times and under all circumstances."

Again commenting upon the contention of the government, he uses this violent expression, highly characteristic:

"But it is insisted that the safety of the country in time of war demands that this broad claim for Martial Law shall be sustained. If this be true it could be well said that a country preserved at the sacrifice of all the cardinal principles of liberty is not worth the cost of preservation."

Chief Justice Chase, voicing the sentiments of the four dissenting judges, said:

"We concur also in what is said of the writ of habeas corpus and of its suspension with two reservations: (1)

That in our judgment when the writ is suspended the Executive is authorized to arrest as well as to detain. (2) That there are cases where the privilege of the writ being suspended, trial and punishment by Military Commission in States where Civil Courts are open may be authorized by Congress as well as arrest and detention:

The Chief Justice said further:

"What we do maintain is it is within the power of Congress to determine in what States or districts such great and imminent public danger exists as justifies the authorization of Military Tribunals for the trial of crimes and offenses against the discipline or security of the army, or against the public safety. . . . We cannot doubt that in such a time of public danger Congress had power under the Constitution to provide for the organization of a Military Commission and for trial by that Commission of persons engaged in this conspiracy. The fact that the Federal Courts were open was regarded by Congress as a sufficient reason for not exercising that power, but the fact could not deprive Congress of the right to exercise it. The courts might be open and undisturbed in the execution of its functions and yet wholly incompetent to avert threatened danger, to punish with adequate promptitude and certainty the guilty conspirators. . . . In times of rebellion and civil war it may often happen indeed that Judges and Marshals will be in

271

active sympathy with the rebels, and courts their most efficient allies."

This voiced the view of the radical leaders in Congress. Upon that view they had determined to erect Military Governments in the southern states, although the "Civil Courts were open."

Generally the opinion, with its magnificent defense of human liberty and Anglo-Saxon land-marks, was hailed with approval. The dictum of the five, which condemned in advance the establishment of Military Tribunals in the South, was bitterly criticized by a few. The case has stood as the guide to presidential action and limitation upon presidential powers in time of war. The presidents at such times may suspend the Writ of habeas corpus throughout the United States. While the courts must still issue the Writ the presidential proclamation is an answer to it. But where the courts are open and functioning, the accused must be presented for indictment to the next Grand Jury and tried with all the forms of law, including the right to a jury. Only in territory which is actually the theater of war, where the courts are closed, where "inter arma silent leges" may Military commissions try and summarily punish offenses against the government without indictment before a court, or trial to a jury.

CHAPTER X.

THE LEGAL TENDER CASES[1]

The decision in the Legal Tender cases is now of little practical interest to working lawyers. With the credit of our government superior to that of any the world ever saw, with every paper dollar at par with gold; the right of the government to make its paper money Legal Tender is of no present importance, but the cases are of profound historical interest. Not more than two or three other cases have excited such bitter animosity, such praise and condemnation, or so completely arrayed the entire country into two hostile camps, one upholding, the other condemning, the decisions which first held the Legal Tender Act invalid, then valid.

In February, 1862, the government was at its wits' end for funds, and the country was almost without a circulating medium, as gold had retired into hiding. State bank bills were greatly discredited and more or less at a discount, no matter how good the bank of issue when presented in another state. Congress,

---

1. Hepburn v. Griswold, 75 U. S. (8 Wall.) 603, 19 L. ed. 513, aff'g 2 Div. (Ky.) 20; over'ld Knox v. Lee, 79 U. S. (12 Wall.) 457, 20 L. ed. 287, aff'g 96 Mass. (14 Allen) 94; Juillard v. Greenman, 110 U. S. 421, 28 L. ed. 204, 4 Sup. Ct. Rep. 122.

therefore, began the issuance of paper money. The question arose whether this paper, which contained merely an indefinite promise to pay in specie, not at any particular time, could be made to circulate on the faith of the government, or whether the Legal Tender quality could lawfully be imparted to it, and would that quality help its circulation and the maintenance of its value.

Secretary Chase, afterwards Chief Justice, then believed that the government had the inherent power to make these bills Legal Tender, and that it would help the circulation of the bills and the maintenance of their value. This view was acquiesced in by the president and the rest of the cabinet, and by a majority in Congress. Accordingly, these bills were made a Legal Tender for all debts, public or private, except customs duties and interest on the public debt. It was thought that by collecting the customs in gold, sufficient gold could be secured to pay the interest on the public debt, and there was, and that would help the flotation of the government's enormous bond issues. This paper money, with the guarantee of the government back of it, used in the payment of taxes, local and federal, and of all debts, became very popular. Enormous quantities of it were issued. The total stood at one time at eight hundred million dollars. Of course, creditors whose contracts had been made before the passage of the Act demanded gold. It seemed inequitable that the man who had borrowed gold should be permitted to pay his obligation in paper, depreciated at times to less than forty per cent of par. New contracts made referably to this paper money stood on a different footing. Many suits were brought seeking to enforce the payment of debts in gold. The courts of Last Resort of fifteen states upheld the validity of the Legal Tender Act, and compelled creditors to accept payment in paper. The sixteenth, Kentucky, in the case of Hepburn vs. Griswold, where the debt was contracted prior to February 25, 1862, refused to compel the creditor to accept payment in green backs, and held that the debt must be paid in gold. The case was appealed to the Supreme Court of the United States and argued in December, 1869, decided February 7, 1870. At that time there were but eight members of the court, and at the outset they were equally divided, four for the validity of the Act and four against it. Judge Grier, who was about to retire under the new Retiring Act, changed his mind and agreed with the Chief Justice; Field, Nelson and Clifford holding the Act invalid, while Judges Miller, Swain, and Davis dissented. The opinion was not delivered until February 7th after Grier had retired, but the Chief Justice stated that he was authorized by Judge Grier to say that the retiring Judge had concurred in the decision holding the Act invalid.

Properly speaking, only one question was before the court; that is, was the Act effectual as to contracts executed before its passage, but the opinion of the court went far beyond this, and held that the government could not make its paper money Legal Tender in payment of any debt, whether contracted before or after the enactment of the law. The country immediately divided into two factions, the creditor class, small but very powerful, commending and upholding the decision, and the debtor class, furiously denouncing it. Immediately creditors began to demand payment of debts in gold, no matter whether contracted when gold was the only currency, or after the Act, when the paper money had greatly depreciated. Gold was then at a premium of one hundred and twenty, and the decision added twenty per cent to every debt in the country at a time when the rapid deflation of the currency was already reducing the price of everything, crippling the debtor-class, and paving the way for the terrible panic of 1873.

On February 7th, the very day on which the decision was made, the appointments to the two vacancies by President Grant, of Strong of Pennsylvania and Bradley of New Jersey, were sent to the Senate, thus restoring the bench to its full membership of nine.

On March 25th, four days after the confirmation of the new judges, Attorney-General Hoar moved that the two Legal Tender cases, Latham vs. United States and Deming vs. United States, then pending, and which involved contracts made after the passage of the Act, be taken up for argument. This disclosed a purpose to seek a rehearing of so much of Hepburn vs. Griswold as referred to these subsequent contracts. A very unusual scene followed. It had been stated that Evarts, who was Attorney-General when Hepburn vs. Griswold was argued, had agreed that the Latham and Deming cases should abide the result of the other case. Attorney-General Hoar denied that there had been any such agreement or order. Chief Justice Chase interrupted him to say that there had been such an order. Judge Miller replied that he knew of no such order; both judges speaking with apparent feeling on the matter. Judge Nelson supported the Chief Justice, and Davis concurred with Miller. The Chief Justice reiterated his statement with great emphasis and apparent passion. Judge Davis said it was idle to bandy words, and the cases went over.

On April 25, 1870, these two cases were dismissed, but on April 30, 1870, the case of Knox vs. Lee,[2] which had been argued in November, 1869, was set down for reargument. In this case Lee had sued Knox for the value of sheep which had been confiscated by the Confederate Government under its Alien Enemy Act, and sold to Knox. The question was raised that the jury should take into consideration in

2. 79 U. S. (12 Wall.) 457, 20 L. ed. 287, aff'g 96 Mass. (14 Allen) 94.

fixing the recovery, the fact that the recovery would be had in depreciated money. The court instructed the jury that the Legal Tender Act was valid, so the case was again brought before the court upon this very point, with the intention of reconsidering the authority of Hepburn vs. Griswold.

Returning to the opinion in Hepburn vs. Griswold, the Chief Justice first takes up the question of the inequity of compelling a creditor who had loaned gold worth par to receive in payment paper money depreciated at times to forty per cent of its face:

"Now it certainly needs no argument to prove that an Act, compelling acceptance, in satisfaction of any other than stipulated payment, alters arbitrarily the terms of the contract and impairs its obligation, and that the extent of impairment is in the proportion of the inequality of the payment accepted under the constraint of the law to the payment due under the contract. Nor does it need argument to prove that the practical operation of such an Act is contrary to justice and equity. It follows that no construction which attributes such practical operation to an Act of Congress is to be favored, or indeed to be admitted, if any other can be reconciled with the manifest intent of the Legislature.

"We confess ourselves unable to perceive any solid distinction between such an Act and an Act compelling all citizens to accept, in satisfaction of all contracts for money, half or three-quarters or any other proportion less than the whole value actually due, according to their terms. It is difficult to conceive what Act would take private property without process of law if such an Act would not.

"We are obliged to conclude that an Act making mere promises to pay dollars a legal tender in payment of debts previously contracted, is not a means appropriate, plainly adapted, really calculated to carry into effect any express power vested in Congress; that such an Act is inconsistent with the spirit of the Constitution and that it is prohibited by the Constitution."

The case of McCulloch vs. Maryland,[3] had stood for more than eighty years as a complete and final definition of implied power. It was cited by the majority and minority; the majority, as authority that the power here contended for cannot be implied because it was not necessary; the minority citing it to prove that, among different measures which might be taken to effectuate an express power, the choice lies with Congress. It is not for the Judiciary to say whether some other measure might have been more adapted to the end; it is sufficient that it is in some manner adapted, and appropriate to the end sought.

This decision has been considered at length in one of these articles, but I will quote again Marshall's celebrated definition of implied power:

3. 17 U. S. (4 Wheat.) 316, 4 L. ed. 579,—discussed, ante, Chapter III.

"Let the end be legitimate, let it be within the scope of the Constitution, and all means which are appropriate, which are plainly adapted to that end, which are not prohibited, but consistent with the letter and spirit of the Constitution, are constitutional."

The Chief Justice then argues that the Legal Tender quality of the notes added nothing to their value, the demand for them and quality of circulation, and did not in any degree tend to maintain their value at or near par. I leave the answer to that to Judge Miller. The Chief Justice undoubtedly anticipated that he would be criticized because he held invalid an act which he had sanctioned while Secretary of the Treasury. He said:

"It is not surprising that amid the tumult of the late Civil War, and under the influence of apprehensions for the safety of the Republic almost universal, different views, never before entertained by American statesmen or jurists, were adopted by many. The time was not favorable to considerate reflection upon the constitutional limits of legislative or executive authority. If power was assumed from patriotic motives, the assumption found ready justification in patriotic hearts. Many who had doubted yielded their doubts; many who did not doubt were silent. Some who were strongly averse to making government notes a legal tender felt themselves constrained to acquiesce in the views of the advocates of the measure. Not a few who then insisted upon its necessity, or acquiesced in that view, have, since the return of peace, and under the influence of the calmer time, reconsidered their conclusion, and now concur in those which we have just announced."

It seems to me that the first part of the majority decision is clearly sound. To compel a creditor to accept payment in depreciated money, in effect, perhaps one-half of what he had loaned, is clearly inequitable, and it would seem that the fifth amendment, "due process of law," covers the Act in that respect. It is true that there is no prohibition against the Federal Government adopting an enactment that violates the obligation of a contract. That explicit prohibition applies only to the states, but good morals and honesty should restrain a government like ours from thus fleecing a large class of its citizens, the creditor class. However, outside of its written promises which it keeps with exactness, our government is not notorious for keeping faith with its creditors at large. It held the money derived from the French Sholiation Claims for fifty years before it disbursed any of it, and many creditors having just claims against this fund died in poverty, because the government was unjust. Over and over again Congress has refused to appropriate money justly due, and on the other hand has paid extravagantly, creditors who had a pull with the law-making body. In truth, payment

281

by the United States is like kissing, it goes by favors. Upon the other hand, it would have been equally inequitable to compel the debtor who borrowed depreciated money, to pay money worth par. The Chief Justice appears not to have considered that side of it.

I pass now to the minority opinion, written by Judge Miller, which in Knox vs. Lee became the majority opinion and settled the law. As the minority held that the Act was valid regardless of whether the contract was entered into before or after its passage, its opinion touches very lightly on the question of good faith. There is a dispute merely as to whether. under the definition given by Marshall in McCulloch vs. Maryland, the Legal Tender provision was necessary, appropriate or fairly conduced to carry out the power to raise money. Judge Miller begins with a lively picture of the condition of the government on February 25, 1862, when the Act became a law:

"All the ordinary powers of rendering efficient the several powers of Congress above mentioned had been employed to their utmost capacity and with the spirit of the rebellion unbroken, with large armies in the field unpaid, with a current expenditure of over a million of dollars per day, the credit of our government nearly exhausted, and the resources of taxation inadequate to pay even the interest on the public debt, Congress was called on to devise some new means of borrowing money on the credit of the nation; for the result of the war was conceded by all thoughtful men to depend on the capacity of the government to raise money in amounts previously unknown. The banks had already loaned their means to the treasury. They had been compelled to suspend the payment of specie on their own notes. The coin in the country, if it could all have been placed within the control of the Secretary of the Treasury, would not have made a circulation sufficient to answer army purposes and army payments, to say nothing of the ordinary business of the country. A general collapse of credit, or payment and of business seemed inevitable, in which faith in the ability of the government would have been destroyed, the rebellion would have triumphed, the States would have been left divided, and the people impoverished. The National Government would have perished, and, with it, the Constitution which we are now called upon to construe with such nice and critical accuracy.

"That the Legal Tender Act prevented these disastrous results and that the tender clause was necessary to prevent them, I entertain no doubt.

"It furnished instantly a means of paying the soldiers in the field, and filled the coffers of the commissary and quartermaster. It furnished a medium for the payment of private debts, as well as public, at a time when gold was being rapidly withdrawn from circulation and the state bank currency was becoming worthless. It furnished the means to the capitalist of buying bonds of the government. It stimulated trade, revived the drooping energies of the country, and restored confidence to the public mind.

"The results which followed the adoption of this measure are beyond dispute. No other adequate cause has ever been assigned for the revival of government credit, the renewed activity of trade, and the facility with which the government borrowed, in two or three years, at reasonable rates of interest, mainly from its own citizens, double the amount of money there was in the country, including coin, bank notes and the notes issued under the Legal Tender Acts."

Discussing the effect of the legal quality so impressed upon these notes, he continued:

"But when by law they were made to discharge the function of paying debts, they had a perpetual credit or value, equal to the amount of all the debts, public and private, in the country. If they were never redeemed, as they never have been, they still paid debts at their par value, and for this purpose were then, and always have been, eagerly sought by the people. To say, then, that this quality of legal tender was not necessary to their usefulness, seems to be unsupported by any sound view of the situation.

"Certainly it seems to the best judgment that I can bring to bear upon the subject that this law was a necessity in the most stringent sense in which that word can be used. But if we adopt the construction of Chief Justice Marshall and the full court over which he presided, a construction which has never to this day been overruled or questioned in this court, how can we avoid this conclusion? Can it be said that this provision did not conduce towards the purpose of borrowing money, of paying debts, of raising armies, of suppressing insurrection? Or that it was not calculated to effect these objects? Or that it was not useful and essential to that end? Can it be said that this was not among the choice of means, not the only means, which were left to Congress to carry on this war for national existence?

"Let us compare the present with other cases decided in this Court.

"If we can say judicially that to declare, as in the case of The United States vs. Fisher, that the debt which a bankrupt owes the government shall have priority of payment over all other debts, is a necessary and proper law to enable the government to pay its own debts, how can we say that the legal tender clause was not necessary and proper to enable the government to borrow money to carry on the war?

"The creation of the United States Bank, and especially the power granted to it to issue notes for circulation as money, was strenuously resisted as without constitutional authority; but this court held that a bank of issue was necessary, in the sense of that word as used in the Constitution, to enable the government to collect, to transfer and to pay out its revenues.

"It was never claimed that the government could find no other means to do this. It could not then be denied, nor has it ever been, that other means more clearly within the competency of Congress existed, nor that a bank of deposit might possibly have answered without a circulation. But because that was the most fitting, usual and efficient mode of doing what Congress was authorized to do, it was held to be necessary by this court. The necessity in that case is much less apparent to me than in the adoption of the legal tender clause."

He sums up the whole matter, in a manner worthy of John Marshall:

"Upon the enactment of these legal tender laws they were received with almost universal acquiescence as valid. Payments were made in the legal tender notes for debts in existence when the law was passed, to the amount of thousands of millions of dollars, though gold was the only lawful tender when the debts were contracted. A great if not larger amount is now due under contracts made since their passage, under the belief that these legal tenders would be valid payment.

"The two houses of Congress, the President who signed the bill, and fifteen state courts, being all but one that has passed upon the question have expressed their belief in the constitutionality of these laws.

"With all this great weight of authority, this strong concurrence of opinion among those who passed upon the question, before we have been called to decide it, whose duty it was as much as it is ours to pass upon it in the light of the Constitution, are we to reverse their action, to disturb contracts, to declare the law void, because the necessity for its enactment does not appear so strong to us as it did to Congress, or so clear as it was to other courts?

"Such is not my idea of the relative functions of the legislative and judicial departments of the government. When there is a choice of means the selection is with Congress; not the court. If the act to be considered is in any sense essential to the execution of an acknowledged power, the degree of that necessity is for the Legislature and not for the court to determine. In the case in Wheaton, from which I have already quoted so fully, the court says that 'Where the law is not prohibited, and is really calculated to effect any of the objects intrusted to the government, to undertake here to inquire into the degree of its necessity, would be to pass the line which circumscribes the Judicial Department, and to tread on legislative ground. This court disclaims all pretenses to such a power.' This sound exposition of the duties of the court in this class of cases, relieves me from any embarrassment or hesitation is the case before me. If I had entertained doubts of the constitutionality of the law, I must have held the law valid until those doubts became convictions. But as I have a very decided opinion that Congress acted within the scope of its authority, I must hold the law to be constitutional, and dissent from the opinion of the court."

It is not worth while to examine the opinion in Knox vs. Lee, written very ably by Judge Strong. It adds nothing to the minority opinion in Hepburn vs. Griswold. It holds, without reservation, the Legal Tender Act valid and applied to all contracts executed before or after the date of the Act. The two new judges, Strong and Bradley, concurred with the minority three who had dissented before. A howl went up that President Grant had packed the court to reverse Hepburn vs. Griswold. That statement has been so often disproven that it is not necessary to discuss it here.

My personal opinion is that the majority opinion in Knox vs. Lee, upholding the sovereign power of the United States to make its paper money Legal Tender, a power inherent in every other sovereignty in the world, is absolutely sound; but I think it should have been restricted to contracts made after the Act was passed. That portion of the decision which compelled creditors who loaned gold to take their payment in depreciated paper, is a stain upon the good faith of the government, and a blot on the records of the Supreme Court. But the Legal Tender cases were not yet completed.

In Juillard vs. Greenman,[4] decided March 3, 1884, the matter again came before the Supreme Court as to United States notes issued in 1878, in time of peace, which were made Legal Tender. The former decision had considered the matter largely from the standpoint of war necessity, but in the last named case, eight of the nine judges then on the bench held that the government had power to make its notes Legal Tender, whether issued in war or in peace. Judge Field, the dogged old fighter, went down with his flag nailed to the mast, and wrote a very bitter opinion in which, as usual, he predicted destruction of the country if his opinion did not prevail.

This case settled for all time and beyond dispute the right of the government to impart to its currency the Legal Tender quality.

4. 110 U. S. 421, 28 L. ed. 204, 4 Sup. Ct. Rep. 122.

CHAPTER XI.

THE SLAUGHTER HOUSE CASES[1]

The career of Samuel Freeman Miller, Justice of the Supreme Court from 1862 till his death in 1890, is unique. He was born in 1816, reared on a farm in Kentucky, clerked in a drug store where he studied medicine, and was a practicing physician for ten years. He did not turn to the bar until he was thirty-one years old, being admitted in Kentucky, in 1847. He loathed slavery, and in 1850 removed to Iowa, where he helped to form the Republican party of that State, and became its leader. He could have had any office in the gift of the people of Iowa, but steadily refused. In 1862, there being two vacancies on the Supreme Bench, the entire bar of Iowa and its judiciary, without regard to party, presented his name to Lincoln, who knew him thoroughly, and he was appointed in July of that year. When appointed he was in his forty-seventh year, and had been at the bar but fifteen years. He was to hold office twenty-eight years, through another very critical and formative period of the Constitution; the post-bellum period, having to do with all the tremendous conflict of reconstruction,

---

1. 83 U. S. (16 Wall.) 36, 21 L. ed. 394, aff'g 22 La. Ann. 545.

negro suffrage, Civil War Amendments, and the enormous growth and development of railroad corporations and their regulation. He wrote more opinions than any Judge who ever sat on that bench, more than seven hundred in all, running through seventy volumes. He wrote more constitutional opinions than any Judge, living or dead. In my opinion he was the ablest Judge who ever sat on the bench with one exception, Marshall, whom he much resembled. He was a pronounced Federalist of Marshall's school, believing in a strong national government, but with the keenest solicitude for the rights of the States and that balance of power which the Founders established. He had the same massive logic as Marshall, overwhelming, unanswerable, conclusive. Marshall at his best was the greatest Judge who ever sat on any bench, at his worst where he was not interested, he was turgid, verbose and discursive. Miller always goes straight to the point, direct, concise, wasting no words. His power to seize and marshal the essential facts, to state them clearly, is extraordinary. On the Circuit, as a trial Judge, he was probably the best loved of all American Judges. His patience, his unfailing courtesy to every lawyer, young and old, his consideration for litigants and witnesses, high or low, and above all his keen sense of justice, his ability to find the kernel in every case, made him the idol of his bar. A strong partisan and union man, the South never had a stronger friend, and not one of his numerous opinions shows the slightest tinge of partisanship. There was something in him of the homely ruggedness of Lincoln, and the two understood and loved each other.

I am glad to pause in these articles to pay this tribute to one of the greatest of Judges, whose character and work are too little appreciated. He justly regarded his decision in the Slaughter-House Cases as his greatest work. It is well that he did not live to see it surreptitiously annulled, not reversed.[2]

There were three of these cases decided in April, 1873, all involving the same question, the validity of an act of the legislature of the state of Louisiana, which had conferred upon the Crescent City Live-Stock Landing and Slaughter House Company the exclusive right to receive and slaughter live-stock for the city of New Orleans and certain parishes connected therewith. The right was given to butchers to slaughter live-stock at the slaughter-house established by this Company, for a reasonable charge and use of the facilities. The Act was passed by the "carpet-bag" legislature of Louisiana, and it was more than suspected that it was procured in part by corruption. Theretofore the landing and slaughter of live-stock had been indiscriminate and unregulated, and, however the Act was passed, its sanitary purpose was approved by the court; but it was claimed that it created

2. See, post, Part III, Chapter XV.

an illegal monopoly, threw many persons out of their occupation as butchers, destroyed their business, and deprived them of their property without "due process of law," under the Fourteenth Amendment. Thus, for the first time, this Amendment which, in the last few years, has received almost as much consideration at the hands of the courts as all the rest of that venerable instrument, was brought to the attention of the Supreme Court of the United States. Judge Miller, who wrote the opinion, thus notes the importance of the question:

"We do not conceal from ourselves the great responsibility which this duty devolves upon us. No questions so far reaching and pervading in their consequences, so profoundly interesting to the people of this country, and so important in their bearing upon the relations of the United States and of the several states to each other, and to the citizens of the states and of the United States, have been before this court during the official life of any of its present members. (Since 1858.)"

He takes up then the question of the object and purposes of the Fourteenth Amendment. He couples it with the Thirteenth and Fifteenth:

"The most cursory glance at these articles discloses a unity of purpose, when taken in connection with the history of the times, which cannot fail to have an important bearing on any question of doubt concerning their true meaning. Nor can such doubts, when any

293

reasonably exist, be safely and rationally solved without a reference to that history; for in it is found the occasion and the necessity for recurring again to the great source of power in this country, the people of the States, for additional guarantees of human rights; additional powers to the Federal Government; additional restraints upon those of the States. Fortunately that history is fresh within the memory of us all, and its leading features, as they bear upon the matter before us, free from doubt."

He discusses slavery, its part in the provocation of the Civil War, and the history of these Amendments. Speaking of the Thirteenth Amendment, he says:

"To withdraw the mind from the contemplation of this grand yet simple declaration of the personal freedom of all the human race within the jurisdiction of this government—a declaration designed to establish the freedom of four millions of slaves—and with a microscopic search endeavor to find in it a reference to servitudes, which may have been attached to property in certain localities, requires an effort, to say the least of it."

He then discusses the meaning of the word "servitude," and shows by the word "involuntary," it was clearly intended to apply solely to personal servitude and not to servitude connected with or attached to property. He shows that, in spite of this Amendment, many of the Southern States lately in rebellion and recently reconstituted, were passing laws which in effect, reduced the black man to a condition worse than his former servitude. They were forbidden to appear in towns in any other character than menial servants. They were required to reside on and cultivate the soil without the right to purchase or own it. They were excluded from occupations of gain, and were not permitted to give testimony in the courts in any case where a white man was a party. These drastic and unjust laws aroused the party then in control of the government. Judge Miller said:

"These circumstances, whatever of falsehood or misconception may have been mingled with their presentation, forced upon the statesmen who had conducted the Federal Government in safety through the crisis of the rebellion, and who supposed that by the 13th Article of amendment they had secured the result of their labors, the conviction that something more was necessary in the way of constitutional protection to the unfortunate race who had suffered so much. They accordingly passed through Congress the proposition for the 14th Amendment, and they declined to treat as restored to their full participation in the Government of the Union the States which had been in insurrection, until they ratified that article by a formal vote of their legislative bodies.

"Before we proceed to examine more critically the provisions of this amendment, on which the plaintiffs in error rely, let us complete and dismiss the history of the recent amendments, as that history relates to the general purpose which pervades them all. A few years' experience satisfied the thoughtful men who had been the authors of the other two Amendments that, notwithstanding the restraints of those articles on the States, and the laws passed under the additional power granted to Congress these were inadequate for the protection of life, liberty and property, without which freedom to the slave was no boon. They were in all those States denied the right of suffrage. The laws were administered by the white man alone. It was urged that a race of men distinctively marked as was the negro, living in the midst of another and dominant race, could never be fully secured in their person and their property without the right of suffrage.

"Hence the 15th Amendment, which declares that 'the right of a citizen of the United States to vote shall not be denied by any State on account of race, color, or previous condition of servitude.' The negro having, by the 14th Amendment, been declared to be a citizen of the United States, is thus made a voter in every State of the Union.

"We repeat, then, in the light of this recapitulation of events, almost too recent to be called history, but which are famliar to us all and on the most casual examination of the language of these amendments, no one can fail to be impressed with the one pervading purpose found in them all, lying at the foundation of each, and without which none of them would have been even suggested; we mean the freedom of the slave race, the security and firm establishment of that freedom, and the protection of the newly made freeman and citizen from the oppressions of those who had formerly exercised unlimited dominion over him. It is true that only the 15th Amendment, in terms, mentions the negro by speaking of his color and his slavery. But it is just as true that each of the other articles was addressed to the grievances of that race, and designed to remedy them as the fifteenth."

It had been strongly contended that the amendment, by its own terms, was not restricted to the negro, but was intended to cover every class of persons whether black or white. It had been generally held, prior to the Fourteenth Amendment, that no person was a citizen of the United States unless he was a citizen of a particular state. Citizenship was a state matter. Each state regulated its own citizenship. That this amendment established a new citizenship, independent of state regulations, was quite clear. Judge Miller shows that these three amendments were parts of a common purpose; the Thirteenth freed the negro, the Fourteenth made him a citizen, placed him under the protection of the Federal Government, and secured his life and liberty from the injustice of the states, the Fifteenth gave him the suffrage. Having thus demonstrated the object and purpose of the Fourteenth Amendment as a part of a comprehensive plan, Judge Miller, admitting that the Thirteenth Amendment would cover Mexican Peonage, or the Chinese Coolie Labor System, if these developed into slavery, says:

"But what we do say, and what we wish to be understood, is that in any fair and just construction of any section or phrase of these amendments, it is necessary to look to the purpose which we have said was the pervading spirit of them all, the evil which they were designed to remedy, and the process of continued addition to the Constitution until that purpose was supposed to be accomplished."

He then discusses, at considerable length and with profound fairness, the contention of the plaintiffs in error that the amendment, in its beneficent purpose, should not be restricted to the colored men alone, but that, under it, whenever a state enactment deprived any individual of life, liberty, or property without "due process of law," the Federal Courts should take jurisdiction and declare such enactment void. To which Judge Miller answered:

"It would be the vainest show of learning to attempt to prove by citations of authority, that up to the adoption of the recent Amendments, no claim or pretense was set up that those rights depended on the Federal Government for their existence or protection beyond the very few express limitations which the Federal

Constitution imposed upon the states—such, for instance, as the prohibition against ex post facto laws, bills of attainder, and laws impairing the obligation of contracts. But with the exception of these and a few other restrictions, the entire domain of the privileges and immunities of citizens of the states, as above defined, lay within the constitutional and legislative power of the States, and without that of the Federal Government. Was it the purpose of the 14th Amendment, by the simple declaration that no State should make or enforce any law which shall abridge the privileges and immunities of citizens of the United States, to transfer the security and protection of all the civil rights which we have mentioned, from the States to the Federal Government? And where it is declared that Congress shall have the power to enforce that article, was it intended to bring within the power of Congress the entire domain of civil rights heretofore belonging exclusively to the States?

"All this and more must follow, if the proposition of the plaintiffs in error be sound. For not only are those rights subject to the control of Congress whenever in its discretion any of them are supposed to be abridged by state legislation, but that body may also pass laws in advance, limiting and restricting the exercise of legislative power by the States, in their most ordinary and usual functions, as in its judgment it may think proper on all such subjects. And still further, such a construction followed by the reversal of the judgments of the Supreme Court of Louisiana in these cases, would constitute this court a perpetual censor upon all legislation of the States, on the civil rights of their own citizens, with authority to nullify such as it did not approve as consistent with those rights, as they existed at the time of the adoption of this Amendment. The argument, we admit, is not always the most conclusive which is drawn from the consequences urged against the adoption of a particular construction of an instrument. But when, as in the case before us, these consequences are so serious, so far reaching and pervading, so great a departure from the structure and spirit of our institutions; when the effect is to fetter and degrade the state governments by subjecting them to the control of Congress, in the exercise of powers heretofore universally conceded to them of the most ordinary and fundamental character; when in fact it radically changes the whole theory of the relations of the state and Federal Governments to each other and of both these governments to the people; the argument has a force that is irresistible, in the absence of language which expresses such a purpose too clearly to admit of doubt.

"We are convinced that no such results were intended by the Congress which proposed these Amendments, nor by the Legislatures of the States which ratified them."

Having thus, to the satisfaction of the majority of the Court, demonstrated that the amendment, in the minds of the people who adopted it, was never intended to revolutionize our form of government, by entrusting to the Federal power and the Federal Courts, rights that had theretofore been deemed wholly of state jurisdiction, he concludes:

"Whatever fluctuations may be seen in the history of public opinion on this subject during the period of our national existence, we think it will be found that this court, so far as its functions required, has always held, with a steady and an even hand, the balance between state and federal power, and we trust that such may continue to be the history of its relation to that subject so long as it shall have duties to perform which demand of it a construction of the Constitution, or of any of its parts."

It was a five to four decision. Chief Justice Chase, Field, Bradley, and Swayne dissented. The dissenting opinions of Field and Bradley were directed mainly to the objection to the Statute on account of its monopolistic character, that no state could thus grant a monopoly in a particular pursuit. In the light of the vast development of the police power of the state, the general trend of legislative and judicial decisions, the learning they expend on this subject has become archaic. It is a common thing for municipalities to grant monopolies, whenever the public health can be

301

best conserved by such grant. They touch but lightly upon the main point in the case, whether the amendment was intended to include all citizens, white or black, but Judge Swayne meets that question boldly. He said:

"These Amendments are all consequences of the late civil war. The prejudices and apprehension as to the central government which prevailed when the Constitution was adopted were dispelled by the light of experience."

He uses this very striking phrase, "the public mind became satisfied that there was less danger of tyranny in the head than of anarchy and tyranny in the members," and that was essentially true at the time the opinion was written. The Civil War was largely the result of the Doctrine of State Rights, carried to a fanatical extreme,—the South Carolina idea. During and following the Civil War, nationalism had become ascendant and completely preponderant, but in the very hour when Judge Swayne was writing this opinion, the pendulum was beginning to swing the other way. The court of which he was a member from the date of the Slaughter-House Decisions, for a period of sixteen years, was steadily resisting the encroachments of federal power, and reconstituting those rights of the state which seemed in danger of destruction.

The decision in the Slaughter-House Cases was the first of a long line of decisions repelling the aggressions of federal power and centralization, and it was not until 1890, when the court had been almost completely reconstituted, that its decisions began to lean steadily, continuously, and increasingly towards aggrandizement of the federal power and the degradation of the states. Judge Swayne continues:

"The provisions of this section are all eminently conservative in their character. They are a bulwark of defense, and can never be made an engine of oppression. The language employed is unqualified in its scope. There is no exception in its terms, and there can be properly none in their application. By the language 'citizens of the United States' was meant all such citizens; and by 'any person' was meant all persons within the jurisdiction of the State. No distinction is intimated on account of race or color. This court has no authority to interpolate a limitation that is neither expressed nor implied. Our duty is to execute the law, not to make it. The protection provided was not intended to be confined to those of any particular race or class, but to embrace equally all races, classes and conditions of men. It is objected that the power conferred is novel and large. The answer is that the novelty was known and the measure deliberately adopted. The power is beneficent in its nature, and cannot be abused. It is such as should exist in every well ordered system of polity. Where could it be more appropriately lodged than in the hands to which it is confided? It is necessary to enable the government of the Nation to secure to every one within its jurisdiction the rights and privileges enumerated, which, according to the plainest considerations of reason and justice and the fundamental principles of the social compact, all are entitled to enjoy. Without such authority any government claiming to be national is glaringly defective."

Thus the issue was clearly drawn by the opinions of these two great Judges, Miller and Swayne. Miller considered it historically. Swayne considered it literally, as though he were interpreting a will or a deed. Miller's method of interpretation was not novel. It is common for courts, in considering Statutes, to take into consideration the circumstances surrounding their enactment, the condition of public affairs, the evil sought to be remedied, and thus ascertain the true intent of the enactment. From the very beginning of the government, the Supreme Court had uniformly held that it would follow the interpretation of a State Statute by the Court of Last Resort of that state. Marshall and his associates, constituting what was known as "the old court," strongly Nationalistic, for thirty-five years held to this principle, and it became firmly fixed in our jurisprudence. So long as a state preserved its Republican form of government, the

National Government could not interfere with its treatment of its own citizens. This, for the plain reason that each state was a sovereignty controlled by its own citizens, and it was not to be assumed that the state would willfully oppress any citizen, and if it did, the citizen's remedy lay with his own court, under his own constitution. If Swayne's interpretation were followed instead of Miller's, the people, by adopting the Fourteenth Amendment, had revolutionized their form of government. They had destroyed that dignity and independence of the several states of which the founders were so jealous, and that balance of power which they so carefully preserved. As Miller suggests, if Swayne's interpretation were the correct one, then in the future all the civil rights of the citizens would depend for their protection upon the National power and the National courts. Can it be thought for a moment, in the light of history, that those who adopted the Amendment dreamed of such a revolution? Again, what was the necessity of such a revolution? For seventy-four years the white citizens of the country had been satisfied with the balance of power as established by the Constitution. They had never thought of appealing to the Federal power unless the Constitution, the laws, or treaties of the United States had been violated by state enactment. The people of each state made their own Constitutions and laws, established their own courts, and chose their in-

305

cumbents. For seventy-four years they had been satisfied with the justice meted out to them by their state courts. At the time this Amendment was adopted, no white citizen was complaining of the oppression of state laws or state courts. The protection of white citizens from state oppression was not in the mind of any human being who voted for that Amendment. It was clearly understood that it was adopted to make a citizen of the negro and to protect that citizenship, no more.

One of the curious things about the case, was the personnel of the counsel who argued it. For the plaintiffs in error, contending for the Nationalist principle, appeared John A. Campbell of Louisiana, who had retired from the United States Supreme Court at the beginning of the War, because he believed in the extreme States-Rights idea. For the defendants in error, contending for the States-Rights principle, appeared Matthew H. Carpenter, of Wisconsin, one of the ablest and strongest Republican statesmen of that period, and Judge Thomas J. Durant, who, before the war, was one of the leaders of the Louisiana Bar, a strong Union man, and the first military Governor of Louisiana appointed by Lincoln. After the War, he moved to Washington. He had been seriously considered for the Supreme Bench when Strong and Bradley were appointed. He was a close friend of my father's and I studied law in his office in Washington for two years. He has told me that he learned from a source which could not be doubted, probably one of the Justices, that the discussion among the Judges in the consultation room was the hottest that any of the Judges had ever known, becoming at times almost bitter, especially between Field and Miller.

Another curious thing was that Field, a Democrat, was for the Nationalist idea and Miller, a Republican, was for the preservation of the rights of the states. The decision was bitterly condemned by many of the Northern Republicans, and hailed with joy by the Southern states.

The manner in which this great decision was quietly annulled without even mentioning it, not reversed but simply destroyed, seventeen years later constitutes the most curious chapter in the history of the Supreme Court of the United States, but it must be reserved for a later article.[3]

3. See, post, Part III, Chapter XV.

CHAPTER XII.

THE CIVIL RIGHTS CASES

These cases were the sequillæ of the Thirteenth, Fourteenth, and Fifteenth amendments and the congressional legislation by which the radical leaders, like Stevens and Sumner, sought to place the Colored Race upon a plane of absolute equality with the White, socially as well as politically. Very much of this legislation was held invalid by the Supreme Court, because it decided that the Fourteenth Amendment, for instance, did not operate upon individuals; prohibit the denial by individuals of equal rights to the Colored race; that its prohibition was solely against the States and their agents; that it was state action that was prohibited, and not the action of individuals. However, even if all those acts of Congress had been upheld, they would have been as futile as the Fifteenth amendment, which has been quite completely annulled all over the South.

The Anglo-Saxon will never permit political control, or social and political equality, with a race so far inferior as the Colored Race then was and as the great mass of it is today.

The wholesale enfranchisement of a servile race, attempted by the Fifteenth Amendment, was a ghastly mistake. Lincoln was for the gradual enfranchisement of the race individually, and not as a class, and only as the individuals became fitted for it by education and experience. In short, in the same manner in which the White Race itself has gradually and very slowly achieved political freedom and the ballot.

This attempted legislation, and the corruption of Carpet Bag Rule, divided the South from the North, kept up the hatred of the Civil War, made the two political parties largely, and one of them completely, sectional. It has required three generations to even measurably repair that mistake.

The first of these cases was United States vs. Reese,[1] a case which came up from Kentucky, where certain inspectors of elections refused to receive and count votes of citizens, because of their race and color. The court said:

"The Fifteenth Amendment does not confer the right of suffrage upon anyone. It prevents the states or the United States, however, from giving preference, in this particular, to one citizen of the United States over another on account of race, color or previous condition of servitude."

It is the popular conception that the Fifteenth Amendment conferred the franchise upon the negro. It did not do this directly, but indirectly. In effect, it struck out of all state constitutions and state laws re-

1. 92 U. S. 214, 23 L. ed. 563.

garding the right to vote, the word "White." If an educational or property qualification is imposed upon the colored voter, the same qualification must be imposed upon the white voter, or the legislation is void. The indictments were dismissed because it was held that the act of Congress did not cover the particular discrimination complained of. The next case was United States vs. Cruikshank[2], which came up from Louisiana, where certain persons were indicted for conspiring to deprive colored citizens of various rights under the constitutions, stated in very large and general terms, and for that reason the court held that the indictments were too vague and indefinite, and sustained a motion in arrest of judgment. The opinion throws little light, except in one respect. The case was decided in 1875, two years after the Slaughter House Cases, and it used this significant language:

"The Fourteenth Amendment prohibits a State from depriving any person of life, liberty or property, without due process of law, and from denying to any person within its jurisdiction the equal protection of the laws; but this provision does not add anything to the fundamental rights of the citizen under the Constitution.

"Every republican government is in duty bound to protect all its citizens in the enjoyment of an equality of right. That duty was originally assumed by the

2. 92 U. S. 542, 23 L. ed. 588.

310

States and it still remains there. The only obligation resting upon the United States is to see that the States do no deny the right. This the amendment guarantees, but no more; the power of the National Government is limited to the enforcement of this guaranty.

"The right of suffrage is not a necessary attribute of national citizenship, but exemption from discrimination in the exercise of that right on account of race, etc., is. The right to vote in the State comes from the States, but the right of exemption from the prohibited discrimination comes from the United States; the former has not been granted or secured by the Constitution of the United States, but the latter has been."

In Strauder vs. West Virginia[3], it was held that the statute of West Virginia, which in effect excluded colored men from jury service, was unconstitutional and void. The defendant had challenged the array for that reason, and it was held that the challenge should have been sustained. The court held that this was a case peculiarly within the scope of the Fourteenth Amendment, and, eight years after the Slaughter-House decisions, thus reiterates and affirms:

"The Fourteenth Amendment of the Federal Constitution is considered and held to be one of a series of constitutional provisions having a common purpose, namely: to secure to a race recently emancipated and held in slavery through many generations, all the civil

3. 100 U. S. 302, 25 L. ed. 664, revers'g 11 W. Va. 745, 27 Am. Rep. 606.

rights that the superior race enjoy, and to give to them the protection of the General Government, in the enjoyment of such rights, whenever they should be denied by the States."

In Ex Parte Virginia, Coles, Petitioner[4], Coles was indicted because, as county judge charged with drawing the jurors, he had willfully refused to draw the names of colored men for service, contrary to the act of 1875. The court held that, in drawing the jurors, the county judge did not act in a judicial but in a ministerial capacity, that so acting he was an agent of the state of Virginia, that the state was acting through him, and that therefore the act came within the purview of the Fourteenth Amendment, which operates, not upon individuals, but only on the states. Judge Field dissented in a very lengthy opinion.

In Virginia vs. Rives[5], two colored men were indicted for murder. The defendants moved the court that the venire, which was composed entirely of the White Race, should be modified so as to allow one-third of the jurors to be colored men. On what theory a demand for just such a proportion of colored men could be sustained does not appear. But this should be noted. The colored people of the South were justly distrustful of a White jury, especially when it was a white man against whom the crime was committed,

4. 100 U. S. 339, 25 L. ed. 676.
5. 100 U. S. 313, 25 L. ed. 667.

or when a white man was the opposing litigant in a civil case. So the right of Negroes to sit on juries in the South was a very precious right; but the court held that it had no jurisdiction in this case because neither the State nor its agents had discriminated against the right of Negroes to sit upon a jury. That it was not a Constitutional right of a Negro to be tried bv a jury wholly or partially composed of Negroes.

In United States vs. Harris[6], certain persons in Tennessee had been indicted for conspiring to deprive colored people of "equal protection of the laws or of equal privileges or immunities under the laws," etc., under an act of Congress. The facts were that two Negroes, charged with a crime, had been taken from the custody of the sheriff, who held them under arrest, and severely ill-treated them. This raised the question involved in the Dyer Anti-Lynching Bill now before Congress. Just how its authors hope to evade this decision in the Harris case is impossible even to guess. The court cites approvingly Virginia vs. Reeves: "These provisions of the Fourteenth Amendment have reference to State action exclusively, and not to any action of private individuals." The indictments were dismissed.

The bitterest of all the cases that arose out of the long struggle over the three amendments, were the Civil Right Cases[7]. The first section of the act of March 1, 1875, was as follows:

6. 106 U. S. 629, 27 L. ed. 290, 1 Sup. Ct. Rep. 601.
7. 109 U. S. 3, 27 L. ed. 835, 3 Sup. Ct. Rep. 18.

313

"That all persons within the jurisdiction of the United States shall be entitled to the full and equal enjoyment of the accommodations, advantages, facilities, and privileges of inns, public conveyances on land or water, theaters, and other places of public amusement; subject only to the conditions and limitations established by law, and applicable alike to citizens of every race and color, regardless of any previous condition of servitude."

Then followed certain drastic penalties. The radical leaders in Congress, like Stevens and Sumner, were determined, not only to raise the negro to political equality with the White, but also to place him upon the same plane socially, by compelling his admission to all public conveyances, hotels and theaters, with the same rights as the White Race. If the enforcement of the Act had been attempted in the South, it probably would have brought on another Civil War. But the first attempts to enforce it were made in the North, and the question came squarely before the Supreme Court whether the Federal Congress could enforce those rights of social equality in states where the legislature had never by law imposed a distinction, where the rights were denied solely by individuals. The question was, as the court stated it: Is the Act constitutional under any one of the three amendments? It is apparent that the opinion of members of Congress who supported the Act as to its constitutionality, must have been urged with a great deal of force, but the court denied that those opinions could have any weight upon such a constitutional question. It was the court that must decide it. The opinions of the members of Congress in favor of an unconstitutional law could have no more weight with this great court than their votes which enacted it. Speaking of the Fourteenth Amendment, the court reiterated the doctrine of Virginia vs. Reeves, and said:

"Individual invasion of individual rights is not the subject-matter of the amendment. It has a deeper and broader scope. It nullifies and makes void all state legislation, and state action of every kind, which impairs the privileges and immunities of citizens of the United States, or which injures them in life, liberty or property without due process of law, or which denies to any of them the equal protection of the laws. It not only does this, but, in order that the national will, thus declared, may not be a mere *brutum fulmen,* the last section of the amendment invests congress with power to enforce it by appropriate legislation. To enforce what? To enforce the prohibition. To adopt appropriate legislation for correction of the effects of such prohibited state law and state acts, and thus to render them effectually null, void and innocuous. This is the legislative power conferred upon congress, and this is the whole of it. It does not invest

congress with power to legislate upon subjects which
are within the domain of state legislation; but to provide modes of relief against state legislation, or state
action, of the kind referred to. It does not authorize
congress to create a code of municipal law for the
regulation of private rights; but to provide modes of
redress against the operation of state laws, and the
action of state officers, executive or judicial, when
these are subversive of the fundamental rights specified in the amendment. Positive rights and privileges
are undoubtedly secured by the fourteenth amendment; but they are secured by way of prohibition
against state laws and state proceedings affecting those
rights and privileges, and by power given to congress
to legislate for the purpose of carrying such prohibition into effect; and such legislation must necessarily
be predicated upon such supposed state laws or state
proceedings and be directed to the correction of their
operation and effect."

The last of the series was Ex Parte Yarbrough[8], generally known as the "Ku Klux Klan" Cases. This was
an appeal of certain defendants, who had been convicted in the Federal court of Georgia of intimidating
certain colored voters from voting, by threats and violence. The prosecution was under a section of the statutes expressly relating to elections, and not to Civil
Rights generally. In considering the old argument

8. 110 U. S. 651, 28 L. ed. 274, 4 Sup. Ct. Rep. 152.

316

that the Constitution does not confer upon Congress, in express terms, the power to protect the federal franchise, and that therefore such power does not exist, the court said that it had never admitted that doctrine: that the rights to protect the purity of the franchise in federal elections, that prevented fraud, intimidation and corruption, were rights inherent in its sovereignty and necessary to its very existence.

"It is as essential to the successful working of this government that the great organisms of its executive and legislative branches should be the free choice of the people, as that the original form of it should be so. In absolute governments, where the monarch is the source of all power, it is still held to be important that the exercise of that power shall be free from the influence of extraneous violence and internal corruption. In a republican government, like ours, where political power is reposed in representatives of the entire body of the people, chosen at short intervals by popular elections, the temptations to control these elections by violence and by corruption is a constant source of danger. Such has been the history of all republics, and though ours has been comparatively free from both these evils in the past, no lover of his country can shut his eyes to the fear of future danger from both sources. If the recurrence of such acts as these prisoners stand convicted of are too common in one quarter of the country, and give omen of danger from lawless violence, the free use of money in elections, arising from the vast growth of recent wealth in other quarters, presents equal cause for anxiety. If the government of the United States has within its constitutional domain no authority to provide against these evils,—if the very source of power may be poisoned by corruption or controlled by violence and outrage, without legal restraint,—then, indeed is the country in danger and its best powers, its highest purposes, the hopes which it inspires, and the love which enshrines it, are at the mercy of the combinations of those who respect no right but brute force on the one hand, and unprincipled corruptionists on the other."

By these cases the full effect of these three amendments was determined. It was settled that Congress could not protect any civil rights of citizens against other citizens. The only exception to this is the protection of the franchise, otherwise the prohibition is against the states, and not against individuals.

CHAPTER XIII.

THE GRANGER CASES

In 1874, upon the death of Chief Justice Chase, President Grant offered the position to Roscoe Conkling, who was wise enough to refuse it. George H. Williams, his Attorney-General, and Caleb Cushing, ex-Attorney-General of the United States, were successively rejected by the Senate. Grant then appointed Morrison R. Waite, of Ohio, who was confirmed. He was unknown outside of the state of Ohio except for one thing, he was one of our Commissioners before the Geneva Arbitration, considering the Alabama Claims, where his speech on the liability of England was decidedly the ablest delivered on either side. He had never argued a case in the Supreme Court of the United States, and, in fact, was only admitted to the bar of that court a few months before his appointment. He was in fact a stranger to the bar of the United States. He presided for fourteen years, and won the universal confidence of the country, although at times bitterly criticized by some for the liberal character of his opinions, and his insistence upon the right of the public to regulate monopolies. His decision in the Munn case was almost revolutionary, although well

319

founded on English precedents. It has stood the test
of fifty years, and, indeed, its principles have been
greatly extended in recent years. Waite was not brilliant but he was sound, thorough, and exact. There
was never anything dubious in his language. One
reads his opinions with absolute certainty of what the
decision means. He ranks among the best of our
Judges.

The deflation, following the Civil War, nearly
ruined the farmers of the Middle West. Most of
them were in debt. They had borrowed dollars, worth,
in index prices, from forty to fifty cents and in the
early 70's were required to pay in dollars worth from
eighty to ninety cents. The dollar had gone up, farm
products down. In addition to that, transportation
was a far more serious burden than it is now. There
was no public control over the railroads, in fact, the
owners of those properties denied absolutely the right
of the public to regulate them in any way, influence
service or control tariffs. In short, the principle of
"the public be damned" was the guiding principle of
railroad managers. Service was poor and rates all the
traffic would bear, except when occasionally competition would bring on a ruinous rate-war. The stocks
and securities were the playthings of Wall Street,—
chips in the great gambling game that was then at its
height. Wholly unscrupulous and remorseless, men
like Jay Gould and Jim Fiske got control of proper-

ties by methods that would today land them in the penitentiary, and ran them, or wrecked them, as best suited their pocketbooks. Nearly everyone traveled on passes,—that is, anyone who had any influence and could make trouble; congressmen and legislators, who might pass unfriendly legislation; judges, before whom railroad litigation would be tried; and every politician down to the very smallest of small fry. It was estimated that, at one time, on the Chicago, Burlington and Quincy Railroad, only one passenger out of four paid fares. There was another grievous burden imposed on the grain growers of the Middle West. Chicago, where the rail and water lines meet, had become the greatest grain center in the world. All the surplus grain of eight great states passed through and was handled at Chicago through a system of elevators, even then enormous in capacity, where the grain was elevated, mixed, re-graded and sent on its way to the markets of the world. The business was a monopoly, controlled by nine men who annually fixed and published the charges for this service, exorbitant, of course, as all monopolistic charges are, and there was absolutely no competition.

These conditions, as was entirely natural, produced a wave of agrarian legislation largely justified. These states enacted laws directly fixing the maximum rates for freight and passengers, or established commissions with full power to fix rates. These laws were immediately and bitterly attacked. Just what business is so impressed with a public interest that it may be regulated had never been determined, or very largely considered, in this country. There was a vague idea, on the part of the people, that the public had the right to regulate monopolies, such as the railways—an idea strenuously denied by those who controlled them. In 1871 the legislature of Illinois, under an Article of its Constitution, provided that all elevators in cities of more than 100,000 inhabitants, where grain was stored and mixed, should be public elevators, and fixed the charges much lower than the existing rate. Munn and other elevator men brought suit to test the validity of this act[1]. Of course, the Fourteenth Amendment was invoked by the plaintiffs in error, but was not considered in the decision. The case turned entirely upon the question of whether this great business was impressed with a public interest. It is a striking proof of the continuity of Anglo-Saxon law,—how far back in the past are the mighty roots from which it draws its strength,—that Chief Justice Waite, who wrote the opinion, did not formulate any new principles for the decision of the case; he simply turned back two hundred years to the opinion of Sir Mathew Hate, in De Portibus Maris[2], prefacing it with this statement on the Fifth Amendment to the Constitution:

---

1. Munn v. Illinois, 94 U. S. 113, 24 L. ed. 77, aff'g 69 Ill. 80.
2. 4 Harg. L. Tr. 78.

"When the people of the United Colonies separated from Great Britain, they changed the form, but not the substance, of their government. They retained for the purposes of government all the power of the British Parliament and, through their State Constitutions or other forms of social compact, undertook to give practical effect to such as they deemed necessary for the common good and the security of life and property. All the powers which they retained they committed to their respective States, unless in express terms or by implication reserved to themselves. Subsequently, when it was found necessary to establish a national government for national purposes, a part of the powers of the States and of the people was granted to the United States and the people of the United States. This grant operated as a further limitation upon the powers of the States, so that now the governments of the States possess all the powers of the Parliament of England, except such as have been delegated to the United States or reserved by the people. The reservations by the people are shown in the prohibitions of the constitutions.

"When one becomes a member of society, he necessarily parts with some right or privileges which, as an individual not affected by his relations to others, he might retain. 'A body politic,' as aptly defined in the preamble of the Constitution of Massachusetts, 'is a social compact by which the whole people covenants

323

with each citizen, and each citizen with the whole
people, that all shall be governed by certain laws for
the common good.' This does not confer power upon
the whole people to control rights which are purely
private[3], but it does authorize the establishment of laws
requiring each citizen to so conduct himself, and so
use his own property as not unnecessarily to injure
another. This is the very essence of government, and
has found expression in the maxim, *Sic utere tuo ut
alienum non laedas.* From this source come the police
powers, which as was said by Chief Justice Taney in
the License Cases, 'are nothing more or less than the
powers of government inherent in every sovereignty
* * * that is to say, * * * the power to govern
men and things.' Under these powers the government
regulates the conduct of its citizens one towards
another, and the manner in which each shall use his
own property, when such regulation becomes necessary for the public good. In their exercise it has been
customary in England from time immemorial, and in
this country from its first colonization, to regulate ferries, common carriers, hackmen, bakers, millers, wharfingers, innkeepers, etc., and in so doing to fix a maximum of charge to be made for services rendered, accommodations furnished and articles sold. To this day
statutes are to be found in many of the States upon
some or all these subjects and we think it has never yet

3. 27 Vt. 143.

been successfully contended that such legislation came within any of the constitutional prohibitions against interference with private property. With the 5th Amendment in force, Congress, in 1820, conferred power upon the City of Washington 'to regulate * * * the rates of wharfage at private wharves, * * * the sweeping of chimneys, and to fix the rates of fees therefor, * * * and the weight and quality of bread'[4]; and in 1848, 'to make all necessary regulations respecting hackney carriages and the rates of fare of the same, and the rates of hauling by cartmen, wagoners, carmen and draymen, and the rates of commission by auctioneers.'

"This brings us to inquire as to the principles upon which this power of regulation rests, in order that we may determine what is within and what without its operative effect. Looking, then, to the common law, from whence came the right which the Constitution protects, we find that when private property is 'affected with a public interest, it ceases to be *juris privati* only.' This was said by Lord Chief Justice Hale more than two hundred years ago in his Treatise De Portibus Maris[5], and has been accepted without objection as an essential element in the law of property ever since. Property does become clothed with a public interest when used in a manner to make it of public conse-

4. 1 Stat. at L. 587, §7.
5. 4 Harg. L. Tr. 78.

quence, and affect the community at large. When, therefore, one devotes his property to a use in which the public has an interest, he, in effect, grants to the public an interest in that use, and must submit to be conrolled by the public for the common good, to the extent of the interest he has thus created. He may withdraw his grant by discontinuing the use; but, so long as he maintains the use he must submit to the control.

"Thus, as to ferries, Lord Hale says, in his treatise De Jure Maris[6], the King has 'a right of franchise or privilege, that no man may set up a common ferry for all passengers, without a prescription time out of mind, or a charter from the King. He may make a ferry for his own use or the use of his family, but not for the common use of all the King's subjects passing that way; because it doth in consequence tend to a common charge, and is become a thing of public interest and use, and every man for his passage pays a toll, which is a common charge, and every ferry ought to be under a public regulation, viz.: that it give attendance at due times, keep a boat in due order, and take but reasonable toll; for if he fail in these he is finable.' So if one owns the soil and landing places on both banks of a stream, he cannot use them for the purposes of a public ferry, except upon such terms and conditions as the body politic may from time to time impose; and this

6. Harg. L. Tr. 6.

because the common good requires that all public ways shall be under the control of the public authorities. This privilege or prerogative of the King, who in this connection only represents and gives another name to the body politic, is not primarily for his profit, but for the protection of the people and the promotion of the general welfare.

"And, again, as to wharves and wharfingers, Lord Hale, in his treatise De Portibus Maris, already cited, says: 'A man, for his own private advantage, may in a port or town set up a wharf or crane and may take what rates he and his customers can agree for cranage, wharfage, housellage, pesage, for he doth no more than is lawful for any man to do, viz.: makes the most of his own. . . . If the King or subject have a public wharf, unto which all persons that come to that port must come and unlade or lade their goods as for the purpose, because they are at the wharfs only licensed by the Queen, . . . or because there is no other wharf in that port, as it may fall out where a port is newly erected; in that case there cannot be taken arbitrary and excessive duties for cranage, wharfage, pesage, etc., neither can they be enhanced to an immoderate rate; but the duties must be reasonable and moderate, though settled by the King's license or charter. For now the wharf, and crane and other conveniences are affected with a public interest, and they cease to be *juris privati* only; as if a man set out

327

a street in new building on his own land, it is now no longer bare private interest, but is affected by a public interest.' "

This statement of the law by Lord Hale was cited with approbation and acted upon by Lord Kenyon at the beginning of the present century, in Bolt vs. Stennett[7].

"And the same has been held as to warehouses and warehousemen. In Allnutt vs. Inglis[8], decided in 1810, it appeared that the London Dock Company had built warehouses in which wines were taken in store at such rates of charge as the company and the owners might agree upon. Afterwards the company obtained authority under the general Warehousing Act, to receive wines from importers before the duties upon the importation were paid; and the question was, whether they could charge arbitrary rates for such storage, or must be content with a reasonable compensation. Upon this point Lord Ellenborough said (p. 537):

" 'There is no doubt that the general principle is favored, both in law and justice, that every man may fix what price he pleases upon his own property, or the use of it; but if for a particular purpose the public have a right to resort to his premises and make use of them, and he have a monopoly in them for that purpose, if he will take the benefit of that monopoly, he

---

7. 8 T. R. 66.
8. 12 East 527.

must, as an equivalent, perform the duty attached to it on reasonable terms. The question then is, whether, circumstanced as this company is, by the combination of the Warehousing Act with the Act by which they were originally constituted, and with the actually existing state of things in the Port of London, whereby they alone have the warehousing of these wines, they be not, according to the doctrine of Lord Hale, obliged to limit themselves to a reasonable compensation, for such warehousing. And, according to him, whenever the accident of time casts upon a party the benefit of having a legal monopoly of landing goods in a public port, as where he is the owner of the only wharf authorized to receive goods which happens to be built in a port newly erected, he is confined to take reasonable compensation only for the use of the wharf.

" 'It is enough that there exists in the place and for the commodity in question a virtual monopoly of the warehouse for this purpose, on which the principle of law attaches, as laid down by Lord Hale in the passage referred to (that from De Portibus Maris already quoted), which includes the good sense as well as the law of the subject.' "

And in the same case Le Blanc, J., said (p. 541) :
"Then admitting these warehouses to be private property, and that the company might discontinue this application of them, or that they might have made what terms they pleased in the first instance, yet hav-

ing, as they now have, this monopoly, the question is, whether the warehouses be not private property clothed with a public right, and if so, the principle of law attaches upon them. The privilege, then, of bonding these wines being at present confined by the Act of Parliament to the company's warehouses, is not the privilege of the public, and shall not that which is for the good of the public attach on the monopoly, that they shall not be bound to pay an arbitrary but a reasonable rent? But upon this record the company resist having their demand for warehouse rent confined within any limit; and, though it does not follow that the rent in fact fixed by them is unreasonable, they do not choose to insist on its being reasonable for the purpose of raising the question. For this purpose, therefore, the question may be taken to be whether they may claim an unreasonable rent. But though this be private property, yet the principle laid down by Lord Hale attaches upon it, that when private property is affected with a public interest it ceases to be *juris privati* only; and in case of its dedication to such a purpose as this, the owners cannot take arbitrary and excessive duties, but the duties must be reasonable."

After citing other authorities, Judge Waite notes that the power to regulate the charges of common carriers was exercised in England as far back as the reign of William and Mary, because their business is "affected with the public interest," within the meaning of

Lord Hale's doctrine. He calls attention to the fact that while there were in Chicago in 1874, 14 elevators, their practices and charges were completely controlled by nine persons in thorough agreement.

"Under such circumstances it is difficult to see why, if the common carrier, or the miller, or the ferryman, or the innkeeper, or the wharfinger, or the baker, or the cartman, or the hackney-coachman, pursues a public employment and exercises 'a sort of public office,' these plaintiffs in error do not. They stand, to use again the language of counsel, in the very 'gateway of commerce,' and take toll from all who pass. Their business most certainly 'tends to a common charge, and is become a thing of public interest and use.' Every bushel of grain for its passage 'pays a toll, which is a common charge,' and, therefore, according to Lord Hale, every such warehouseman 'ought to be under public regulation, viz.: that he . . . take but reasonable toll.' Certainly, if any business can be clothed 'with a public interest, and cease to be *juris privati* only,' this has been. It may not be made so by the operation of the Constitution of Illinois or this statute, but it is by the facts.

"It is insisted, however, that the owner of property is entitled to a reasonable compensation for its use, even though it be clothed with a public interest, and that what is reasonable is a judicial and not a legislative question.

331

"As has already been shown, the practice has been otherwise. In countries where the common law prevails, it has been customary from time immemorial for the Legislature to declare what shall be a reasonable compensation under such circumstances, or, perhaps more properly speaking, to fix a maximum beyond which any charge would be unreasonable. Undoubtedly, in mere private contracts, relating to matters in which the public has no interest, what is reasonable must be ascertained judicially. But this is because the Legislature has no control over such a contract. So, too, in matters which do affect the public interest, and as to which legislative control may be exercised, if there are no statutory regulations upon the subject, the courts must determine what is reasonable. The controlling fact is the power to regulate at all. If that exists, the right to establish the maximum of charge, as one of the means of regulation, is implied. In fact, the common law rule, which requires the charge to be reasonable, is itself a regulation as to price. Without it the owner could make his rates at will, and compel the public to yield to his terms, or forego the use.

"But a mere common law regulation of trade or business may be changed by statute. A person has no property, no vested interest, in any rule of the common law. That is only one of the forms of municipal law, and is no more sacred than any other. Rights of property which have been created by the common law cannot be taken away with due process; but the law itself, as a rule of conduct, may be changed at the will, or even at the whim, of the Legislature, unless prevented by constitutional limitations. Indeed, the great office of statutes is to remedy defects in the common law as they are developed, and to adapt it to the changes of time and circumstances. To limit the rate of charge for services rendered in a public employment, or for the use of property in which the public has an interest, is only changing a regulation which existed before. It establishes no new principle in the law, but only gives a new effect to an old one.

"We know that this is a power which may be abused; but that is no argument against its existence. For protection against abuses by Legislatures the people must resort to the polls, not to the courts."

The court was here laying down the principle upon which it decided the Railroad Rate Cases which immediately follows this case, namely, that the right to fix maximum rates for public utilities was legislative right over which the courts have no control, a doctrine soon abandoned by the court. Judge Field and Judge Strong dissented. The dissenting opinion of Judge Field is wholly unworthy of that great jurist. For instance, he says:

"The receipt and storage of grain in a building erected by private means for that purpose does not

333

constitute the building a public warehouse. There is no magic in the language, though used by a constitutional convention, which can change a private business into a public one, or alter the character of the building in which the business is transacted. A tailor's or a shoemaker's shop would still retain its private character, even though the assembled wisdom of the State should declare, by organic Act or legislative ordinance, that such a place was a public workshop, and that the workmen were public tailors or public shoemakers. One might as well attempt to change the nature of colors, by giving them a new designation. The defendants were no more public warehousemen, as justly observed by counsel, than the merchant who sells his merchandise to the public is a public merchant, or the blacksmith who shoes horses for the public is a public blacksmith; and it was a strange notion that by calling them so they would be brought under legislative control.

"If this be sound law, if there be no protection, either in the principles upon which our republican government is founded, or in the prohibitions of the Constitution against such invasion of private rights, all property and all business in the State are held at the mercy of a majority of its Legislature. The public has no greater interest in the use of buildings for the storage of grain than it has in the use of buildings for the residences of families, nor, indeed, anything like so great an interest; and, according to the doctrine announced, the Legislature may fix the rent of all tenements used for residences, without reference to the cost of their erection."

To say that the business of a tailor or a shoemaker is just as much impressed with the public interest as this great monopoly with its stranglehold on the grain buiness of eight great states, controlling in fact the price of their surplus to both producer and consumer, is simply childish. The same question came before the court in Budd vs. New York[9], decided in 1892, where a similar act of the New York Legislature was attacked. Munn vs. Illinois was fully approved and affirmed, and the opinion collates a number of decisions since the Munn case, following its principles. Judge Brewer, the nephew of Judge Field, who was then on the bench, wrote a dissenting opinion in which his uncle, Judge Field, joined. In the course of that decision Judge Brewer announced that every form of paternalism was odious to him. Both of them believed that the states could not regulate any monopoly, that the states had not created by law. That every other form of business is private with which the state has no concern, no matter how oppressive its operation may be. Munn vs. Illinois was an out-post case. Many lawyers believed it would be withdrawn, but it was

---

9. 143 U. S. 517, 36 L. ed. 247, 12 Sup. Ct. Rep. 468, aff'g 117 N. Y. 1, 126, 15 Am. St. Rep. 469, 5 L. R. A. 559, 22 N. E. 670.

affirmed fifteen years later in the Budd case, and vastly extended a generation later, in German Alliance Insurance Company vs. Lewis[10].

The four other Granger cases, which immediately followed the Munn Case, are: Chicago, Burlington and Quincy Railroad Company vs. Cutts; Peik vs. Chicago and North Western Railroad Company; Chicago, Milwaukee and St. Paul Railroad Company vs. Ackley; Railroad Company vs. Blake, all cases attacking the validity of maximum rates established by law or by the orders of railroad commissions authorized thereto. The court held that until Congress had established interstate rates, State Legislatures had complete control over rates, within the boundary of the State, even though the traffic was a part of interstate traffic,— a doctrine which it was compelled to renounce in St. Louis and Pacific Railroad Company vs. Illinois[11]. It reiterated the doctrine of the Munn case and applied it to railroads, that a Legislature in rate-making was omnipotent; that even though rates were confiscatory, the courts could not interfere. This the court soon renounced, holding that where the rate was confiscatory the court would interfere; and the reasonableness of a rate is always a judicial question, thus, opening up a vast new field of litigation. Practically nothing is

10. 233 U. S. 389,   L. ed.   , 34 Sup. Ct. Rep. 612.

11. Wabash, St. L. & P. R. Co. v. Illinois, 118 U. S. 551, 557, 30 L. ed. 244, 7 Sup. Ct. Rep. 4, revr'ng 105 Ill. 236.

now left of the last four decisions; but the Munn Case, in its main features, is still the law of the land.

Not only that, but it has been considerably extended. In the Munn decision, some stress was laid upon the fact that these elevators were located at a great terminal point where rail and water lines connect, but in Brass vs. North Dakota[12], an act making all buildings, elevators, and warehouses used for the handling of grain for profit, public warehouses, and fixing the storage rates, was completely upheld. The doctrine of public interest in all such warehouses, so upheld, has been applied by legislation in nearly every state."

In German Alliance Co. vs. Lewis[13], rejecting the theory that the business must be a monopoly in order to its regulations, the court said:

"This difference in conditions is 'for those who make and not those who interpret, the laws.' And considering the expression in the other cases which, it was said, went rather to the expediency of the laws than to their validity, yet, it was further said, the expressions had their value because the 'obvious aim of the reasoning that prevailed was to show that the subject matter of these enactments fell within the legitimate sphere of legislative power, and that so far as the laws and Constitution of the United States were concerned, the leg-

12. 153 U. S. 391, 38 L. ed. 757, 14 Sup. Ct. Rep. 857, aff'g 2 N. D. 482, 52 N. W. 408.

13. 233 U. S. 389,   L. ed.   , 34 Sup. Ct. Rep. 612.

islation in question deprived no person of his property without due process of law.' "

The court then cited approvingly the language used by Judge Andrews in the Budd Case[14]:

"The attempts made to place the right of public regulation in the cases in which it has been exerted, and of which we have given examples, upon the grounds of special privilege conferred by the public on those affected, cannot be supported. 'The underlying principle is that business of certain kinds holds such a peculiar relation to the public interest that there is superinduced upon it the right of public regulation.'

The court then discussed the proportions to which the fire insurance business of the country has grown, and the manner of its operation. The ratio of loss to insurance has been so accurately determined by experts that there is practically a fixed rate made by rating bureaus, so that there is no more competition than there is in railroad rates, no more freedom of contract between the insurer and the insured than there is between the shipper and the railroad company. The insured must take the contract that the insurer tenders. Again, the court points out that fire insurance has become almost universal. No merchant can secure credit without insuring his stock. The lender compels the borrower to insure the mortgaged property for the

14. 117 N. Y. 27, 5 L. R. A. 559, 15 Am. St. Rep. 460, 22 N. E. 670.

338

interest of the mortgagee. To a large extent the entire fabric of credit in this country thus depends upon fire insurance, and the courts hold that it is therefore so impressed with the public interest that the state may not only regulate all of its other practices,—form of policy, investment of funds which has long since been done in most states,—but may also regulate the rates.

The case was a shock to the Bar of the country. It had been generally thought by the Bar that such regulation was only legal where there was a monopoly created by the state, or in those functions where the public may demand the service, where the corporation must give the service without discrimination to everyone who applies; that, in other words, the right to regulate was correlative to the right to demand service. The court brushes that aside and, in upholding the act, finally says:

"The attempts made to place the right of public regulation in the cases in which it has been exerted, and of which we have given examples, upon the ground of special privilege conferred by the public on those affected, cannot be supported. 'The underlying principle is that business of certain kinds holds such a peculiar relation to the public interest that there is superinduced upon it the right of public regulation.' Is the business of insurance within the principle? It would be a bold thing to say that the principle is fixed, inelastic, in the precedents of the past, and cannot be applied though modern economic conditions may make necessary or beneficial its application. In other words, to say that government possessed at one time a greater power to recognize the public interest in a business and its regulation to promote the general welfare than government possesses today."

Here was a warning that the extension of this power derived from public interest had not yet reached its limitations in the view of the court that it might be still further extended, and it was. In Block vs. Hirsh[15], the court upheld the New York Statute fixing rents, setting aside rental contracts already entered into, on the ground that it was "emergency legislation."

It is to be hoped that the court will not continue to take the view that the Constitution may be warped, twisted, or swayed to meet emergencies. That is an extremely dangerous doctrine, and it is doubtful if Block vs. Hirsh will ever be followed. It is one outpost case that will probably be withdrawn.

15. 254 U. S. 640, 65 L. ed. 452, 41 Sup. Ct. Rep. 13, dny'g certiorari to 50 App. D. C. 56, 207 Fed. 614, 11 A. L. R. 1238.

CHAPTER XIV.

THE ELEVENTH AMENDMENT

When the case of Chisholm vs. Georgia[1] was decided, holding that a state could be sued in the Supreme Court by a citizen of another state, the decision aroused a storm of fury. Under the original constitution, the decision could not have been otherwise, as it clearly provided for the jurisdiction in such cases. But these states which had but recently declared their sovereignty against Great Britain, conquered and established it at the bitter cost of nine years of destructive and desolating warfare, and but recently surrendered a portion of it to the Federal government, were extraordinarily proud and jealous of that sovereignty. Each felt that its achieved independence made it as completely a sovereign as Great Britain. That, as a state, it inherited all the privileges, rights, and immunities of the British Crown, among which was immunity from suit by a private citizen without its consent. The immediate consequence of that decision was the speedy adoption of the Eleventh Amendment, which provided that "the judicial power of the United States shall not be construed to extend to any suit in

1. 2 U. S. (2 Dall.) 419, 1 L. ed. 440.

341

the United States by citizens of another state or by law or equity instituted or prosecuted against one of citizens or subjects of any foreign state." The opinion in the Chisholm case by Chief Justice Jay, who resigned that position because he believed the court was powerless and would always be a nonentity, is the only one of his decisions that has left its mark. In considering the Eleventh Amendment, the general oppression and dishonesty of the states it authorized and sanctioned, it is well to re-read one paragraph from that decision.

"The extension of the judiciary power of the United States to such controversies, appears to me to be wise, because it is honest, and because it is useful. It is honest, because it provides for doing justice without respect of persons, and by securing individual citizens as well as states. in their respective rights, performs the promise which every free government makes to every free citizen, of equal justice and protection. It is useful, because it is honest, because it leaves not even the most obscure and friendless citizen without means of obtaining justice from a neighboring state; because it obviates occasions of quarrels between states on account of the claims of their respective citizens; because it recognizes and strongly rests on this great moral truth, than justice is the same whether due from one man to a million, or from a million to one man; because it teaches and greatly appreciates the value of our free republican national government, which places all our citizens on an equal footing, and enables each and every one of them to obtain justice without any danger of being overborne by the weight and number of their opponents; and, because it brings into action, and enforces this great and glorious principle, that the people are the sovereign of this country, and consequently that fellow citizens and joint sovereigns cannot be degraded by appearing with each other in their own courts to have their controversies determined."

The Eleventh Amendment slumbered without further action until 1819. The state of Ohio passed an act taxing the branch banks of the United States Bank, $50,000 annually, and, in spite of the decision of Bank vs. McCulloch, undertook to enforce the tax. Four days before the date of the tax-levy, the bank, in the Federal Circuit Court, obtained an injunction against Osborn, the state auditor, prohibiting the collection of the tax. Disregarding the injunction, Osborn delivered a warrant to the State Treasurer, Harper, who went to the branch office of the Bank, entered the vaults and forcibly took away more than $120,000 and placed it in the state treasury. The case came up on contempt proceedings against Harper, and to recover the money. The Bank recovered, in the Circuit Court, a decree ordering Osborn and the State Treasurer, Sullivan, to restore the money taken with interest, and enjoining collection of the tax. Sullivan refused to obey. He was attached and committed to prison. Commissioners appointed by the court took the keys of the State Treasury from Sullivan and removed $98,-000, all they could find. The case was appealed to the Supreme Court and argued twice by the most noted lawyers of the time, among them Webster and Clay, and was decided in 1823[2]. It was urged by Osborn's counsel that the state of Ohio was the real party in interest, that in fact it was a suit against the state of Ohio, forbidden by the Eleventh Amendment. The court held (opinion by Marshall) that the Ohio law, like the Maryland law, was void, that the State Treasurer, when he forcibly took the money from the bank, was a trespasser, and that he could not justify his act under a void law of the state of Ohio; that the state was not a necessary party and that it was not a suit against the state of Ohio. Ohio was much excited at first and threatened armed resistance, but finally subsided.

The question seems not to have been mooted again for more than sixty years. In Louisiana vs. Jumel[3], bondholders of Louisiana had sought to compel, by mandamus, the proper officers of the state to apply certain funds in the state treasury to the payment of state bonds, a duty clearly imposed upon them by the

2. Osborn v. Bank of United States, 22 U. S. (9 Wheat.) 738, 6 L. ed. 204.
3. 107 U. S. 711, 27 L. ed. 448, 2 Sup. Ct. Rep. 128.

law of the state. But the mandamus was denied under the Eleventh Amendment. In Cunningham vs. Macon, etc., Railroad[4], where bondholders sought to foreclose on a railroad, possession of which had been taken by the state of Georgia, relief was again denied under this Amendment. And when creditors of Louisiana, living in New Hampshire, assigned their claims to that state and it brought suit on the claims against Louisiana[5], the court refused jurisdiction.

So stood the matter when the great case of United States vs. Lee[6] was decided, in 1882. In that case the Arlington estate, consisting of about 1,100 acres lying across the Potomac river from Washington, which the plaintiff, the son of Robert E. Lee, deraigned from his maternal grandfather, had been sold for taxes, bid in by the government, a national cemetery established on it, and it was then in the possession of Kaufman and Strong, officers of the government. Lee brought suit in the State court against Kaufman and Strong for possession. The case was removed to the Federal court where a jury found the tax-sale void, because a tender of the taxes had been made by the plaintiff's agent. Throughout the case, the Attorney-General of

4. 109 U. S. 446, 27 L. ed. 992, 3 Sup. Ct. Rep. 292, 609.

5. New Hampshire v. Louisiana, 108 U. S. 763, 27 L. ed. 656, 2 Sup. Ct. Rep. 176.

6. 106 U. S. 196, 27 L. ed. 171, 1 Sup. Ct. Rep. 240, aff'g 3 Hughes, 139 Fed. Cas. No. 8, 192.

345

the United States had continuously objected that the United States was the real defendant, the real party in interest, that it had not consented to be sued, and that, therefore, the case should be dismissed.

The issue was thus perfectly clear. The government had seized private property without the slightest authority of law, had established upon it a national cemetery and fort, excluded the owner from possession, and when reparation was sought, admitted the wrongful seizure, held it in defiance of law and right on the mediæval prerogative of the British Crown,— that no matter what wrong the King had committed against a subject he could not be sued to right the wrong without his own consent; and the rule in this country contended for was much harsher than in England, because, as Judge Miller pointed out, for generations English citizens so wronged, by a Petition of Right, could secure the consent of the crown to be sued and have justice, and in modern times that Petition is seldom if ever denied. Again, the act of the government was in absolute derogation of the Fifth Amendment to the Constitution, which provides that private property shall not be taken for public use without compensation. The government then was denying a solemn right created by the very instrument which gave it existence. It was a situation that would appeal most powerfully to that great jurist, Judge Miller, second in ability only to Marshall, and he handled it in characteristic fashion. With irresistible logic he strips away the kingly tradition, shows how utterly inapplicable it is to a republican form of government created by a written constitution with its strict limitations. It must be noted that he applied the decision impartially to the federal government and the states, despite the Eleventh Amendment. Every part of the decision applied to both, and it has been so accepted. He says:

"It is obvious that in our system of jurisprudence the principle is as applicable to each of the states as it is to the United States, except in those cases when by the constitution a state of the Union may be sued in this court.

"Under our system the people, who are there called subjects, are the sovereign. Their rights, whether collective or individual, are not bound to give way to a sentiment of loyalty to the person of the monarch. The citizen here knows no person, however near to those in power, or however powerful himself, to whom he need yield the rights which the law secures to him when it is well administered. When he, in one of the courts of competent jurisdiction, has established his right to property, there is no reason why deference to any person, natural or artificial, not even the United States, should prevent him from using the means which the law gives him for the protection and enforcement of that right."

347

He then cites the early case of United States vs. Peters[7], where it was held that on a judgment of an individual against the treasurer of the state of Pennsylvania for money wrongfully held in the state treasury could be recovered, although the state held and claimed the money; a case which nearly led to an armed conflict between the federal authorities and the state of Pennsylvania. He cites at some length the case of Osborn vs. Bank[8], and Brown vs. Huger[9], where a suit for the possession of the military arsenal of the United States at Harper's Ferry was sustained. Citing the Fifth Amendment with its several provisions for the protection of the liberty of the citizens, he says:

"If this constitutional provision is a sufficient authority for the court to interfere to rescue a prisoner from the hands of those holding him under the asserted authority of the government, what reason is there that the same courts shall not give remedy to the citizen whose property has been seized without due process of law and devoted to public use without just compensation?

"Looking at the question upon principle, and apart from the authority of adjudged cases, we think it still clearer that this branch of the defense cannot be maintained. It seems to be opposed to all the principles

7. 9 U. S. (5 Cr.) 115, 3 L. ed. 53.
8. 22 U. S. (9 Wheat.) 738, 6 L. ed. 204.
9. 62 U. S. (21 How.) 305, 16 L. ed. 125.

upon which the rights of the citizen, when brought in collision with the acts of the government, must be determined. In such cases there is no safety for the citizen, except in the protection of the judicial tribunals, for rights which have been invaded by the officers of the government, professing to act in its name. There remains to him but the alternative of resistance, which may amount to crime. The position assumed here is that, however clear his rights, no remedy can be afforded to him when it is seen that his opponent is an officer of the United States, claiming to act under its authority; for, as Chief Justice Marshall says, to examine whether this authority is rightfully assumed is the exercise of jurisdiction, and must lead to the decision of the merits of the question. The objection of the plaintiffs in error necessarily forbids any inquiry into the truth of the assumption that the parties setting up such authority are lawfully possessed of it, for the argument is that the formal suggestion of the existence of such authority forbids any inquiry into the truth of the suggestion. But why should not the truth of the suggestion and the lawfulness of the authority be made the subject of judicial investigation? In the case supposed the court has before it a plaintiff capable of suing, a defendant who has no personal exemption from suit, and a cause of action cognizable in the court —a case within the meaning of the term, as employed in the constitution and defined by the decisions of this court. It is to be presumed in favor of the jurisdiction of the court that the plaintiff may be able to prove the right which he asserts in his declaration. What is that right as established by the verdict of the jury in this case? It is the right to the possession of the homestead of plaintiff—a right to recover that which has been taken from him by force and violence, and detained by the strong hand. This right being clearly established, we are told that the court can proceed no further, because it appears that certain military officers, acting under the orders of the president, have seized this estate, and converted one part of it into a military fort and another into a cemetery. It is not pretended, as the case now stands, that the president had any lawful authority to do this, or that the legislative body could give him any such authority except upon the payment of just compensation. The defense stands here solely upon the absolute immunity from judicial inquiry of every one who asserts authority from the executive branch of the government, however clear it may be made that the executive possessed no such power. Not only that no such power is given, but that it is absolutely prohibited, both to the executive and the legislative, to deprive any one of life, liberty or property without due process of law, or to take private property without just compensation.

"These provisions for the security of the rights of the citizen stand in the constitution in the same connection and upon the same ground as they regard his liberty and his property. It cannot be denied that both were intended to be enforced by the judiciary as one of the departments of the government established by that constitution. As we have already said, the writ of habeas corpus has been often used to defend the liberty of the citizen, and even his life, against the assertion of unlawful authority on the part of the executive and legislative branches of the government. See Ex Parte Milligan[10], and the case of Kilbourn, discharged from the custody of the sergeant-at-arms of the house of representatives by Chief Justice Carter. Kilbourn vs. Thompson[11].

"No man in this country is so high that he is above the law. No officer of the law may set that law at defiance with impunity. All the officers of the government, from the highest to the lowest, are creatures of the law and are bound to obey it. It is the only supreme power in our system of government, and every man who by accepting office participates in its functions is only the more strongly bound to submit to that supremacy, and to observe the limitations which it imposes upon the exercise of the authority which it gives.

"Courts of justice are established, not only to decide upon the controverted rights of the citizens as against each other, but also upon rights in controversy between

10. 71 U. S. (4 Wall.) 2, 18 L. ed. 281. Discussed, ante, Chapter IX.
11. 103 U. S. 168, 26 L. ed. 377.

them and the government, and the docket of this court is crowded with controversies of the latter class. Shall it be said, in the face of all this, and of the acknowledged right of the judiciary to decide in proper cases, statutes which have been passed by both branches of congress and approved by the president to be unconstitutional, that the courts cannot give remedy when the citizen has been deprived of his property by force, his estate seized and converted to the use of the government without any lawful authority, without any process of law, and without any compensation? If such be the law of this country, it sanctions a tyranny which has no existence in the monarchies of Europe, nor in any other government which has a just claim to well-regulated liberty and the protection of personal rights. It cannot be, then, that when in a suit between two citizens for the ownership of real estate, one of them has established his right to the possession of the property according to all the forms of judicial procedure, and by the verdict of a jury and the judgment of the court, the wrongful possessor can say successfully to the court, 'Stop, here I hold by order of the president, and the progress of justice must be stayed.' That, though the nature of the controversy is one peculiarly appropriate to the judicial function, though the United States is no party to the suit, though one of the three great branches of the government to which by the constitution this duty has been assigned has declared its judgment after a fair trial, the unsuccessful party can interpose an absolute veto upon that judgment by the production of an order of the secretary of war, which that officer had no more authority to make than the humblest private citizen."

Judge Miller concludes with a striking description of that independent branch of the government, the Judiciary.

"If it be said that the proposition here established may subject the property, the officers of the United States, and the performance of their indispensable functions to hostile proceedings in the state courts, the answer is that no case can arise in a state court where the interests, the property, the rights, or the authority of the federal government may come in question, which cannot be removed into a court of the United States under existing laws. In all cases, therefore, where such questions can arise, they are to be decided, at the option of the parties representing the United States, in courts which are the creation of the federal government. The slightest consideration of the nature, the character, the organization, and the powers of these courts will dispel any fear of serious injury to the government at their hands. While by the constitution the judicial department is recognized as one of the three great branches among which all the powers and functions of the government are distributed, it is inherently the weakest of them all. Dependent as its courts are for the enforcement of their judgments upon officers appointed by the executive, and removable at his pleasure, with no patronage and no control of purse or sword, their power and influence rests solely upon the public sense of the necessity for the existence of a tribunal to which all may appeal for the assertion and protection of rights guaranteed by the constitution and by the laws of the land, and on the confidence reposed in the soundness of their decisions and the purity of their motives. From such a tribunal no well-founded fear can be entertained of injustice to the government or purpose to obstruct or diminish its just authority."

It was a 5 to 4 opinion, the Chief Justice, Gray, Bradley and Woods dissenting. The opinion by Judge Gray is largely taken up with considerations of the English precedents, and wholly fails to notice the differences in form of the two governments. He says:

"To maintain an action for the recovery of possession of property held by the sovereign through its agents, not claiming any title or rights in themselves, but only as the representatives of the sovereign and in its behalf, is to maintain an action to recover possession of the property against the sovereign; and to invade such possession of the agents, by execution or other judicial process, is to invade the possession of the sovereign and to violate the fundamental maxim, that the sovereign cannot be sued. That maxim is not limited to a monarchy, but is of equal force in a republic. In the one, as in the other, it is essential to the common defense and general welfare, that the sovereign should not, without its consent, be dispossessed by judicial process of forts, arsenals, military posts, and ships of war necessary to guard the national existence against insurrection and invasion, of custom houses and revenue cutters, employed in the collection of the revenue; or of light-houses and light-ships, established for the security of commerce with foreign nations and among the different parts of the country."

It would seem that a sufficient answer to this is, that the government, before it erects a fort, arsenal, custom-house or light-house, should take that ordinary precaution of inquiring, through an abstract of title, whether it has title to the ground on which the public improvement is to be made. According to the opinion of the four dissenting judges, the government may seize any piece of realty without even a color of right, erect thereon a public building, refuse the owner compensation, and contemptuously disregard his suit for relief. This is simple tyranny, violating the very instrument which creates the government itself. The fact that four such eminent judges should entertain this view, shows to what extent a certain order of legal mind clings to the mouldering past.

In the course of the argument, one of the judges asked this question of Judge Shipman, one of the counsel for Lee: "Do I understand your position to be that if the title to a piece of land on which the government has set up a light-house should be disputed, the claimant might bring an action of ejectment, and if successful, remove the light-house?" The intrepid judge replied: "Certainly, that is my position. Far better extinguish all the light-houses there are, rather than put out the light of the law."

So once more this great court stood as the guardian of the rights of the individual against the aggression of any power, even that of the state. This was followed in 1885 by the case of Poindexter vs. Greenhow.[12] Virginia, in 1870, had refunded its debt and issued new certificates of indebtedness, the interest coupons on which were made receivable for taxes. Later, the Mahone-Riddleberger Legislature had repudiated this contract by repealing the redeemability of the coupons. Poindexter tendered to Greenhow, the city Treasurer of the city of Richmond, who was tax-collector, one of these coupons in part payment of his state taxes. Greenhow refused to receive it. Distraint was levied on Poindexter's property for the whole amount of the tax, and he brought suit in detinue against Greenhow for the property distrained. The defense was made that the suit was against the state

12. 114 U. S. 270, 29 L. ed. 185, 5 Sup. Ct. Rep. 903, 962.

and therefore not maintainable. In a lengthy opinion by Judge Field, the decisions in Osborn vs. Bank and United States vs. Lee, were applied, and the plaintiff recovered.

Since then these decisions have been applied to prevent the oppression of the individual in any form by officers of the state or federal government, acting under void legislation. So much of the Eleventh Amendment remains that the state cannot be directly sued, but none of its officers or agents can justify wrong to individuals by pleading the authority of the government, when such authority is illegal.

CHAPTER XV.

The Revolution.

In the preceding fourteen chapters I have covered
almost exactly one hundred years of the life of the
Supreme Court, considering those decisions which
seem to me epochal and formative. Surveying these
decisions as a whole, it is clear that the formative influence of the Supreme Court has been controlling in retaining the structure of the Government as the Fathers
intended it. While the Court has at times been
strongly Nationalistic, and at other times preponder-
atingly for the rights of the States; nevertheless the
statement of Judge Miller, in the Slaughter-House
cases, is unqualifiedly true:

"Whatever fluctuations may be seen in the history
of public opinion on this subject during the period of
our national existence, we think it will be found that
this court, so far as its functions required, has always
held, with a steady and even hand, the balance between state and federal power, and we trust that such
may continue to be the history of its relation to that
subject so long as it shall have duties to perform which
demand of it a construction of the Constitution, or of
any of its parts."

358

Marshall, the strongest of Federalists, respected the rights of the States with the utmost care. It was early established that the State Courts were supreme within their own sphere. That whenever a State Court had interpreted its own Constitution or laws or procedure, such determination was binding upon the Supreme Court of the United States. Marshall brooked no interference in the exercise of national jurisdiction in interpreting "the Constitution, laws, and treaties of the United States." But he was equally sedulous to preserve the independence of the States from Federal interference. He saw with the broad vision of a statesman what the founders clearly saw, that a careful maintenance of the just balance of power between these two sovereignties was necessary for the prosperity and continuity of this Republic. So, under the guidance of this great court, the centrifugal power of the Federal Government, and the centripetal force of the State Governments, had been held in absolute balance.

At the end of a hundred years the Federal power had been firmly consolidated and the power of the States remained undiminished. We approach now a Revolution in our form of government, accomplished by the Supreme Court of the United States, so startling that it seems almost incredible, and this Revolution was completed so silently that it has passed almost unnoticed, even by the careful historians of the Constitution and of the Court.

If there was anything definitely decided by the Slaughter-House Cases, it was that the Supreme Court of the United States had no power to interfere with the domestic concerns, Constitutions and Statutes of the States. The doctrine was repeatedly affirmed in the next fifteen years, in the Civil Rights and other cases, but from the hour that decision was announced, litigants began a continuous and persistent assault upon the doctrine of the Slaughter-House Cases. Appeals from state decisions under the Fourteenth Amendment, claims that the party had been deprived of his property by state legislation and state decisions "without due process of law," poured in upon the court. These cases became so numerous that the court, at one time, somewhat petulantly reproved lawyers who were bringing these cases up from the State Courts, and begged them to read again the Slaughter-House decision.

That corporations should seek the protection of the Federal Courts wherever possible, is natural. There is, among the great mass of our people, a deep rooted hostility to corporations, born partly of fear of these great aggregations of capital, nourished, more or less, by demagogues, but partly growing out of evil practices, corruption and oppression of corporate bodies. To reach the Federal Court and especially the equity side, thereby evading a trial by jury generally prejudiced against it, is the natural aim of every corporate litigant.

If the Slaughter-House Cases could be reversed or annulled, and if the Fourteenth Amendment could be so interpreted as to include within its protection, not only colored men, but all persons; and if a corporation could be held to be a person within the meaning of this Amendment, it would be an enormous gain for corporate litigants, thus escaping not only state courts but jury trial,—as such protection would always be exercised on the equity side.

Therefore lawyers for corporations continuously and skillfully assaulted the court to break down the force of the Slaughter-House decision. In this they had a powerful advocate on the Supreme Bench, in Judge Field, who was not only a vigorous Nationalist, but believed thoroughly that the Federal Courts were instituted largely to protect invested wealth from confiscatory assaults by any agency of the state.

Five years after the Slaughter-House Cases, in 1877, the case of Davidson vs. New Orleans[1] was decided, and Judge Miller wrote the opinion. The case involved the validity of the assessment of certain taxes by the city of New Orleans, but the court held that inasmuch as the law providing for these taxes gave the taxpayer a hearing in the state courts which decided against her on appeal, that thereby she had had

1. 96 U. S. 97, 24 L. ed. 616, aff'g 27 La. Ann. 20.

"due process of law." The court did not undertake to investigate the decision of the Supreme Court of Louisiana. It merely examined the Statute, and having found that the defendant had had her day in court, that she could not bring herself within the Fourteenth Amendment. The fact that the court considered her claim, showed a tendency to extend the doctrine of the Slaughter-House Cases to other persons than those of color. Comparing the language of the Fifth Amendment, which is identical with that used in the Fourteenth Amendment, Judge Miller remarks:

"It is not a little remarkable, that while this provision (taken from the Fifth Amendment), has been in the Constitution of the United States, as a restraint upon the authority of the Federal Government, for nearly a century, and while, during all that time, the manner in which the powers of that Government have been exercised has been watched with jealousy, and subjected to the most rigid criticism in all its branches, this special limitation upon its powers has rarely been invoked in the judicial forum or the more enlarged theater of public discussion. But while it has been a part of the Constitution, as a restraint upon the power of the States, only a very few years, the docket of this court is crowded with cases in which we are asked to hold that State Courts and State Legislatures have deprived their own citizens of life, liberty or property without due process of law. There is here abundant evidence that there exists some strange misconception of the scope of this provision as found in the Fourteenth Amendment. In fact, it would seem, from the character of many of the cases before us, and the arguments made in them, that the clause under consideration is looked upon as a means of bringing to the test of the decisions of this court the abstract opinions of every unsuccessful litigant in a State Court of the justice of the decision against him, and of the merits of the legislation on which such a decision may be founded. If, therefore, it were possible to define what it is for a State to deprive a person of life, liberty or property without due process of law, in terms which would cover every exercise of power thus forbidden to the State, and exclude those which are not, no more useful construction could be furnished by this or any other court to any part of the fundamental law."

He then lays down the fundamental proposition that where a person has had his day in court, by the ordinary procedure of the state where the case is tried, that is due process of law with which the Supreme Court will not interfere, he says:

"That whenever by the laws of a State, or by state authority, a tax, assessment, servitude, or other burden is imposed upon property for the public use, whether it be of the whole State or of some more limited portion of the community, and those laws provide for a

363

mode of confirming or contesting the charge thus imposed, in the ordinary courts of justice, with such notice to the person, or such proceeding in regard to the property as is appropriate to the nature of the case, the judgment in such proceedings cannot be said to deprive the owner of his property without due process of law, however obnoxious it may be to other objections.

"It may violate some provision of the State Constitution against unequal taxation; but the Federal Consitution imposes no restraints on the States in that regard. If private property be taken for public uses without just compensation, it must be remembered that, when the Fourteenth Amendment was adopted, the provision on that subject, in immediate juxtaposition in the Fifth Amendment, with the one we are construing, was left out, and this was taken. It may possibly violate some of those principles of general constitutional law, which if we were sitting in review of a Circuit Court of the United States, as we were in the Topeka Case[2], we could take jurisdiction of. But however this may be, or under whatever other clause of the Federal Constitution we may review the case, it is not possible to hold that whereby the laws of the State the party aggrieved has, as regards the issues affecting his property, a fair trial in a court of justice, according to the modes of proceeding applicable to such case,

2. Citizens Sav. & L. Assoc. v. Topeka, 87 U. S. (20 Wall.) 655, 22 L. ed. 455, aff'g 3 Dill. 376, Fed. Cas. No. 2, 734.

that he has been deprived of that property without due process of law. This was clearly stated by this court, speaking by the Chief Justice, in the case of Kennard vs. Morgan[3], and repeated, in substance, in the case of McMillan vs. Anderson[4].

"This proposition covers the present case. Before the assessment could be collected, or become effectual, the statute required that the tableau of assessments should be filed in the proper District Court of the State; that personal service of notice, with reasonable time to object, should be served on all owners who were known and within reach of process, and due advertisement made as to those who were unknown, or could not be found. This was complied with; and the party complaining here appeared, and had a full and fair hearing in the court of the first instance, and afterwards in the Supreme Court. If this be not due process of law, then the words can have no definite meaning as used in the Constitution."

This doctrine of the independence of the state, wherever their legislation or decisions did not interfere with the national concerns, was first announced in 1798 in the case of Calder vs. Bull[5], and continuously affirmed and reinforced in almost every possible sort of a case for nearly one hundred years.

3. 92 U. S. 480, 23 L. ed. 478, aff'g 25 La. Ann. 238.
4. 95 U. S. 37, 24 L. ed. 335, aff'g 27 La. Ann. 18.
5. 3 U. S. (3 Dall.) 386, 1 L. ed. 648, aff'g 2 Root (Conn.) 350.

In Galpin vs. Page[6], decided in 1874, four years after the Fourteenth Amendment was adopted, the question of the conclusiveness of the finding of a state court as to its own jurisdiction, came squarely before the Supreme Court. The finding of the lower and Supreme State Court upon the question of jurisdiction was collaterally attacked in the Federal Court. Judge Field said:

"The adjudication of the appellate court (of California) constitutes the law of that case upon the points adjudged, and is binding upon the Circuit Court and every other court, when brought before it for consideration. The Circuit Court possesses no revisory power over the decisions of the Supreme Court of the State, and any argument to show that that court mistook the law and misjudged the jurisdictional fact, would have been out of place. There were no facts before the Circuit Court which were not before the Supreme Court of the State when its judgment was pronounced."

Note the language, "any argument to show that that court mistook the law and misjudged the jurisdictional fact, would have been out of place." Such then was the law down to 1894; in other words, for twenty years after the decision in the Slaughter-House Cases. During those years the court had been completely reorganized. The Judges who concurred in the Slaughter-

6. 85 U. S. (18 Wall.) 350, 21 L. ed. 959, rev'g 1 Sawy. 309, Fed. Cas. No. 5, 205.

House Decision had died or retired, and their places taken by Judges of vastly different training, views and leanings.

We have just noted that in the decision of Galpin vs. Paige, the finding of a state court as to its own jurisdiction is final and binding upon the Federal Courts. I turn now to Scott vs. McNeal[7], decided in 1894. In that case the plaintiff Scott, living in the state of Washington, had disappeared from his home. After an absence of more than seven years, with nothing heard from him, his wife applied to the Probate Court in the proper county setting forth the facts of his disappearance and the length of time that had elapsed, and the Probate Court, following the presumption arising from seven years' absence, found that Scott was dead, and appointed an administrator. The administrator duly applied for authority to sell the real estate of Scott. A piece of land was sold, and the title passed by mesne conveyances to the defendant, McNeal. Scott re-appeared, forcefully denied that he was dead or ever had been, and brought ejectment against McNeal for the possession of this land. It was conceded that all of the proceedings connected with the sale of the land had been regular and according to law. It was a collateral attack and Scott relied upon the Fourteenth Amendment to invalidate these transfers of his land; that, inasmuch as he was alive when

7. 154 U. S. 34, 38 L. ed. 896, 14 Sup. Ct. Rep. 1109, rev'g 5 Wash. 309, 34 Am. St. Rep. 863, 31 Pac. 873.

the administration was had, he had been deprived of his property without due process of law. The lower court held that the proceedings were regular, that the presumption of death arising from seven years' absence under the Washington Law was conclusive as to the property rights involved, and denied the plaintiff any relief. He appealed to the Supreme Court at Washington[8], which affirmed the decision of the lower court, and denied the plaintiff any relief; he then appealed to the Supreme Court of the United States. The Supreme Court held that, under the Fourteenth Amendment, Scott had been deprived of his property without due process of law, and reversed the case. It disregarded the findings of the lower court as to its jurisdiction; ignored all of its previous decisions from the Slaughter-House Cases on, and held that wherever the question of jurisdiction was raised the Supreme Court, under the Fourteenth Amendment, could examine the jurisdiction of the state court, and that it was not bound as held in Galpin vs. Page, by the finding of the state court upon this jurisdictional matter.

The amazing thing about the case is that, while it reverses in effect the doctrine of at least eight of its own decisions, not the slightest reference is made to any of them. So far as the court's opinion is concerned, the great decisions in the Slaughter-House Cases and Davidson vs. New Orleans, might have been

8. 5 Wash. 309, 34 Am. Rep. 863, 31 Pac. 873.

so much waste paper. It ignores the fact that Scott had had his day in court, had had a fair trial with all the forms of law, and that therefore either he had had due process of law, or else the decision in Davidson vs. New Orleans was not the law of the Supreme Court,—but no reference is made to that case. The court cites some of the Civil Rights Cases which, I have noted in a previous chapter[9], such as Ex Parte Virginia, that the provisions of the Fourteenth Amendment "extend to the acts of the state, whether through its legislative, its executive, or its judicial authorities." None of these decisions are authority in any way for the decision in Scott vs. McNeal. For instance, in Ex Parte Virginia, which was the colored Jurors case, the court expressly held that the County Judge, in drawing the Jury, was not acting in a judicial capacity. In fact, down to the decision of Scott vs. McNeal, no decision had yet held that the Fourteenth Amendment applied to judicial acts performed in the due course of the law of the state, in a trial where the party complaining had had full opportunity to defend and right of appeal. Such cases had been uniformly held to be outside the purview of the Fourteenth Amendment, however else it might be interpreted.

By this decision the court, in effect, constituted itself a court of appeal and errors from every decision of the State Supreme Court, where the question of jurisdic-

9. See, ante, Part III, Chapter XII.

369

tion was involved. This opened a whole new field of jurisdiction, that has been largely occupied by litigants, and has greatly increased the labors of the court. That it was revolutionary in its character, no candid mind can doubt.

I turn now to another phase of this Revolution, equally remarkable. The Railroad corporations were continuously appealing to the Supreme Court from various restrictions, burdens, and servitudes imposed by the State Legislatures, invoking always the Fourteenth Amendment. The Court uniformly considered these appeals, and as uniformly denied them. One of the crucial cases was Stone vs. Farmers Loan & Trust Company[10], decided in 1886, where the Mobile and Ohio Railroad Company appealed from a law of Mississippi establishing a Railroad Commission, with power to regulate rates. The railroad company relied upon its charter as a perpetual grant of power to fix its own rates. The Supreme Court held that the Legislature could not thus part with its police power of rate-regulation, unless it was shown by the charter in the plainest and most specific terms, and the claim was denied. Upon the question of the Fourteenth Amendment, the court held that the state had a right to establish a Railroad Commission with power to fix rates, but as the Commission had not as yet fixed rates, no

10. 116 U. S. 307, 29 P. ed. 636, 11 Sup. Ct. Rep. 334, 388, 1191, revs'g 20 Fed. 270.

right of the railroad company had been impaired, and the appeal was dismissed, but in the course of the decision, the court used this language, after upholding the power of regulation:

"From what has thus been said, it is not to be inferred that this power of limitation or regulation is itself without limit. This power to regulate is not a power to destroy, and limitation is not the equivalent of confiscation. Under pretense of regulating fares and freights, the state cannot require a railroad corporation to carry persons or property without reward; neither can it do that which, in law, amounts to a taking of private property for public use without just compensation, or without due process of law. What would have this effect, we need not now say, because no tariff has yet been fixed by the commission, and the statute of Mississippi expressly provides "that in all trials of cases brought for a violation of any tariff of charges, as fixed by the commission, it may be shown in defense that such tariff so fixed is unjust."

This was pure dictum, unnecessary to the decision of the case, but it expressed the views of the court. It was a warning that railroad property could not be confiscated by the will of the state Legislature. The court had already overruled its decision in the Granger Cases, holding that the power to fix rates was purely legislative, with which the courts could not interfere. It will be noted that, in the paragraph just quoted, the

371

court held that a rate that did not give the railroad
company a return upon its investments would amount
to the taking of private property for public use without compensation. A most righteous decision, applicable to all these statutes in all courts.

In all of these cases the question of whether a cor-
portion is a person under the Fourteenth Amendment,
had not been discussed by the court. In Minneapolis
Railroad Company vs. Beckwith[11], decided in 1889,
this momentous proposition was thus disposed of by
the court, in the opinion of Judge Field, considering
the Fourteenth Amendment:

"It is contended by counsel, as the basis of his argument, and we admit the soundness of his position, that
corporations are persons within the meaning of the
clause in question. It was so held in Santa Clara
County vs. Southern Pacific Railroad Co.[12], and the
doctrine was reasserted in Mining Co. vs. Pennsylvania[13]. We admit also, as contended by him, that corporations can invoke the benefits of provisions of the
Constitution and laws which guarantee to persons the
enjoyment of property or afford to them the means for
its protection, or prohibit legislation injuriously affecting it."

11. 129 U. S. 26, 32 L. ed. 585, 9 Sup. Ct. Rep. 207.

12. 118 U. S. 394, 396, 30 L. ed. 118, 6 Sup. Ct. Rep. 1132, aff'g 9 Sawy.
165, 18 Fed. 385.

13. 125 U. S. 181, 189, 31 L. ed. 650, 8 Sup. Ct. Rep. 737.

It will be noted that there is here no discussion, no reasoning in favor of this proposition. Judge Field said that it was so held in Santa Clara County vs. Southern Pacific Railroad Company. When we turn to that case, we find that nothing of the sort was held. The question of whether the word person in the Fourteenth Amendment included corporations, was not even mentioned in the Santa Clara County Case. In that case, the law of California provided that real estate and improvements should be assessed separately, and that among the various kinds of improvements were fences. The state attempted to assess the fences as part of the railroad right of way. The company paid the tax under protest, and brought suit in the Federal Court to recover. Judge Field, sitting in Circuit, decided in favor of the Railroad Company, and held that the word person included corporations. When it came to the Supreme Court of the United States on appeal the court, after noting the constitutional question raised by the railroad, said:

"The propositions embodied in the conclusions reached in the Circuit Court were discussed with marked ability by counsel who appeared in this court for the respective parties. Their importance cannot well be over-estimated; for they not only involve a construction of the recent amendments to the national constitution in their application to the constitution and the legislation of a state, but upon their determination, if it were necessary to consider them, would depend the system of taxation devised by that state for raising revenue, from certain corporations, for the support of her government. These questions belong to a class which this court should not decide, unless their determination is essential to the disposal of the case in which they arise. Whether the present cases require a decision of them depends upon the soundness of another proposition, upon which the court below, in view of its conclusions upon other issues, did not deem it necessary to pass."

It then proceeds to discuss the law of California, decides that, under that law, the fences are not part of the roadbed and could not be assessed, under the state law, and affirms the decision of the Circuit Court upon that ground, wholly ignoring the question of the Fourteenth Amendment. The court says:

"It results that the court below might have given judgment in each case for the defendant upon the ground that the assessment, which was the foundation of the action, included property of material value which the state board was without jurisdiction to assess, and the tax levied upon which cannot, from the record, be separated from that imposed upon other property embraced in the same assessment. As the judgment can be sustained upon this ground, it is not necessary to consider any other questions raised by the pleadings and the facts found by the court."

It is apparent that Judge Field had mistaken his own opinion in the Circuit Court for the opinion of the Supreme Court on appeal—probably one of the most curious mistakes ever made by a Judge of the Supreme Court.

Turning to the case of Pembina Consolidated Silver Mining and Milling Company vs. Pennsylvania,[14] decided in 1888, we find that the court was there considering the question of whether the state could impose a license-tax upon a non-resident corporation, for the privilege of maintaining an office and doing business in the state. The court held that a state had a right to exclude or admit foreign corporations at its pleasure, and in admitting such corporations it could impose conditions which were entirely valid, if they were uniform as to all corporations. The question of whether a corporation was a person was not before the court. It was not argued, it was not discussed. The court does say, however:

"Under the designation of person there is no doubt that a private corporation is included."

To begin with, this general statement of the law is not a correct statement, as I shall show later. In this case it was pure dictum. That was equally true of the statement in the Beckwith case, because the court there held that the Iowa Statute, under consideration, was valid, and it was not necessary to consider whether

14. 125 U. S. 181, 31 L. ed. 650, 8 Sup. Ct. Rep. 737.

375

the Fourteenth Amendment would apply. From thence on, without any further discussion in treating these cases as having settled the matter, the Supreme Court has uniformly held that the word "person" includes "corporations," under the Fourteenth Amendment.

Considering the vast mass of litigation which this doctrine has created, and which now overwhelms the court, it is certainly an astonishing thing that the principle should have been adopted thus without discussion, without reasoning, without considering binding precedents in the past decisions of the court.

I propose now to discuss the reasonableness of this classification. In so doing it will be understood that I am not discussing the abstract justice of this inclusion. Of course, corporations should have every legal right for the protection of their property that is given to individuals. That is not the question here. The question is, did Congress, in submitting the Fourteenth Amendment, and the states in adopting it, intend to change the form of the Constitution, destroy the power of the states and of state courts, as they had existed under the Constitution for a hundred years? It will be observed that these decisions completely nullify the doctrine of the Slaughter-House cases, without even alluding to that decision. So, in considering the propriety of extending the word "person" to include "corporations," we will disregard, for the moment, the decision of the Slaughter-House cases, as the Supreme Court has done and consider the Amendment itself.

It is true that very frequently the courts hold that the word person includes corporations. It has been so held in many penal as well as civil Statutes. There is much confusion, however, as to when this inclusion should be applied. Some courts, in fact many courts, hold that the inclusion will not be made unless it was the plain intent of the Legislature that it should be. Probably the best test of such inclusion is to be found in a decision of the Supreme Court itself, Beaston vs. Farmers Bank.[15] In that case the court had under consideration a Statute which made the Government a preferred creditor where a "person" indebted to the Government became insolvent. The question was whether, as there used, the word person included corporations, the suit being against a corporation. Judge McKinley thus expresses the test:

"Corporations are to be deemed and considered persons when the circumstances in which they are placed are identical with those of natural persons expressly included in such Statutes."

The court finds that the corporate defendant in that case was placed in circumstances identical with those of a person who had become insolvent, and holds that

---

15. 37 U. S. (12 Pet.) 102, 9 L. ed. 1017, aff'g 7 Gill & J. (Md.) 421, 28 Am. Dec. 236.

in such case the word person includes corporations. This is the clear and logical test, and it is a test which the Supreme Court has set up, although no allusion was made to this case by Judge Field.

Turning to the Fourteenth Amendment, the first section contains two propositions, the second dependent upon the first. The first is, "all persons born or naturalized in the United States and subject to the jurisdiction thereof, are citizens of the United States and of the state wherein they reside." Certainly this cannot include corporations, as corporations can neither be born nor naturalized. The intention of this provision, as decided in the Slaughter-House Cases, was to make every person born in the United States a citizen of the United States, regardless of whether he was at a particular time a citizen of any particular state under its law. It created, in effect, a national citizenship, citizenship theretofore having been entirely a matter for the states to regulate.

It then proceeds with the provision that has been so often and so much mooted, that "no state shall make or enforce any law which shall abridge the privileges or immunities of the citizens of the United States." The word "citizen," as here used, undoubtedly refers back to the citizenship created by the preceding paragraph, a citizenship composed of persons either born in the United States or naturalized; and the court, as late as

378

1869, in the case of Paul vs. Virginia,[16] had expressly held that a corporation was not a citizen under the second section of the Fourth Article of the Constitution, from which this language is taken verbatim. Follows a semicolon, and then: "nor shall any state deprive any person of life, liberty, or property, etc." The privileges and the immunities of the citizen, and the protection of the person, are thus inclosed in one paragraph.

It is to me extraordinary that anyone can hold that it was ever the intention, in adopting this amendment, that the word "person," as last used above, was intended to include anything but a natural person, because the entire section, up to that point, clearly speaks of natural persons and no others. The second section provides for the apportionment of representatives among the several states, according to their respective numbers, "counting the whole number of persons in each state." The third section provides "no person, etc., shall be eligible to office who has been engaged in insurrection against the United States."

It will not do, in construing this great Amendment, to wrench a single paragraph from its context and interpret its meaning when thus isolated. Like a will, it must be read from the four corners, to obtain the intent of whoever framed it. So read, the Amendment speaks of persons five times. In four of them

16. 75 U. S. (8 Wall.) 168, 19 L. ed. 357.

the reference cannot be to any one but natural persons. Are we to say then that the word "person" as used in the last paragraph of the first section, meant something other and different from its meaning in the other four places? If we adopt the test of the Supreme Court itself, we shall find it difficult to think so. Are corporations placed in circumstances identical with those of natural persons expressly included throughout the amendment? Certainly that cannot be. The prohibition in the very language of the paragraph we speak of, includes not only deprivation of property but of life and liberty. Certainly a corporation has neither life nor liberty which is here mentioned. Life, as used here, means physical life, liberty means personal liberty. In order to meet the Supreme Court's views, the paragraph would have to read like this: "nor shall any state deprive any person of life or liberty, or any person or corporation of property." That is the meaning which Judge Field's decision gives to the expression, which in the Amendment is: "nor shall any state deprive any person of life, liberty or property."

No court, outside of the Supreme Court of the United States, has ever held a corporation to be a person under a Statute similar in language, or in intent, to this. If we consider the entire amendment, regardless of its history and the political events which impelled its adoption, the conclusion is irresistible that the Amendment throughout speaks of, and was intended to be confined to, natural persons. Throughout it deals exclusively with natural persons, with their citizenship, their life, their liberty, their enumeration for representative purposes, and their disfranchisement for insurrection; and yet the court says, in spite of that, that the word person, when it comes to property and property alone, is intended to include corporations.

Judge Field did not undertake, nor has any other Judge of the Supreme Court undertaken, to analyze this Amendment and give any sort of a reason why it was intended to include corporations. No Judge has done so simply because no Judge can. I submit to any candid mind that these decisions—and there are some that I have yet to cite—have amended the Constitution of the United States by the act of the judiciary alone, without any vote of the people who made, and who alone can alter, the Constitution.

The testimony of Judge Miller and his associates in his review of the events which led up to the adoption of the Fourteenth Amendment, a chronicle of events which is in no wise challenged or disputed by the minority opinions, ought to be sufficient; but a further test may be applied. Will any candid student of our political history assert that the states would have adopted this amendment, clearly phrased as it is, if they had known that the Supreme Court would ulti-

381

mately place its present construction on it; that in adopting this amendment they were surrendering a large portion of that independence of the states, which they had enjoyed from the beginning, that they were degrading the dignity and jurisdiction of their own Supreme Courts, making them in effect mere intermediate courts of appeal on the way to the final tribunal; that, as Miller predicted, they were placing the Supreme Court as a Board of Censors to sit in judgment upon every state enactment that affects corporations; that their action was to paralyze and render of the slightest value all future state regulations of public utilities, and orders of public utility commissions? No sane and candid student will make such an assertion. If that be true, then either the adoption of the amendment was procured by false pretenses on the part of Congress, or the intention of the people has been thwarted by the will of the Supreme Court. But Congress no more dreamed of such a construction, when it suggested the amendment, than did the states when they adopted it. All contemporary discussion at the time of the adoption, by public men and the press, shows clearly that the Fourteenth Amendment was supposed to be a mere corollary of the Thirteenth Amendment, conferring citizenship upon the blacks just emancipated and protecting that citizenship, and but for that belief the amendment never would have been adopted.

Indeed the Supreme Court very early established the historical rule of interpretation. In Rhode Island vs. Massachusetts,[17] the court said:

"In the construction of the Constitution we must look to the history of the times and examine the state of things existing when it was framed and adopted."

And in the income tax cases, Pollock vs. Farmers Loan and Trust Company,[18] the court said:

"In construing the Constitution, the court is at liberty to refer to the historical circumstances attending the framing and adoption of the Constitution as well as the entire frame and scheme of the instrument, and the consequence naturally attendant upon the one construction or the other."

To pursue the story of the Revolution. In Chicago, Milwaukee and Saint Paul Railway Company vs. Minnesota,[19] decided in 1890, which came up on writ of error to the Supreme Court of Minnesota, the rate law of Minnesota was called in question. It established a Railroad Commission, with power to fix rates, but made its findings conclusive, and made it the duty of the Supreme Court of the state, when the Commission should apply to it by mandamus, to impose these

17. 37 U. S. (12 Pet.) 657, 9 L. ed. 1233.

18. 157 U. S. 429, 39 L. ed. 759, 15 Sup. Ct. Rep. 673, reversed 158 U. S. 601, 39 L. ed. 1108, 15 Sup. Ct. Rep. 912.

19. 134 U. S. 418, 33 L. ed. 970, 10 Sup. Ct. Rep. 462, 702, revers'g 28 Minn. 281, 37 N. W. 782.

rates upon the carriers. The court held the law invalid, because it deprived the carriers of a right to a judicial review of the reasonableness of the rates. This was in entire harmony with Davidson vs. New Orleans.

A series of cases immediately followed, beginning with the Texas Railroad Commission cases,[20] by which very shortly the Supreme Court assumed and still retains complete control of the rate-making of every public utility whether interstate or intrastate. In the much-discussed case of Smyth vs. Ames,[21] the court established the basis of rate-making upon "reproduction value." Several speculative elements,—such as "going value," loss during preliminary period, etc.,— have since been added, so that today the basis of rate-making, so far from being scientific, is as puzzling and distracting as the famous "rule of reason" in the Anti-Trust Cases.

The Revolution was now complete. It has resulted in an enormous increase in the business of the court. In the last twenty-five years more than two thousand of these cases have been taken to the Supreme Court, and more than eight hundred decided, the others being dismissed for want of merit, and three hundred forty-five state statutes annulled. A curious thing about this

20. Regan v. Farmers' Loan & Trust Co., 154 U. S. 362, 38 L. ed. 1014, 14 Sup. Ct. Rep. 1047.

21. 169 U. S. 466, 42 L. ed. 819, 18 Sup. Ct. Rep. 418, aff'g 64 Fed. 165.

Revolution, is the fact that all the historians of the Supreme Court,—that I have been able to examine,—make no illusion to this vast change in our form of government. All of them leave the impression that the doctrine of the Slaughter-House Cases is still in full force. There seems to be a conspiracy of silence on the subject. Undoubtedly every lawyer whose practice is corporate, or chiefly so, will approve of this Revolution. That is natural. "The dyer's hand is subdued to that which it works in." But, to the thoughtful and impartial lawyer, there is a question whether it is worth while to prevent occasional injustice to corporations by completely destroying that balance of power between the nation and the states that was so carefully established by the founders, and so sedulously guarded by the Supreme Court for more than a hundred years.

The Supreme Court itself took the first step towards centralization, and Congress and the Executive have been swift to follow. As a result, the states have lost their old robust vigor and independence. They have been degraded, in effect, to mere geographical expressions. Their Supreme Courts are no longer courts of last resort, but intermediate tribunals, and the Supreme Court of the United States sits as a Board of Censors upon every enactment that affects corporations, whether local or interstate. This is precisely what Miller predicted would happen if the present interpretation of the Fourteenth Amendment were adopted. The result of this centralization has been to build up a great Bureaucracy in Washington, with more than seven hundred thousand members, constantly increasing. The greatest danger to this country is not from below, but from above; not from the Reds and Anarchists, but from the Bureaucrats. It is profoundly significant, although apparently unnoted by the public, that the scandals that have been rife in Washington have not touched the elective servants of the people, Congress and the President. All the slime and filth of corruption, bribery, and malversation is confined and absolutely limited to the Bureaucracy. Such has it been in all history. It was the corruption and inefficiency of the Bureaucracy, and not Tzarism, that destroyed the great Russian Empire. It was the corruption and inefficiency of the Italian Bureaucracy, as much as Bolshevism, that drove Italy into the arms of Fascisti. It was the corruption and inefficiency of the Spanish Bureaucracy that compelled a Dictatorship. And the Washington Bureaucracy, with its strangle-hold on the government, its corruption and inefficiency, is running true to historical form. A Bureaucracy is the most odious of all tyrannies, because it is anonymous. While we have been pursuing this course, our English cousins have been decentralizing; not only granting full self-government to their Colonies and to Ireland, but decentralizing at home by establishing such local governmental bodies, as the London County Council, with legislative and administrative powers almost equal to our states.

It will be observed that I am against any Revolution, whether from below or above. I am opposed to any Amendment to the Constitution that is not adopted by the people. In short, upon the question of the Constitution, I am a Counter-Revolutionalist, a reactionary. I would replace the ancient land-marks and re-light the old beacons that burned, with an illumining power, for more than a hundred years. While the present court has no outstanding figures like Marshall, Taney, and Miller, in the average of its ability, in its composite character, it has not been surpassed by any in our history. It seems to me that I see signs of a reaction in its decisions, a tendency of the pendulum to swing towards State Rights. I hope this is true. If I did not hope so, I should fear for this Republic.

I do not think that I exaggerate the immeasurable importance of the Federative principle and the independence of the States. I quote from the greatest American historian of our times, John Fiske, in The Critical Period of American History:

"If the day should ever arrive (which God forbid!) when the people of the different parts of our country shall allow their local affairs to be administered by prefects sent from Washington, and when the self-government of the states shall have been so far lost as that of the departments of France, or even so far as that of the counties of England,—on that day the progressive political career of the American people will have come to an end, and the hopes that have been built upon it for the future happiness and prosperity of mankind will be wrecked forever."

CHAPTER XVI.

CONCLUSION

Those who have followed these pages so far, have seen a rude, barbaric people, with the instinct of freedom and self-government gradually emerge, through long struggle and bitter travail, into the highest civilization, and the best form of government, that humanity has yet evolved. The task is now to preserve that government. Can it be improved upon? Doubtless, but not hastily. Such hasty, ill-considered Amendments as the Fourteenth, Fifteenth, Seventeenth, Eighteenth, and Nineteenth have weakened the great edifice, and a few more such will destroy it. The Fourteenth was well meant and, if it had been confined to the protection of the black man, as it was intended, it would have done no harm, although, in that regard, it has done little good. As Senator Thomas, of Colorado, once expressed it: "The Fourteenth Amendment was adopted to protect the negro, and it has been used to protect everyone else but the negro." The Fifteenth Amendment was the most ghastly mistake in our history, since the Constitution left slavery unchecked. The Anglo-Saxon achieved suffrage, and the qualifications for it, by centuries of

389

bitter struggle, that educated him to its use. Suffrage is a privilege, not a right. It should be granted by the state only to those who can intelligently use it, and by its use contribute to the strength and welfare of the state. As well conscript children from the cradle to bear arms, as to grant suffrage to the ignorant. Stripped of the subterfuge of the time, we know that the radicals in Congress granted suffrage to the black man to overwhelm and submerge the political power of the white Anglo-Saxon and make the Southern States Republican. They failed, because the Anglo-Saxon will never submit to the domination of an inferior race. By methods that must be deplored, the Anglo-Saxon wrested from this inferior race his inborn and unconquerable mastery.

That amendment continued indefinitely the old Mason and Dixon Line. It made the two great political parties, one entirely and the other partially, sectional; divided, not upon natural political issues, economic like the tariff, but based on an artificial difference created by fear in the South of the domination of the negro. It split the White Anglo-Saxons of our country into hostile camps, and made it impossible for them to unite against the rising flood of foreign immigration, with its ignorant and corruptible vote,— one of the imminent dangers to the country. Its evil influence has lasted for fifty years, and there will be no end to it until the Republican Party has courage enough to remit to the several states the control of the franchise, where the Founders placed it, and where, for the safety of the Republic, it must always remain.

In this consideration I pass by the terrible immediate consequences of that black domination in the Southern States; the welter of corruption, peculation, crime, and infamy never surpassed in any country. It is an astonishing thing that this historical lesson has had so little effect upon our public men. They solemnly propose independence for the Filipinos, who are no more capable of self-government than an American child of ten years. They still think that the black-and-tan races, south of us, can be self-governing: when, in fact, every one of them is a "despotism, tempered by assination." England is making the same terrible mistake with Egypt and India. You cannot make a Republic on paper, or create a self-governing people by a treaty. Enough of this.

The Sixteenth Amendment was made necessary by a most unfortunate decision of the Supreme Court, reversing a precedent that had stood for a hundred years, by the over-night change of the opinion of one Judge, Shiras[1]. It brought as much odium on that court as the Dred Scott Decision. The Federal government, being a complete sovereignty within its limits, should of course have the power to levy an income

---

1. Pollock v. Farmers' Loan & Trust Co., 158 U. S. 601, 39 L. ed. 1108, 15 Sup. Ct. Rep. 912, revers'g 157 U. S. 429, 39 L. ed. 759, 15 Sup. Ct. Rep. 673.

391

tax, a power possessed by every sovereign in the world, and undoubtedly included by the Founders in its implied powers. For lack of that power the Confederacy failed. Without that power we could not have won the Great War. Whatever evils and inequality may exist in its administration, its principle is sound, a part of national sovereignty, and the Sixteenth Amendment should never have been necessary.

The increasing corruption in the election of United States Senators by the legislatures of the states, compelled the adoption of the Seventeenth Amendment, providing for the election of United States Senators by popular vote. That it cured this evil is undoubted; that it has lowered the level of intelligence and distinction in the Senate is equally undoubted. The cure for this is quite simple. Restore nomination by convention. Not the old corrupt, boss-ridden conventions, whose delegates were picked in the back room of a saloon or a country law office, but a primary election for delegates surrounded by all the safeguards that are now provided by the direct primary, so that the delegates, coming to the convention directly from the grass-rots, shall not represent bosses, but the people.

The enormous expense of the modern primary, which makes it a rich man's pastime; the uncertainty, the indifference of the people which results generally in a candidate chosen by a small minority of the people—all condemn it. If this Republic is to be saved alive, we must return to the representative principle, purged and purified by the light of experience.

The Eighteenth Amendment remains, and will always remain, controversial. I place myself upon safe ground. Sumptuary laws that are suited to pastoral states, like South Dakota and Nebraska, and there easily enforcible, are utterly unsuited to states with great cities, like New York, Chicago, and San Francisco, where the Eighteenth Amendment never has and will never be enforced. It has created a vast addition to the Washington Bureaucracy, an addition both corrupt and inefficient,—so that the term, "federal enforcement officer," has become a by-word, an expression of reproach and contempt. Such laws should be left to the state, such reforms relegated to the growing consciousness of the people that the saloon is as much an enemy to humanity as slavery. It is impossible to enforce any law where public opinion is not back of it. The perfectly well-known result is that the Volstead Act is enforced only in those states, and to the same extent, where it was enforced by state prohibition before its enactment. In the wet states it remains a joke, a farce. The Volstead Act has set back and delayed the real growth of the temperance movement for more years than any one can now predict. I condemn it because it takes from the states a subject of legislation that naturally belongs to them, degrades them, and confers upon the national government powers that were never intended to belong to the central authority. It has weakened the states without accomplishing its object. And it has added to the numbers of that corrupt and inefficient Washington Bureaucracy.

The Nineteenth Amendment, conferring suffrage upon women, is another invasion upon the rights of the states. The women in one state may be sufficiently enfranchised, sufficiently educated, to vote with fair intelligence, though never, in the mass, as intelligently as men. In another state they may be as backward, politically, as they were in the Middle Ages. It would be invidious to name examples. Therefore, each state, as provided originally, should prescribe the qualifications for the franchise.

Woman Suffrage has accomplished nothing governmentally. It has given a few ambitious self-seeking ladies publicity and the spot-light. That was what they wanted; that was what they got; and that is all anybody has gotten from the amendment. The great mass of women are indifferent to the franchise, and either do not vote, or vote as their men-folks advise them—or else wholly at random. Their antics in the last national convention of one of the great political parties were simply pitiful.

There is now an orgy for amending the Constitution. In the last Congress there were 107 propositions of amendment; some of them, of course, duplicates; but all of them intended to degrade local self-government and exaggerate centralization of government. Open bribes were held out to the states, such as that contained in the proposal for a Federal Department of Education, with an enormous appropriation distributed among the states that surrendered their control of education to the federal government. The Shephard-Townley Bill, which would place maternity and childbirth under federal supervision, with another enormous bureau, a myriad agents meddling in every home where the stork is expected. The Child-Labor Amendment already submitted, which will place every mill, manufactory, and mine directly under federal control, with another horde of federal agents entering every home of the industrial class, questioning parents and neighbors and searching the family Bible, to find infractions of the law.

In this country today one man in every twelve is employed and paid by the government, the other eleven support him. Yet a little while, if we continue these amendments, and it will be, in the language of the street, "fifty-fifty." Every producer will support one parasite. There is one sure test to be applied to every constitutional amendment; will it, if adopted, disturb that exquisite balance of power upon whose continuance the future of this great country depends? If it tends to degrade the state and aggrandize the Federal Government, increase the members of the Washington Bureaucracy, then it should be condemned and rejected. Local injustices, where they exist, may, and should, await the healing and the awakening conscience of the state, rather than destroy our form of government, by constitutional amendment. The larger this country grows, the more extended its dominions, the denser its population, the more absolutely necessary is the preservation of local self-government. There is a vast and just complaint against the increasing, cumbrous-inefficiency of the Federal Government. It is the fault of the people. They have overloaded the machine, till it can no longer function properly. The task before thoughtful men is to decentralize that government, reduce it to its proper functions, and thus restore its old time efficiency.

PART IV.

PART IV.

ENCROACHMENT BY THE FEDERAL GOVERNMENT UPON THE POWERS OF THE STATES.

CHAPTER I.

PRELIMINARY MATTERS.

As the guest of the California State Bar Association, Hon. F. Dumont Smith spent some weeks in the fall of 1924 at the Hotel St. Catherine, Avalon, Santa Catalina Island, off the southwestern coast of California, in proximity to Los Angeles, and delivered the Annual Address for that year to the Bar Association on September 12, taking for his subject The Story of the Constitution.

One of the "live" questions engaging the attention of the Bar of the Union, and thoughtful people generally, is the tendency in the political world of the country for the last two decades or more toward Centralization and Paternalism: raising the inquiry— Shall we continue the process of Centralization, destroying the sovereignty of the states, together with the genius and form of our government, or shall we decentralize?

While in California, Mr. Smith delivered yeoman strokes in that cause which lies along the course of the one great thought in the minds of earnest and patriotic citizens everywhere: Bringing Back to the American People the Federal Constitution as it Left the Hands of the Fathers,—that greatest assemblage of statesmen and political wisdom ever brought together under one roof in the history of the world, in the Constitutional Convention which met at Philadelphia in 1787.

During his stay at Avalon, Mr. Smith was invited by the San Francisco Bar Association to address that body at the first luncheon of the season, given at the Palace Hotel on September 3; the subject selected for the address being: "Encroachments of the Federal Government on the Powers of the States." This address was taken in shorthand and printed in The Recorder, the law paper of San Francisco.

To render more complete Mr. Smith's discussion of constitutional questions, the publishers have taken it upon themselves to incorporate in this volume the San Francisco address as given in The Recorder, together with the thoughtful and able comment thereon.

In introducing the speaker, Mr. Hodgehead, president of the Association, said, among other things:

"The Federal Constitution is an instrument which is not altogether static. Its growth and development

400

have not been entirely symmetrical. The granted powers have outgrown and outstripped the reserved powers.

"We have nineteen amendments if we count the Eighteenth. But there has been no amendment since the original ten guaranteeing or enlarging the rights of the states. We have been constitution-making ever since the original instrument was ratified. There has been a continual attrition and depletion of the powers of the states; attrition through interpretation, and depletion through positive enactment. If we take stock now after a period of 135 years of operation, the question is: What are the present atrophied powers of our sovereign and subject states? Is the tendency toward Centralization a wise policy?"

CHAPTER II.

ADDRESS OF MR. SMITH.

I may be somewhat trite, I may tell you things that you already know in discussing these constitutional limitations, and the balance of power in the Federal Government and the states, but, as a matter of fact, I know of many lawyers who get by and make money, who have not even a speaking acquaintance with the Constitution. I do not suppose there are any such here, but I am going to flatter you by assuming that you know as much about this subject as I did when I began to study it, and no more. (Laughter.)

To understand how far and to what extent our Constitution has been changed and distorted, how considerably that exquisite balance of power between the Federal Government and the states, that the fathers intended, has been disturbed, we must go back to the beginning and consider what the rights of the states were at the outset. To begin with, when the thirteen colonies had declared their independence of Great Britain and achieved it with the sword, each became an independent sovereign, with every attribute of sovereignty that belonged to great powers like Great Britain and France, power to make peace and war, to raise armies and build navies, and all of the other attributes of independent and sovereign states. As such they formed a league, the confederation whose legislative body, as Marshall expressed it, was a mere congress of ambassadors from independent states. The Confederation did not operate upon a people of the United States. It operated solely upon its constituent members, and each state voted and had one vote. This league, as you all recall, was a lamentable failure. It resulted in total chaos and anarchy.

And so the Constitutional Convention, initiated by a conference at Mt. Vernon to consider the building of a canal to connect the headwaters of the Potomac and the Ohio broadened into the Annapolis Convention, which resulted in a recommendation, drawn by Hamilton, asking the Continental Congress of the Confederation to call a convention to amend the Articles of Confederation.

Instead of Amending the Articles of Confederation they struck out an entirely new document, and much of the opposition to the Constitution was based upon the fact that the convention had exceeded its power, which, of course, was no argument at all because the convention merely suggested a Constitution, and it was the people who adopted it.

But here were thirteen sovereign independent states —one of them, Rhode Island, not represented in the convention—each jealous of its sovereignty, proud of its gallant and romantic past and its history, and each reluctant to surrender any of these attributes of sovereignty.

It happened that in this country at that time, with barely four millions of people, there were gathered in that convention more statesmen of the first rank than have ever been produced in any country in a single generation. (Applause.) And they were not chosen by a direct primary. (Laughter and applause.) If they had been chosen by a direct primary we never would have had any Constitution. In these jealousies of the states the fathers saw the germ of the federated principle. Theretofore all of the federations that the world had ever seen, the Dutch Republic, the League of Hanseatic Cities, the Swiss Federation, had been merely leagues, operating upon the membership of the league alone. It remained for these statesmen to adopt a new plan, absolutely novel in the political history of the world, that is, a league, a federation of independent states, but which, in its national powers, operated not upon the states, but directly upon the people.

Marshall harped upon this idea over and over again, in his great decisions, that the Federal Constitution was not adopted by the states, but by all of the people. "We, the people of the United States," for certain purposes make the Constitution. It became necessary, then to rob these states of various sovereign attributes and powers, in order to confer them upon the national government, to make it an efficient instrument.

404

They took from the states forty-five powers which are now forbidden to the states, and they granted, expressly, sixty-three powers to the Federal Government, and eighteen of these sixty-three are concurrent and may be exercised both by the Federal Government and the states. But such was their jealousy of the central power, such their dread of centralization, that there are seventy-nine absolute prohibitions, seventy-nine attributes of sovereignty that belong to all other nations, which are forbidden to our nation.

The fathers knew that every republic or democracy that had theretofore existed had been destroyed, either by the centrifugal or centripetal influence. Either it had been reduced to anarchy or chaos or had sunk into a despotism. They saw, in this federated principle, that which they believed would prevent centralization, and, jealous as they were of the central power, they were very careful to limit the Federal Government absolutely to those things that are national in their scope, those objects which affect all of the people of the United States alike, and to leave all other powers in the hands of the state governments or the people themselves.

Very early in our constitutional history, I think it was in 1829, in Calder vs. Bull[1] the Supreme Court of the United States held that the decision of the court of last resort of the state interpreting its own statutes

1. 3 U. S. (3 Dall.) 386, 1 L. ed. 4448, aff'g 2 Root (Conn.) 350.

and constitution, was binding upon the Supreme Court of the United States. And this judicially established the independence of the states in their local matters.

And that principle was followed for almost a hundred years. The Eleventh Amendment, as you recall, was adopted because of the case of Chisholm vs. Georgia[2], providing that a state could not be sued without its own consent, an amendment which has been, very largely, nullified by the Supreme Court of the United States in United States vs. Lee[3], in the Virginia coupon cases. So that now a state, through its officers, can be sued in almost any case, except a suit on a contract.

The Twelfth Amendment was necessitated by the mix-up of the election of Jefferson in the House.

Then we pass along for seventy years without any amendments whatever. During practically all of that time all of the political parties, and all of the political conflicts, were based upon this very proposition of the rights of the states. One school contended that this Constitution of ours was merely a league created by the states. The other school of Marshall held it created a true sovereignty, a true national sovereignty. The one group thought that this league might be dissolved at any time, at the will of any of the parties; that it was a contract that could be denounced by any

2. 2 U. S. (2 Dall.) 419, 1 L. ed. 440.
3. 106 U. S. 196, 27 L. ed. 171, 1 Sup. Ct. Rep. 240, aff'g 3 Hughes 139, Fed. Cas. No. 8, 192.

of the parties to the contract. The other school held that it was an indissoluble union of indestructible states.

Then came the war, brought on, very largely, mark you, probably more largely by the extreme assertion of the doctrine of state rights than by slavery itself, that destroyed, for the time being, this idea of state rights, made it odious, and exalted enormously the national power.

Then came the three war amendments, the Thirteenth, which freed the slaves, the Fourteenth, which was supposed, at the time, to be the black man's charter of liberty, and which, as Senator Walsh of Colorado once expressed it, was intended for the protection of the black man, but has been used to protect everybody else on earth but the black man, and the Fifteenth Amendment, conferring the suffrage upon the negro.

I think all candid men today regardless of politics, will admit that the Fifteenth Amendment was a ghastly mistake. Aside from the odious nature of the carpet bag rule that it imposed upon the southern states, it has created and kept alive the lines of cleavage between the north and the south. It has made two great political parties, one largely sectional and the other completely so. It has kept alive the passions and the animosities of the war, and it has not conferred suffrage upon the colored man in the south so that you can notice it.

407

The Fourteenth Amendment came before the Supreme Court of the United States first in the Slaughter-House cases,[4] with which you are doubtless familiar, but, as I said before, I am not going to take it for granted that you know too much. In those cases the gist of it was that a certain statute, enacted by the carpet-bag legislature of Louisiana, and not without some suspicion of corrupion had deprived these plaintiffs of their livelihood, of their property, without due process of law. Mr. Justice Miller wrote the opinion. He examined, historically, the origin and reason for these amendments. And let me say here that, while the dissenting opinion is a very powerful one, and there were four dissenting judges, none of them has disputed, nor has anyone since disputed, that the reason for the Fourteenth Amendment was the fact that the negro was not being permitted to use his newfound freedom in the southern states, but was being reduced to a state of peonage by various state enactments, and the Fourteenth Amendment was passed for the purpose of protecting that grant of freedom.

In considering the question of whether this statute did deprive these plaintiffs of their property without due process of law, Mr. Justice Miller carefully considered what the effect of the decision would be, if in favor of the plaintiffs, that is to say, if the Supreme Court examined this state statute and reversed the deci-

4. 77 U. S. (10 Wall.) 273, 19 L. ed. 915.

sion of the supreme court of Louisiana, if it examined the statute for the purpose of seeing whether it conformed to the Constitution of the State of Louisiana, and if the court established that precedent, from that time on, the Supreme Court of the United States would have to sit in consorship of every state statute that imposed a burden or a servitude upon anybody who objected to it; that it would completely destroy the balance of power established and fixed by the founders; that it would center power in the National Government that had always been held by the state, and that the result would be such that nothing, except an absolute compulsion upon the reason of the court, would compel them to make such a decision or to hold such a view.

Now, if there was anything on earth decided in that case, it was that Calder vs. Bull was still the law of the land, that whenever the Supreme Court of a state had interpreted its own statute under its own Constitution, it was binding upon the Supreme Court of the United States, and that the Fourteenth Amendment was not intended to make the Supreme Court of the United States a board of censors to sit in judgment upon state enactments unless the state enactment conflicted with the Constitution, a law or a treaty of the United States.

Four years later, in Davidson vs. New Orleans[5], a similar question came before the court, and Mr. Justice Miller wrote the opinion. In that case the woman plaintiff complained that a certain scheme of taxation, adopted in Louisiana, deprived her of her property without due process of law. Miller said that the court would not make a definition of what would be considered "due process of law" that would serve in all cases, that the court would have to proceed by a process of inclusion and exclusion. But he laid down this rule: That, wherever the plaintiff complaining of the burden or servitude had a day in court, according to the forms of law of the state, and an appeal to the court of last resort of the state, that then he had had due process of law, and that the Supreme Court of the United States would not consider any appeal from such a decision.

The curious thing is that these two cases, the Slaughter-House case, and Davidson vs. New Orleans[5], have never been overruled, they have never been criticized, they remain, so far as any decision—and now mark what I am going to say, gentlemen—they remain, so far as any decided case is concerned by the Supreme Court of the United States, they remain the law of that court today. Neither one of them has ever been overruled.

5. 96 U. S. 92, 24 L. ed. 616, aff'g 27 La. Ann. 20.

This remained the law, then, for nearly twenty-two years. During those twenty years we saw the greatest development of railroad and corporate investments that the world had ever seen anywhere, far greater than the whole hundred years preceding that. It is true that injustice was done here and there to corporations in some of the states, but that injustice brought its own punishment because, wherever capital was denied protection, capital withdrew and the state suffered. Finally, in Minneapolis Railway Company vs. Beckwith[6], Mr. Justice Field—and it was not necessary to that decision, there was complaint of a state law—but the court, in the upshot, in considering that, held that the state law was valid under the state constitution, and it was not necessary to consider the paricular question. Mr. Justice Field let drop this remark: "We have no doubt"—I do not know that I quote it exactly, but this is the substance of it—"We have no doubt that, under the Fourteenth Amendment, the word 'person' includes a corporation. It was so held in Santa Clara County vs. The Southern Pacific Railroad Company[7]."

Now, if you will examine the text writers, like Taylor on "Due process of Law," if you will examine the historians like Carson and Warren, you will not find any allusion to the fact that, by that remark, the doc-

6. 129 U. S. 26, 32 L. ed. 585, 9 Sup. Ct. Rep. 207.

7. 118 U. S. 394, 30 L. ed. 118, 6 Sup. Ct. Rep. 1132, aff'g 9 Sawy. 165, 18 Fed. 385.

trine of the Slaughter House , and of Davidson vs. New Orleans , was absolutely nullified and destroyed. And the curious thing is that, when we turn to the Santa Clara County case[8], we find that nothing of the sort was decided. The question was raised there whether the word "person," under the Fourteenth Amendment, includes a corporation, and Mr. Justice Harlan, who wrote the opinion, declared that it was a matter of such importance that the court would not pass upon that unless it was absolutely necessary to the determination of the case. And he found that, under the California law, the tax attempted to be levied by the State of California was invalid under the state law, without reference to the Fourteenth Amendment.

The fact was that Mr. Justice Field, sitting in circuit, had held that the word "person" included a corporation. But the Supreme Court of the United States absolutely refused to consider that question, and did not pass upon it and never has. This may sound like a startling assertion, but I say, without any qualification, that the Supreme Court of the United States has never yet decided—mark you, it has dropped a dictum —but I pause here for a moment to say this much: there is a tradition (and I have been told that the remark appears in the first edition of the Supreme Court Reports, it certainly does not in any of the later ones), that, when the argument opened in the Santa

8. 75 U. S. (Wall.) 168, 19 L. ed. 357.

Clara County case, Judge Waite, from the bench, said to the lawyers: "You need not discuss the question of whether the word 'person' includes a corporation, the court is of the opinion that it does."

Assuming that to be correct, that that remark was made—and I have no doubt that it was—it was pure dictum, not necessary to the determination of the case. It was not even a dictum that went into the printed report and became part of the opinion. It was a remark expressing the opinion of the court, apparently, at that time. Marshall has probably given the best definition of dictum of anybody, and he held, absolutely, that the court is not bound by a dictum, that it is not bound by anything but what is necessary to the decision of the case. And Marshall, over and over again, unblushingly rejected his own dicta whenever it suited him in the trial of a case. And it has been held by the Supreme Court over and over again, that these expressions of opinions, parallels and illustrations, do not bind the court in any future decision.

So I say that this, one of the most important decisions probably ever rendered by the Supreme Court of the United States, was rendered as a mere dictum, an expression from the bench and not directly decided. And, as a matter of fact, if, today, the court were of the opinion that the word "person" does not include a corporation, as used in the Fourteenth Amendment, it could so decide without overruling any decided case.

413

It would be simply brushing away a mere dictum. Now, understand, I am not speaking of the abstract justice of that dictum. Certainly, everyone will agree that corporations should have every protection under the law that a person has. The question that I am discussing is, how shall that protection be given? Is it worth while, for the sake of preventing an injustice to a corporation here and there, when burdened with some servitude that it objects to, to disturb this exquisite balance of power and destroy the independence of state tribunals, as has been done by this line of decisions? I presume that lawyers with corporate practice, or largely so, will disagree with me. That is natural. But the question for thoughtful students is this: Is it worth while? Because this was the first step, mark you now, that was taken in this federalization of power in Washington that we are today complaining of. The first step toward the amendment of the Constitution of the United States was taken by the Supreme Court of the United States without discussion, without being directly decided. And Congress has been swift to follow.

If one will consider the Fourteenth Amendment, its history, the reasons that actuated its adoption, he will find it very difficult to believe that the word "person" as there used, was intended to cover corporations. The opening sentence declared that "All persons born or naturalized in the United States and subject to the jurisdiction thereof, are citizens of the United States and of the state wherein they reside." Therefore citizenship had been a creature of the state purely. This created a national citizenship over which the state had no control.

Then, after a comma, comes the phrase, "No state shall make or enforce any law which shall abridge the privileges or immunities of citizens of the United States." That, certainly, applies to the citizenship just repeated. It is taken bodily from the Fourth Article of the Constitution, and under that article the Supreme Court of the United States in Paul vs. Virginia[8] already had held that a corporation was not a citizen within the purview of that protective section. Then comes the clause that has been so often quoted: "Nor shall any state deprive any person of life, liberty or property without due process of law."

The "life" here spoken of is physical life. "Liberty" is personal liberty. To make this clause express the sense Judge Field gives it, it should read thus, "nor shall any state deprive any person of life or liberty or any person (or corporation) of property." The second section dealing with the apportionment of representatives in Congress certainly does not refer to corporations nor does the third section which disfranchises those who have borne arms against the United States. The word "person" is used five times; four times it cannot possibly refer to any but natural born persons.

415

If we are to adopt the rule in this matter fixed by the Supreme Court itself, we must reject the inclusion of corporations. That court has held that the word "person" can only include corporations when they are in exactly the same situation. Under this rule Judge Field is clearly in error.

Well, as a result, what has happened? The Supreme Court of the United States does sit as a board of censors over every legislative enactment. More than two thousand cases under this particular clause have been decided by the Supreme Court since then. More than five hundred state laws have been held invalid solely under that proposition, reversing decisions of the supreme courts of states which had, theretofore, been held sacred, with the result that today the docket of the Supreme Court of the United States is clogged with these cases. Every corporation upon whom a burden of servitude is imposed, or a tax levied, immediately rushes into the Supreme Court with a plea that it is not "due process of law," and these cases now constitute about one-fourth of the business of the court. That has accustomed the general public, and accustomed Congress to this aggrandizement of the national sovereignty, and we see how swiftly that has been followed.

Take, for instance, an amendment like the Eighteenth,—I know that that is a very tender subject to all lawyers, and I only mention it briefly. If it had been supposed by the fathers, who all took their toddy regularly, that, in establishing this Constitution, the time would ever come when this particular police power, this power of the states over sumptuary legislation, would be conferred upon the National Government, I have no hesitation in saying that this Constitution of ours would never have been adopted.

But here is the courious thing about it: there is something logical, so profoundly inevitable in the relationship established by the fathers between the states and the nation, that, whenever you disturb it, you accomplish nothing. For instance, you practically accomplished nothing when you passed the Fifteenth Amendment, conferring the franchise upon the black. He has the franchise now where he would have gotten it from the states in the north, and nowhere else.

So, as to the Eighteenth Amendment and the Volstead Act, I believe this is a fair statement: That, wherever, and in every state where they had prohibition before the Eighteenth Amendment, the Volstead Act is enforced just about as well, and no more so, than were the old state prohibitory enactments. While, in every state that was wet before, that refused to pass prohibitory laws, the act is not enforced. I think that is a fair statement. In other words, whenever the Federal Government undertakes to usurp the police power that is naturally local, that can only be enforced by the states themselves, that enactment, that constitutional amendment fails, necessarily, because of the very circumstances.

As a matter of abstract justice, I have always thought, and have wondered what would have happened if, in the old days, when three-quarters of the states were wet, they had undertaken to pass a constitutional amendment providing something like this: That no state should ever make and enforce any law forbidding the manufacture, sale or importation of intoxicating liquor. There would have been a great howl go up from states like Kansas. And yet, as a matter of abstract justice, I do not know of any more reason why Kansas should force the citizens of New York to drink water, than there is why the citizens of New York should force the people of Kansas to drink whiskey, whether they want to or not. As a matter of abstract justice, and balance of power, they are the same.

I come now to a very tender subject, the Nineteenth Amendment, by which the ladies, God bless them, got the right to vote, which they do not seem to care about using. Before that right of suffrage was purely a state matter, and properly so, because the women of one state might be intelligent enough to vote, while the women of another state were not sufficiently equipped, mentally or by training, for the franchise. But at one sweep we enfranchised the ignorant women of the slums, the foreign women, the negro women, along with the intelligent white women of the other states. And the result of that is operating just the same. The statistics show that not over thirty per cent, on the average, throughout the United States, of the women vote. It is quite evident the great majority of them do no desire the suffrage at all.

So now we have got a mania for constitutional amendments. There were one hundred and nine propositions to amend the Constitution offered in the last Congress. Some of these were, in effect, ludicrous. But, with three or four exceptions, every one of them was in derogation of the rights of the states, intensifying and increasing the centralization of power at Washington, and every one of them involved an enormous increase of that bureaucracy, which is rapidly getting a strangle hold on the Government of the United States.

Of all tyrannies that of a bureaucracy is the most odious because it is anonymous. You will recall that, with all that welter of scandal in Washington, not a breath of it touched an elective officer of the United States. It was centered, absolutely, in the bureaucracy, which is running true to form with every other bureaucracy that the world ever saw, corrupt and inefficient. It was the corruption and inefficiency of the Russian bureaucracy, and not Tzarism, that destroyed the Russian Empire; it was the corruption and not inefficiency of the Italian bureaucracy and not bolshevism that drove the people into the hands of the Fascisti, and has established a dictatorship in Spain. And ours is running true to form.

Now, let us see some of these propositions. Mr. Coolidge, who is a lawyer of some repute, wants to have a cabinet officer known as a Minister of Education, or something like that. Along with that is a hundred million dollars to be appropriated as a bribe to the states in order that we may turn all of our educational institutions over to the Federal Government to be run from Washington. Mr. Davis, who is a lawyer of great repute—Mr. John W. Davis criticises Mr. Coolidge for that because it would tend to increase the bureaucracy at Washington, and, in the same breath, advocates the Child Labor Amendment.

Now, what would happen if we had the Child Labor Amendment? There would be an army of inspectors, necessarily, going through every mill, factory, mine, store, and farm in the country to ascertain whether this Federal law passed by virtue of this constitutional amendment, if it is adopted, is enforced— going into the home of every laboring man who has a child employed, to investigate the family Bible and take evidence as to the age of the child. Another horde of government employees interfering with business, seeking for more power and adding more and more to that bulky, unwieldy machine which we are building up there in Washington. Another bill would have a government man around in every home in America where the stork is expected. No child could be legally born unless there was a Federal inspector present. (Laughter.)

Among the things that it is proposed to do are to take from the power of the states sanitation, health, schools, until, as a matter of fact, we are reducing the states to mere geographical expressions.

There were more than twenty thousand bills and resolutions introduced in the last Congress. Of course, not one per cent of them received the slightest consideration. But measures of vast importance received no consideration whatever because we have imposed too great a burden upon Congress. If Congress legislates upon national concerns alone, as it did for more than a hundred years, there would be some degree of efficiency, but we are gradually imposing upon them, not only all these, but also matters of purely local concern.

Now, this Child Labor Amendment is proposed— and certainly I am as much opposed to child labor as anybody—because, in five states, I believe at the most, in the south they permit child labor, and so we are to take the whole subject and commit it to Washington because the five states are backward in this humanitarian matter.

I believe there was a time when San Francisco was rather badly governed. I presume you would all like to forget it, but I mention it merely for a parallel. There was corruption and graft, and it seemed as though the people of San Francisco were unable to throw off these chains. Was it suggested by anybody that, because San Francisco was misgoverned, that you should take the charter from every city in California and govern them all from Sacramento because they would be better governed there? Or if such a proposal had been made, how much support would it have received from any sane or intelligent man?

And yet that is the tendency of the time because, here and there, a state is backward in education, backward in sanitation, backward in the matter of child labor, we propose to deprive all of the states of those attributes of sovereignty that were theirs from the foundation, and were always deemed sacred and necessary to the preservation of this country.

My friends, the curious thing is that, while we are proceeding with this process of centralization our English cousins are decentralizing. They are granting to bodies like the London County Council, for instance, powers equal to our state legislatures. Decentralizing in every direction, while we are taking the contrary course, and taking a course that, if persisted in, can lead to only one thing. I am thoroughly aware of the fate of the late lamented Casandra, and I do not want to prophesy, but if there be anything in history, if there be anything in the lessons of the past, that the fathers so carefully considered when they formed our Constitution, the path that we are treading of centralization, of building up a vast bureaucracy in Washington, responsible to nobody, can end but in one thing: The creation of an autocracy or a despotism and the downfall of the country.

CHAPTER III.

ATTRITION.

The comments of the editor of The Recorder represent the view of the intelligent and thoughtful lay mind on the question, the editor not being a lawyer. The editorial is as follows:

There is much food for thought in the address delivered by F. Dumont Smith of Kansas before the Bar Association of San Francisco at its luncheon on Wednesday last and published in full in "The Recorder" this morning. The layman as well as the lawyer is interested in the preservation, not alone of the letter of the Constitution, but of its spirit as well.

Constitutions, like statutes, should change with the changing necessities of times so long as the changes do not affect the principles underlying the fundamental law; but the evils sought to be guarded against should still be watched with vigilance lest in some way they should be forgotten and eventually supersede the safeguards set up, as a protection against them.

It will be remembered that one of the great subjects of debate during the Constitutional Convention was the preservation of the rights of the states and their protection from the possibility of usurpation by the Federal Government created by the Constitution.

424

In order that the states might be reassured that their sovereignty would be protected, the Constitution makers provided checks and balances, granting to the Federal Government and to Congress only such powers as were purely national, while reserving to the states all matters of purely local concern.

It was because of this division of authority—this endeavor to so balance the powers of the states and the Federal Government that the rights of the states in the disposal of local matters would be preserved—that the states were persuaded to accept and adopt the Constitution.

These facts are elementary; they are known to every student of the Constitution who has taken the trouble to read Madison's Debates, Farrand's History of the Constitutional Conventions, those illuminating papers generally referred to as "The Federalist," and the history of the period.

Prior to the Civil War the rights of the states were generally recognized and preserved. After the Civil War came the rise of the Federal power and the gradual usurpation by the Federal Government of state powers, either through amendments to the Constitution or the interpretation of those amendments by the Supreme Court of the United States.

The power of the states over citizenship has been annulled in favor of Federal control, the right of the states to control the manufacture and sale of intoxicating liquors has been transferred to the Federal jurisdiction; in various ways the Federal police power is being extended to include matters formerly considered as appertaining solely to the states.

Now the Federal Government, through congressional enactment and constitutional amendment is endeavoring to transfer to its own jurisdiction control over education and child labor; and it will not be long before public health and sanitation will be added to the powers that the Federal bureaucracy at Washington desires to control.

One does not have to be an alarmist to see in this trend away from the original principles of the Constitution a condition that is not altogether good for the country at large. We are centralizing the functions of government at Washington and are erecting there a vast bureau of employees responsible, as Senator Smith pointed out, to nobody but engaged in the making of regulations that eventually will interfere with the private life of every citizen.

Each act that takes from the states powers reserved to them by the Constitution and confers those powers upon the Federal Government adds another unit to the army of inspectors and agents of the Government charged by law with power of interference with the daily activities of citizens of the United States and piles another straw upon the already heavy load of taxation borne by the people for the support of the Federal Government.

It must be borne in mind that the men who are calling these things to the attention of the people and counselling them to be careful lest the powers of the states be taken from them and centered in the Federal Government are not demagogues or alarmists but are lawyers learned in the law and imbued with the idea that it is in the public interest that the safeguards established by the framers of the Constitution for the protection of the states be preserved.

The framers of the Constitution were students of government; they knew wherein and wherefore other federations of states had failed; they knew the feeling and the jealousies of the states for which they were called upon to legislate; and they endeavored to set up a system of checks and balances as between the states and the Federal power that would prevent the very centralization of power in the Federal Government that is now the cause of serious alarm.

The people, who in that distant day were jealous of the prerogative of their individual commonwealths and who took an interest in their preservation, have become apathetic. So long as they are materially prosperous they give little heed to the business of government, even neglecting to participate in the election of public officials and in the determination of public questions submitted to them for decision.

427

It is small wonder, then, that the American Bar Association has sounded a clarion call designed to turn the country back to the Constitution and to the principles upon which it was founded. We have run far in our pursuit of strange gods; it is high time that we returned to our old allegiance and the altars builded by the men who framed the Constitution and gave us a charter that will continue to be the bulwark of our liberties only so long as we do not permit its principles and purposes to be perverted in the interest of an extended and overpowering Federal power that will destroy what remains of liberty before it, too. is destroyed.

PART V.

PART V.

CHAPTER I.

ORIGIN OF CONSTITUTION—CORRESPONDENCE

The following correspondence may serve to help clear away some of the questions heretofore troubling many students regarding the particular source, or sources, from which the Federal Constitution was derived—if indeed it is a derivative document, as some claim, indigenous in the country and time, as others maintain, or a gradual growth and development through long ages of suffering and struggle for freedom, as the author maintains. The publisher adds this chapter, believing it is not only interesting, but may be helpful to those interested in and studying the question.

Chicago, April 15, 1924.

Mr. F. DuMont Smith,
Attorney at Law,
First National Bank Building,
Hutchinson, Kansas.
Dear Sir:

I thank you for sending to me the copy of your "Story of the Constitution." It is beautifully written, in a flowing and clear style; but in two or three essen-

431

tials it does not seem to me to be sound history. In the next printing the text might be somewhat modified.

My exceptions are directed (1) to your drawing our constitutional system too much from German and English origins; (2) to your overlooking the real source-ground of our government, the century and three-quarters of American experimentation in all sorts of circumstances and conditions before the Constitution was written, a period which, because of the influence of our Constitution on the governments of the world, I believe to have been the most important epoch in the civil history of mankind; and (3) to your failure to recognize the contributions of other peoples, notably of the Romans, the formulators of principles which not only modified very markedly for the better English law, but which also govern half the civilized peoples of the world today, men fitly described by Lord Byron as "those dead but sceptered sovereigns who still rule us from their urns."

No one appreciates more than I do, as is evidenced by my book, "THE CONSTITUTION OF THE UNITED STATES: Its Sources and Its Application," our debt to the English for law in behalf of the man and his property. The world has seen no braver picture than that of the Englishman fighting for centuries to get his government off his back. But I believe that the constitutional government of the United States is American, and that this should be taught with em-

432

phasis to young America. It seems to me as unnecessary to labor to trace back our government to European sources as it would be to find European origin for the American steel building, that expression of light, cleanliness and comfort which has become the admiration and the pattern of all countries. While many kinds of building had existed in Europe, and while it cannot be said that the modern office building in this country is not like in some respects (as in the matter of windows and doors) European buildings, still no well-informed architect would endeavor to write a book showing that our steel building originated in Europe. In government, as in buildings, we are of course the heirs of time, but America stated and applied principles for the control of power which were new to men and which have changed most of the systems of the world.

Napoleon described history as "a fable agreed upon"; and Voltaire warned against our believing "ancient history in particular," because he said that it is the work of fabulists. The historians "make" too much history. Many works once standard have been entirely discredited by research. It was fabulists who worked out the theory that the Saxon took a polity to England and that the English brought or sent it to America. We have no real definite information about those times. Yet, since the German house of Hanover went upon the English throne, a great deal has been written with positiveness by sycophants to show that constitutional government in Great Britain and in the United States are owing to the Germans—a people who never had such a government themselves before 1871, and who spent the centuries down to 1914 in submission to a succession of incomparable tyrants and autocracies.

As said, the history of early Germany and of Saxon England is very indefinite. I have studied Tacitus carefully, and I never could find anything in "Germania" to justify even remotely what German and English historians have based upon it. Tacitus says no more about government among German tribes than could be said of any of our highest Indian tribes. All tribes have government. Self-defense is an instinct. But on such a commonplace fact as tribal order we cannot predicate the proposition that the British government proceeded from it and ours from that. When the Germans began gathering in cities they found Roman law ready, Walton says, and adopted it and have since used it. Germany has always been one of the most Roman of Continental countries. Its constitution of 1871 was borrowed largely from ours.

What has been built up on a few statements in the "Germania" of Tacitus and on Caesar's "Commentaries" reminds me of the construction by "scientists" of the Neanderthal man out of a small piece of the top of a skull. They deal with him as cocksurely as though they had lived with him.

In "The Puritan in Holland, England and America" Douglas Campbell not only rejects the theory of the British origin of our system, but he also takes the position that our Constitution and our federative plan both came from Holland, where Puritanism as a political force began. His theory is fully as good as the other. He wrote a two-volume work of a thousand pages on this subject and his manuscript was read in whole or in part by the Rev. Dr. Charles A. Briggs of the Union Theological Seminary, Prof. C. C. Langdell of the Harvard Law School, and Prof. A. M. Wheeler of Yale. He shows that New York and New Jersey were settled by the Dutch West India Company, that William Penn was half Dutchman, that Roger Williams of Rhode Island was a Dutch scholar, that Thomas Hooker, who gave life to Connecticut, was from Holland, and that the so-called New England institutions were found in New York when it was a Dutch colony—notwithstanding all of which, and more, he adds, "we are continually told that we are an English people, with English institutions." That, he says, is because our historians have been "almost exclusively Englishmen, or descendants of Englishmen." He, too, believes that history is sometimes made by historians.

With the doctors of history who are seeking to find the origin of the American government in foreign countries thus in hopeless disagreement, what becomes of the sound education of the American youth? No wonder he hasn't any. The thing to do is to reject all those theories as historically untenable (since they are) and to teach that our government is the product of American experience and intelligence applied for over a century and a half under the pressure of American circumstances—which it is.

At page 21, Story of the Constitution, a pamphlet issued and distributed by American Bar Association Committee, you say:

"With the revolution of 1688 the British constitution very speedily took on its present form; and, as it is more or less the model from which our Constitution was formed, it is necessary to know just what that constitution was."

"More or less the model" is too vague for historic value. As Lord Bryce pointed out, the British really have no constitution. All that they possess could be set aside by Parliament, he wrote, "as quickly as it could repeal the last Explosives Act." Our legislative body cannot do anything like that, which is a good illustration of the fact that fundamentally—very fundamentally—our Fathers did not follow "more or less" a British model.

A comparison of the British government in 1787 with our Constitution is enough to show that it served our forefathers, not as a model, but as an example of what a government in a new and clean world ought not to be. Thus they created an Executive Department without the absolute veto power, without the power to convoke and dismiss Congress, without the power to declare war or make treaties, and without many other powers which the Executive in England had possessed.

They created a Congress consisting of a Senate made up of men representing States as political organizations, which body could, of course, bear no resemblance to anything that existed in Europe; and a House of Representatives composed of members elected directly by the people, as the members of the House of Commons in England never had been. The present-day apology of the English people for the acts which brought on our Revolution is that Parliament did not represent the people. That is true. The House of Commons did not become a popular body according to our understanding of that term until after our Civil War, when manhood suffrage was extended quite widely, though not to all. Our Fathers placed twenty-nine direct and many indirect restrictions upon the Senate and the House of Representatives, whereas the House of Commons was then and is yet absolute in power. Did space permit other illustrations might be given to show the fundamental dissimilarity of the Legislative Department in England and that which our Fathers set up.

The framers of our Constitution provided a third department, the Judicial, the like of which did not exist in England then and does not now. It was intended to pass upon constitutional questions and to restrain the other departments and keep them within their designated spheres. It was particularly designed to prevent in the United States the erection of a legislative despotism like that which they saw and had felt in Great Britain. "A legislative despotism," said Jefferson, "was not the government we fought for."

The Executive with specified powers; the Senate containing representatives of self-governing States; the House with carefully defined powers and powers carefully denied; the Judicial Department, with authority and duties which never had existed in the world before; and the National authority acting directly upon and receiving allegiance from the individuals in each of the federated States—none of these was modeled after the so-called British constitution. Those fundamentals (the whole body of our system) are American. That is what we should teach. For who can doubt that, after nearly two centuries of strenuous experience in government, greatly original work was done by a body of administrators and scholars which Gladstone and other foreign writers have declared to have been the most remarkable that ever assembled? No writer disputes that our judicial system and the Senate are wholly American inventions.

438

In Fisher's "Evolution of the Constitution" he shows twenty-three documents in illustration of the development of the federalism in America. Along with the development of federalism was the growth of administrative parts. The New England Confederacy of 1643 was made up of Massachusetts, Plymouth, Connecticut, and New Haven, the people of those Colonies being alike in politics and religion and differing in those particulars from the people of Maryland and Virginia. They were remote from other Colonies and were fearful of the Dutch on the Hudson River, and of the French, and they were in constant peril from the Indians. Naturally they confederated.

In 1698 Penn formulated a plan of union with two delegates from each Colony to constitute a "congress," the first use of the word for an intercolonial assembly.

In 1754 Franklin drafted a plan of union.

In 1765 the Stamp Act Congress spoke collectively for the Colonies, and so did the first Continental Congress in 1774. The second Continental Congress (1775) considered Franklin's form of confederacy and used the term "United Colonies of North America." Other plans of union or confederation might be mentioned, but those are enough to illustrate the compelling pressure of tremendous circumstances which made the Colonies instinctively to form a circle of defense, as it were, and face outward against common perils. First there were the loose colonial unions, then the impromptu congresses made necessary by the war, the last of which appointed a committee to draft the Articles of Confederation, the first constitution of the United States, which proved in practice to be a failure. The Confederacy was succeeded by the present federal system, the like of which never had existed in England or in any other land, doubtless because the circumstances which created or compelled our federal system never had precedent. Under the Articles of Confederation the States maintained their independence. Therefore, the problem of our Constitutional Convention was, not to form a federal *government,* but to *create* a federal *state,* a new entity acting as directly upon the people of each of the State entities as the States themselves act, a co-ordination of two separate systems, each of the members of which must be "wholly independent in those matters which concern each member only," and all of the members of which "must be subject to a common power in those matters which concern the whole body of members collectively."

That cannot be traced back to the time of Julius Caesar, or of Tacitus, or of the Saxon Chronicles. That is American. Let us make all this plain to the boys and girls. The great trouble in the United States today is that education is very deficient in showing whence our government came, what it cost, and therefore what it is worth. And the most fruitful century

and a half in the whole life of the world is practically
an unknown age in the history studied by American
youth. Instead of bringing into the schoolroom and
glorifying the works of that time, all of which are of
authentic record, we have hitherto searched for an
alien beginning through the fogs of legend.

At page 5 [pamphlet issued by American Bar Association Committee] you write:

"When suffrage was granted to women in this coun·
try by the Nineteenth Constitutional Amendment we
merely restored woman to the same position she held
among our ancestors in the German forests two thousand years ago."

Of course it is not historic to indicate that the
American woman, who had been voting in some of the
States for nearly half a century, had been backward in
comparison with the woman of Germany, who never
had and has not now any political power. As neither
man nor woman in Germany had suffrage as we understand it down to the German constitution of 1871, the
best features of which were American, and as the German woman did not get it then, it requires an extraordinary exertion of the imagination to connect across
so many centuries the constitutional position of the
American woman today with that of the tribal woman
in the German forests. Even were we to concede that
the seeds of popular constitutional government existed
in the Germany of Tacitus or in the Britain of the

Saxons, how could that affect America when those seeds never had come to fruition in either of those countries up to 1787? And how can the early House of Commons be traced to the Folkmote of the Saxon when a House by popular election never existed in England prior to the time of our Civil War? The House of Commons is British, not German, the product of centuries of experience ending in revolution. The government of the United States is American, not German or British.

You have collected a great deal of interesting and valuable matter and presented it in a very spirited and engaging way, but I believe that in the particulars mentioned you have followed too closely writers using German sources to the disregard of our country's history, and of the influence of other peoples.

Yours very truly,

T. J. NORTON,
Hutchinson, Kansas,
May 13, 1924.

Mr. Thomas J. Norton
Railway Exchange Building
Chicago, Ill.

Dear Sir:

In your first letter to me criticizing my pamphlet, The Story of the Constitution, I recall that you complimented the style but told me that it was poetry and not history. I wrote you that your indictment was too general, that I could not plead to it unless it was made more definite. I have now to thank you for your letter of April 15, for the many kind expressions in it and for the definite nature of its criticism which amounts to this.

That I draw too much from and give too much credit to early Germanic sources of our free institutions and American Constitution, ignoring other sources, principally Dutch impressed upon the Puritan residents in Holland, and Roman Law. This is an old controversy. Senator Beveridge some time ago raised the particular question as to the Dutch sources, quoting as you do from Douglas Campbell's book.

Let me at the outset make my position clear. I hold that there are four fundamentals of free government and only four—four essentials upon which all the others depend, from which they draw life and support. These four are: first, the right of the people to choose their own rulers; second, the right to make their own

laws by representatives freely chosen; third, the right
to tax themselves; fourth, trial by Jury. These are the
four cornerstones of our Constitution and of the English Constitution. The superstructure may vary, it
may have many doors and windows for light and access, it may have many different rooms for convenience of the government, but upon these four cornerstones rests the whole temple of free government. If
the people have the right to choose their own rulers,
if they have the right to make their own laws by representatives freely chosen, if they have the right to tax
themselves, if they may have their civil and criminal
causes tried before a Jury of their Peers chosen from
the body of their fellow citizens, they have a free government. Without any of these essentials they have
not. (Of course to some extent with the modern independence of the Judiciary of both the Executive and
the Legislative branches, trial by Jury is not the sacred
thing that it was with our fathers, and yet it is so hal-
lowed by precedent, it has fulfilled so important an
office in the safeguarding of our liberties, that it has
become a fetish of the Anglo-Saxon people.)

Given these four essentials there can be no tyranny,
no usurpation of power. All of the other rights so
meticulously set forth in the Ten Amendments, flow
from these fundamentals are, religious liberty, freedom of speech, freedom from unlawful search and
seizure, the right to bear arms, the right of petition,

the right to peaceably assemble, and all of the other great rights which have been established and safeguarded by these four fundamentals. Every one of these rights are Anglo-Saxon. (I use this term because it is the common expression, hardly descriptive but by common acceptance everyone knows what it means.) Not one of these can be traced to Dutch, Roman or any other origin. I quite agree with you that until the close of the 18th Century there was very little real history written. History was largely fable because it was written to please the government in power, a dynasty or a ruling class. The history of Charles XII by Voltaire is perhaps the first example of modern history, speedily followed by Gibbon, and Hume. But the historians that I shall cite, English historians of the Victorian Era such as Stubbs, Greene, Freeman, Lecky, Hallam, and May, can hardly be said to be toadies of the Hanoverian sovereign.

To begin with I will cite one historian, John Fiske, whom you will hesitate to impugn; born in Connecticut, utterly free from foreign influence of any kind, indefatigable in research, clear, lucid, analytical, and above all philosophical. He may well be crowned one of the first of American historians not below Motley, Prescott or Parkman. In his work on "The Beginnings of New England" in the opening chapter he describes the three forms of government which have successfully governed large territories. The Asiatic,

445

a despotism which, conquering subject peoples, reduced them to slavery, governed by Satraps, without a human right. The Roman, conquering wide territories and alien peoples, submitting all of them to the rule of Roman Law, granting them eventually the status of Roman citizens, so that to say "Romanus Sum" became the proudest boast even of St. Paul, but governed despotically, ruling them tyrannically from Rome, taxing them at will with no right except the right to be judged among themselves by Roman Law. And last of all the representative government invented by the Anglo-Saxon, never heard or dreamed of until our English forefathers in Saxon times devised and established it. Thus and thus only have the modern English world, the great British Empire with "its far flung battle line" on which the sun never sets, and the American Federal Union, developed. He points out that the conflict between little England and mighty Spain in which England won and a hundred years later between England and the Empire of Louis XIV, was a contest between these two systems. Spain and France typified the Roman system as against the English free representative government, not as free then of course as it is now but emerging swiftly from Feudal despotism.

If you reply to this. I shall be glad to have you tell me where you can find in the Dutch Republic or anywhere in the Roman Empire or where from any continental source we derive any of these four essential principles of free government and their sequillæ. You will be bound to admit that every one of them is an Anglo-Saxon invention. They existed in Saxon Enggland because there was the representative assembly, the Shiremote, and the Saxons at will chose their own rulers, and Harold, the last of the Saxon Kings, was elected and the heirs of Edward, the Confessor, were set aside. When Norman Baron and Saxon Franklin confronted King John at Runnymede the demand of the people who had by amalgamation become English, was not for a new thing but for a return to the "laws of Edward the Confessor," the last but one of the Saxon Kings.

Let us turn first to Dutch sources. You quote Douglas Campbell, whose book I have never read, but you say on his authority "that our Constitution came from Holland where Puritanism as a political force began." Puritanism as a political force, the rejection of the divine right of kings, the right of a king to impose a form of worship upon his people, the demand for religious liberty, began with Wycliff and the Lollards two centuries before Puritanism was heard of. It slumbered for a while but revived under Elizabeth and grew to a living flame under James.

The Puritans went to Holland in 1606, a few of them. After fourteen years residence there they began to fear that the Dutch toleration of all religions, intimate contact with the many strange forms of worship, would contaminate their members and in 1620 a small body of them emigrated to New England and landed at Plymouth. More than one-half of those who came over on the Mayflower died the first winter. At the end of nine years when the Plymouth Charter was granted, there were less than three hundred of them. In that same year the real settlement of New England began under the leadership of John Winthrop, founding the Massachusetts Bay Colony which became Massachusetts and into which later the little Colony of Plymouth was merged. In the next ten years more than fifteen thousand of these Puritans emigrated to Massachusetts, not one of whom ever saw the shores of Holland. It was the greatest exodus that the world has ever seen since the Israelites left Egypt. No such selected body in character, education and substance ever went from one country to another. They founded Puritan New England. They were "Separatists," "Independents." They rejected not only the church of England but the Presbyterian church. They rejected all church government except the government of each congregation and lived by the Word of God alone.

It must be admitted that they did not found at the outset a Democracy. Their ideal was a Theocratic government modeled after the Israelites under Moses, Joshua and Samuel. What they did establish was a very narrow, rigid Hierarchy, governed absolutely by the ministers of the Independent Church, what I suppose we would now call Congregationalists. Neither Catholic nor Protestant, unless he belonged to that church, could vote. They persecuted the Quakers, branded them, whipped them at the cartstail and hung four of them including one woman, Mrs. Fisher. Did they get that from tolerant Holland? And yet that sturdy Independent spirit built up the most powerful commonwealth on the American continent, the chief obstacle and stumbling block to kingly power, the colony that initiated the Revolution. If you will read carefully Fiske's story you will find that he derives every one of their institutions, their assembly, their courts, their laws from English tradition.

You speak of Hooker. Hooker was a minister of the Independent church. He was silenced by Archbishop Laud for denying the right of the kind in matters of conscience. He taught a grammar school for two years and then went to Holland where he preached at Delft for three years and then went to New England. Very shortly he fell out with John Cotton and the other Puritans because of their narrowness and their persecution of other sects. With his flock, shortly followed by other liberal churchmen, he went to Hartford and founded the Connecticut Colony. It was there in his first sermon that he announced the doctrine that the people were the sole repositories of political power, that neither an anointed king, a consecrated bishop, nor an ordained minister had any more political right than the plain common citizen. It was the first time that this doctrine was openly pronounced on American soil. The people of Connecticut formed their own Constitution with religious freedom although they restricted the franchise to members of the Independent church. They never had a Charter from the English Crown and everyone is familiar with the romantic story of that charter which Andros attempted to seize, the candles were blown out, and it was smuggled away and hidden in the famous Charter Oak and that Constitution lasted until 1818. Hooker had spent forty years in England. He spent three years in Holland. When Mr. Campbell or anyone else tells me that he got his idea of political freedom from his three years in Holland and not in his forty years in England, that he got those ideas from Holland, those ideas for the preaching of which he had been silenced by Laud in England, he insults my intelligence and falsifies history.

You speak of Roger Williams as a Dutch scholar. Roger Williams was the son of a London tailor, who fell under the admiring observation of Sir Edward Coke, who procured him an education. He never saw Holland. He emigrated direct from England to New England. He fell immediately into a controversy with the New England Hierarchy, fled from a sentence of banishment, took refuge with the Indian Chief Massasoit and founded the Narragansett Bay Colony which later became Rhode Island, where for the first time on American soil absolute religious freedom was established. Since he never was in Holland, he could hardly have brought that idea from there. In 1663 he procured a charter from Charles II which among its fundamentals provided for religious freedom. Charles II at that time, because he wanted toleration for the Catholics, was granting toleration to all other sects. That was one of the complaints against him.

You say, apparently quoting Campbell, "that the so-called New England institutions were found in New York when it was a Dutch Colony." I call your attention to Thorpe's American Charters and Constitutions which you should study. It contains the Charter and Constitution authentically reprinted, of every American Colony and state. Under the head of New York you will find that New Amsterdam was despotically governed by Governors appointed by the Dutch West India Company, such men as Van Twiller, Kieft and Stuyvesant. There was no representative assembly but these Governors occasionally appointed burghers as members of his Council and as frequently removed them. In 1649 the settlers of New Amsterdam held a convention and petitioned the Holland government to grant them a "suitable burgher government." The Directors of the West India Company said to them, "We have already connived for the many impertinences of some restless spirits in the hope that they might be shamed by our discreetness and benevolence but perceiving that all the kindnesses do not avail, we accordingly hereby charge and command your Honor (meaning the Governor) that whenever you shall certainly discover any clandestine meetings, conventical or machinations against our government or that of our country, that you proceed against such malignants in proportion to their crimes." That is the kind of a government that the Dutch had in New Amsterdam when the English were founding Connecticut and Rhode Island. New York never had a representative Assembly until it came under the English Crown.

You say that the Dutch settled New Jersey. My histories say that New Jersey was settled by the Swedes and that afterwards the Dutch overflowed into it. Probably my histories are wrong. At any rate New Jersey never had a Constitution or a charter until 1664 after it had been taken from the Dutch.

You speak of William Penn as half Dutch. His mother was a Dutch woman. Penn's father, the Admiral, had been the close personal friend of Charles II and he granted Pennsylvania to William Penn with autocratic power and in 1681 Penn, who had never been in Holland and was a Quaker, gave his Colony a government with an Assembly, an English Assembly, and gave the franchise "to all free men and planters," the first example of universal suffrage in America, which was later withdrawn and the property qualification instituted after the Colony had bought out Penn's rights. But Penn as Lord Proprietor, retained the Governorship and right of veto, governed usually by his deputies and his heirs continued to be Governors until Pennsylvania bought out his heirs for the sum of $500,000.00.

Turning back to the Dutch Constitution. At the time the Puritans lived there, it was as far from being a Democracy as Venice, in fact it was a pure Oligarchy, controlled by hereditary nobles like the Prince of Orange, great land owners and wealthy merchants, shipowners and heads of the various guilds. Each city, like Amsterdam, was a pure aristocracy. And note this, at the present day, the suffrage in Holland is confined to those who pay certain communal duties and office holding is confined strictly to certain classes. No laboring man can be either a voter or an office holder in Holland as he is in England. Holland was a Republic but it never was a Democracy. The myth of Dutch influence on our institutions is absolutely unsupported by any historical fact.

I might easily sidestep your allusion to Roman Law because I was not writing a history of the municipal law of England and America but of the Constitution. However, since you present the issue, let us consider it.

You assert the powerful influence of Roman law upon our Constitution. I think you will hardly say

that John Norton Pomeroy, author of "Equity Jurisprudence," is either a "fabulist" or a "toady" of the
Hanoverian Kings. In the first volume of his Fourth
Edition, if you will examine it, he gives the beginnings of equity jurisprudence in England. After a
history of the Roman law and its administration on
page thirteen, he notes that the Saxon law was largely
customary. "The Saxon local folk court and even the
supreme tribunal, the Witenagamote, not being composed of professional judges were certainly guided in
their decisions of particular controversies by customs
which were established and certainly were considered
as having the same obligatory character which we give
to positive law." Then he goes on to say that in the
reign of William the Conqueror, the local folk courts
of the Saxon polity together with the manor courts of
the Normans were the courts of first resort. Very
gradually the common law courts grew up under
which the *"lex non scriptae"* became the *"lex scriptae"*
as the courts began to give their decisions in writing.
He bemoans the immediate commencement of that
rigid adherence to precedent which finally compelled
the establishment of the equity jurisdiction of the Chancellor with principles borrowed from the Roman law
to relieve the rigidity and injustice of the common law.
He points out that it was not until Holt's time and
very late in that time and in fact not to any considerable extent until the time of Mansfield, that the Eng-

454

lish Judges began to borrow from the Roman law, about the beginning of the eighteenth century. I have never shared the blind reverence for the English common law. The Professors of Civil Law on the continent viewed the English common law with its rigidity and adherence to precedent, with contempt. Unquestionably the great body of the Roman law with its continuous free growth and what we now call Civil Law succeeding, is the greatest contribution to the jurisprudence of the world that the law knows. It is for that very reason that today it rules more than half of the civilized world, but when English Judges began to borrow from it, when the King's Chancellor began to issue writs in equity, the Roman law was a graft upon our system, not a root, mark that. The Anglo-Saxons never borrowed from the Roman Law a single fundamental Constitutional principle. I defy you to show me in any part of the fundamentals of our Constitution or the English Constitution, one single feature that we derive from the Roman or Civil law. Enough of that.

You allude to the adoption by Germany of the Civil law as an argument that the Anglo-Saxon does not owe his institutions to his Germanic ancestors. You speak of the Germans, in their conquests of cities, finding the Roman law which they adopted. That is quite true on the continent but in the conquest of Britain, unless Greene, Freeman, and every other historian of England is wrong, when our Germanic ancestors con-

quered England they destroyed every trace of Roman
civilization. They destroyed alike, Roman temples,
Christian churches, Roman law and Druidic worship,
as they destroyed or drove out all of the then inhabitants of England. Unless all historians are wrong
these Germanic tribes planted themselves, their religion, and institutions upon that which they had made
a vacant soil. The Roman law never knew of a trial
by Jury. The Saxons established it in a crude form.
The Roman law never knew of a ruler elected by the
suffrages of all the people, yet such in effect were the
Saxon Kings. The Roman law never knew such a
thing as a representative law-making body (I speak
now of that Rome which conquered the world), the
Saxon Folkmote. As the country increased in population, this changed into the representative assembly
of the Shiremote which became the model of the
House of Commons, so say Freeman, Greene, Stubbs
and May. They say also that the Witenagamote became the King's Council and later the House of Peers.
I leave you to quarrel with them. Perhaps they too
are "fabulists" and "toadies." The Roman law ultimately and beginning with the eighteenth century
powerfully influenced the English law but it never in
any degree influenced the English or American Constitutions.

You say that England has no Constitution because
Parliament is omnipotent and may at any time change

the English Constitution by a bill duly enacted. I do not understand that a Constitution depends upon the machinery by which it may be changed. My dictionaries, and I have several, thus define a Constitution: "the fundamental organic law or government of a nation, state, or other organized body of men embodied in written documents (as in the United States) or implied in the institutions and customs of the country (as in England)." "The British Constitution belongs to what is called customary or unwritten Constitutions." "The Constitution of the United States belongs to what are often called rigid Constitutions which cannot be changed except through such processes as the Constitution itself ordains." Lord Bryce never said, as you suggest, that there was no British Constitution. He simply said what everyone knows, that Parliament can at any time change the Constitution. What is Parliament? It is the representative body of the British people freely chosen. If Parliament tomorrow should abolish the Crown, as it could, it would be done by the representatives of the people and if the people were not satisfied with this act of their representatives they would at the next election choose a body that would re-establish the Crown. How do we change our Constitution? Two-thirds of a quorum of the House and the Senate propose a Constitutional Amendment. They are not chosen specially for that purpose, it is simply a part of their functions.

If two-thirds of the Legislatures of the different states by a majority of a quorum in each House adopt the Amendment, it then becomes a part of our fundamental law and these Legislatures are not chosen especially for that purpose. The people do not in any case vote upon this change in the Constitution. They change their Constitution, first through their representatives in Congress, and second, through their representatives in the state Legislatures. The British change their Constitution by a single act through their representatives in Parliament. The difference is not in principle but in machinery. Ours is slower, more difficult, but in each case, it is accomplished not by the people themselves voting directly but by their representatives and it is worth noting here that in spite of the circumlocution by which we must accomplish a change, we have amended our Constitution nine times since 1792 and in that time the British have amended their Constitution once, restricting the veto power of the Peers to one adverse vote on a bill passed by the Commons. If it is passed the second time it becomes a law.

You mention certain novelties in our Constitution to show that it is purely an American product, for instance, that the House of Representatives is chosen according to numbers, while in the Senate each state, however small, has two members. Surely you know that that was not an act of conscious prevision, it was purely a compromise. Four times the convention had voted for a Senate representing population exactly like the lower House. The fifth time, early in July, 1777, when it came up again, the vote was a tie. Delaware openly declared it would leave the Convention and hinted that it would form a foreign alliance. It was apparent that the smaller states would secede. A committee of eleven was appointed with Franklin as chairman, which on July 5, 1777, recommended what was called the Connecticut plan although it had been very early suggested by James Wilson of Pennsylvania. A lower house chosen on the basis of population and a Senate with two members from each state and that provision was made irrevocable. This was the turning point in the Constitution and saved the day, but mark this, this as well as the compromise on slavery by which Georgia and South Carolina secured the relegation of slavery to the separate states and in return combined with New England for the adoption of the Commerce clause, was simply one of the many compromises in the machinery by which the new government was established. You apparently confuse fundamental rights with governmental machinery. We established a new machinery of government out of the necessities of our situation. For what? For the protection of those fundamental rights that were the birthright of these English Colonists, derived from the mother country. Two things in our government were novel and are above praise. A Federal system that respecting the independence of its various members in their local affairs, yet operates directly upon the people. The only model for that is the Iroquois Republic, The Six Nations, which endured longer than any Federation that the world ever saw and which Jefferson says was the model of our system. Certainly it was not modeled from the Achaian League of the Greek cities, the League of Italian cities against the Emperor Henry, the Swiss Cantons, or the Dutch Republic. The other and most remarkable point in our Constitution is the independent Judiciary, clothed with power to restrain the other departments of government within their granted powers. This is the great and distinctive contribution of America to the governmental systems of the world without which this country would have long since dissolved into "dissevered discordant and belligerent fragments."

I turn now to an authority which you will agree with me is indisputable. It is a book entitled, "The Constitution of the United States, Its Sources and Its Application" (mark that, its sources) by Thomas J. Norton. Now I appeal "from Philip Drunk to Philip Sober." I appeal from Norton, the critic of my little pamphlet, to Norton the authentic historian. Examining that book carefully I find that in considering the sources of the Constitution you have alluded to British sources forty-eight times. You have alluded to the

460

Roman law twice; once, with reference to bankruptcy, certainly not a fundamental Constitutional right, and once to the taking of private property. You have alluded to Colonial precedents five times and every one of these are about the time of the Revolution. You have not anywhere alluded to the Connecticut, Rhode Island, or Pennsylvania Constitutions. If, as you say now, we owe our Constitution largely to Dutch and Roman sources, why did you not in this book which was intended for a text-book for the young, give these sources? You were writing then as a diligent, studious historian. I think I can answer the question. You were unable to find any such sources and I challenge you now in concluding this too long letter to cite me to one single precedent in the Constitution of the Dutch Republic, or in Roman law from which we could have drawn the four fundamentals of the English and American Constitutions and of the Bill of Rights contained in the ten Amendments. I do not care to quarrel with you about the truthfulness of Tacitus. His statements are confirmed by all of his contemporaries, Pliny, Livy and Julius Caesar. Probably their government was simply a tribal government, perhaps not much better than the government of the Indian tribes but they took it with them to England when they conquered it. Out of those seeds of freedom grew the government of the Saxon Kingdom with a law crude but suited to the time, laws made by the

461

people and binding both upon the King and the citizen. Rude courts and a crude form of trial by Jury on which were based and out of which grew eventually the English Constitution.

You continually allude to the modern Constitution of Germany as though that had anything to do with our controversy. The Germanic tribe who conquered Rome adopted Roman laws and to some extent the Roman language and the modern Germanic Constitution grew out of that. It was the happy isolation of our forefathers on the little isle of England that enabled them to develop their free institutions, uncontaminated by the Roman polity. You might as well cite the French Constitution under Louis XIV. It would be quite as applicable to our very pleasant little controversy.

In concluding this too long letter, let me say that it has always seemed to me that if the American child could be taught what I conceive to be the truth, that our Constitution was of slow growth, the result of a long, continuous and bitter struggle lasting for more than a thousand years, bought and paid for by our fathers with a heavy price, it would give them a more appreciative sense of its value[1]. I am,

Respectfully yours
F. DUMONT SMITH.

1. The Constitution of the United States: Its Sources and Application. Little, Brown & Co., Boston.

In the XXth Article of the Federalist, page 115, Lodge's edition, written by Madison and Hamilton jointly, they take up, describe and consider the form of government of the United Provinces, that is, the Dutch Republic. They criticize it mercilessly, show its weakness, how utterly unsuited it would be for our country at that time, and demonstrate that it was never considered in the slightest degree as a model for our Constitution, or followed in a single particular. As between Mr. Campbell, whoever he is, and Hamilton and Madison, I prefer the later as authorities.

May 27, 1924.

Mr. F. DuMont Smith,
Hutchinson, Kansas.
Dear Sir:

In reply let me first point out that I made no claim that the framers of our Constitution borrowed anything from Holland. Campbell's two-volume work was referred to for the purpose of illustrating how widely apart theorists may wander when they write without basis of ascertained fact. I said that Campbell's theory (that our Constitution is of Dutch origin) is as good as yours (that it is of German-Saxon origin); and I added that "the thing to do is to reject all those theories as historically unreliable" and teach true American history, a very badly neglected subject. I therefore pass by all your comments on what I drew (but did not adopt) from Campbell's volumes.

But as an interesting fact of governmental history it may be remarked that in 1582, over two centuries before our Constitution was written, a constitution was prepared under which William of Orange would have become (but for his death) Count of Holland. Motley says ("Rise of the Dutch Republic," Vol. 3, Ch. 5, p. 589) that in the year before "his Majesty * * * held in his hands the supreme power, *legislative, judicial, executive*" (italics Motley's), and that under the new constitution William "exchanged substance for shadow, for the new state now constituted a free commonwealth—a republic in all but name." Motley further says that instead of exercising all the powers (Madison's definition of absolute tyranny, Federalist, No. 47) William "was content with those especially conferred upon him." He could not declare war, his appointing power was limited, he was in many ways restricted. "As to his judicial authority," says Motley, "it has ceased to exist. The Count of Holland was now the guardian of the laws, but the judges were to administer them." Do not those divisions of and limitations upon power give a Hollander a better basis for arguing our indebtedness to the Dutch than you have for your Anglo-Saxon theory? William's death made a federal republic where it had been planned to have a constitutional monarchy.

I decline to discuss matters not related to my the-
orem, which is that the American (not the Teuton or
the Briton) invented the Constitutional mechanism by
which the man became the master of his government
instead of its victim. At the time our Constitution
was written he was generally throughout the world the
victim of his government. No matter what ideals were
entertained in England or in any other country as to
jury trial, due process, habeas corpus, and the like, the
man was the victim of his government.

We could not have borrowed from England the religious freedom really protected by the First Amendment when intolerance at home drove Pilgrims, Puritans, Quakers and others to America. The idea was
in England, but the freedom was not. We established
the freedom by writing and set up a Judicial Department to guard it. Nor could the framers of the Constitution have gone there for trial by jury when by bill
of attainder Parliament sent 969 exiles to become a
convict colony in Australia at the very time our Constitutional Convention was sitting, many of them
people of the highest type and learning, whose descendants were second to no men that set foot in France
during the World War. Nor could our Fathers have
gone there for what you call "the right of the people
to choose their own rulers," since heredity generally
determined that in Britain when edge-tools or revolution did not. Nor could they have gone there for your
"right to make their own laws by representatives freely

chosen," because anything like the right of manhood suffrage did not come to pass in England until after our Civil War. As to a people's "right to tax themselves,'" the British idea on this was so unacceptable to Americans that they carried on a successful war against it.

The last four sentences contain all I care to say about your "four fundamentals of free government, and only four," which you consider the four cornerstones of the English constitution and of our own.

The Constitution of the United States was the instrument by which the longings of Englishmen and the ideals of other peoples were, after centuries of effort, realized in daily life—that the crushing weight of government should be lifted from the back of the man. No way had been devised to keep the government from breaking the man when it found him in the way of its machinations or otherwise undesirable. While there had been centuries of controversy and conflict which had accomplished much to the glory of English thought, it was still a fact when our Constitution was written that the government could crush the man—could deny religious freedom, could deny jury trial, could deny due process of law, could condemn to death or penal servitude by act of the legislature and without accusation, without counsel, without hearing.

All that was changed by an American invention in government. That invention put in three departments the governmental powers, each department a protection against the other two, the Judicial Department to pass upon the validity of any act of government that the man affected might see fit to challenge. Professor Dicey of Oxford quoted at pages 180 *et seq.* of my book, grants this in the most complimentary way. Ours he declared to be "the only adequate safeguard which has hitherto been invented against unconstitutional legislation"—that is to say, in other words, legislation tending toward that usurping or blending of powers which was always found where the government held the man as victim.

Before Dicey wrote, the two greatest of British dependencies, Canada (1867) and Australia (1900), had paid the supreme tribute of framing constitutions very like our own, including the all-saving Judicial Department—which the unlearned and the vicious in our country today find so much to their disliking.

You ask me to show "one single feature" of our Constitution which was derived from Rome. I do not claim that anything was derived directly. My contention is for American derivation. But doubtless Rome had influence. The records of the Convention show that the delegates discussed with remarkable familiarity every important government that had ever existed; and we know that Rome was the first great central government operating over a large number of subordinate and widely separated provinces or states. It very carefully and very wisely let local governments alone as far as possible, from which our National government today may re-learn the mostly forgotten lesson taught by our Fathers, and so carefully crystallized in the Tenth Amendment. In Herbert S. Hadley's illuminating "Rome and the World Today," written to recommend Roman methods to the bettering of present times, it is said (p. 349) :

"Roman law * * * became the basis of the legal codes of half the world, and Rome's form of government influenced the organization of the republics and constitutional monarchies of Europe and America."

In a special message to Congress asking for relief to sufferers from earthquake, President Roosevelt spoke of "the debt which civilization owes to Italy." As Roosevelt's greatest ability was shown in the field of history, he doubtless had in mind achievements in law and government as well as in music, painting, sculpture, and the other arts.

My idea is that a historical booklet intended to introduce young people in school to our Constitutional history should take the widest outlook upon the great governments of mankind. It should not strive to find in Saxon polity what is not clearly there—or what is clearly not there. Of the impossibility of drawing anything definite from Saxon times Bagehot, the ablest Englishman that has written on the subject, says in the last chapter of "The English Constitution" (p. 213) :

"I cannot presume to speak of the time before the Conquest, and the exact nature even of all Anglo-Norman institutions is perhaps dubious; at least, in nearly all cases there have been many controversies. Political zeal, whether Whig or Tory, has wanted to find a model in the past; and the whole state of society being confused, the precedents altering with the caprice of men and the chance of events, ingenious advocacy has had a happy field."

The first two chapters of Stubbs' "Constitutional History of England," dealing with early times, cites thirteen German works, one of them (Waitz: Deutsche Verfassongs-Geschichte on every page, on some pages frequently. I do not regard that favorably as English history. Bagehot is better.

The trial by jury, one of the four cornerstones which you laid, and which you trace to the Saxon, was to him probably unknown, according to Sergeant Stephen's Blackstone (Vol. 3, p. 588, note z) ; and Forsyth, a distinguished English scholar, in "Trial by Jury" (p. 45), goes farther and says that "it may be confidently asserted that trial by jury was unknown to our Anglo-Saxon ancestors."

You question my statement that Bryce said that the British really have no constitution. I quote from "Studies in History and Jurisprudence" (Vol. 1, p. 133) :

"There is no British Constitution. That is to say, there are no laws which can be definitely marked off as fundamental laws, defining and distributing the powers of government, the mode of creating public authorities, the rights and immunities of the citizen."

Space does not permit an explanation of the contents of the British Constitution.

Of course I show in my book[1], as you say, that the English colonists brought with them much of English law. They also rejected much. They brought some set and very practicable ideas of government. Many of the colonists were here because of government at home objectionable or intolerable to them. England is the source of a great deal of matter in our Constitution, most of which had been "glittering generalities" at home, but all of which became living actuality under our plan of government.

"In questions of power, then," wrote Jefferson, "let no more be heard of confidence in man, but bind him down from mischief by the chains of the Constitution."

That is the great American idea. There, in one sentence, we have the complete history of the world's failures in government. Whatever may have been *thought* in other lands, it was first *done* in the United States. The nations have been copying our method.

The success of it in the Spanish and the Portuguese countries of South America, as well as in other countries, shows that the genius for government does not belong to one race. All races can do well when they bind down from mischief the man in power. That is what America taught the world to do. The world has been better so far as it has done it. Germany will do it now.

While instructing youth we should give full credit to other peoples for what we definitely know we owe them, but our great endeavor should be to show forth and glorify the unprecedented achievements of Colonial and of later America, now, unfortunately, so little understood.

Yours truly,

T. J. NORTON.

CHAPTER II.

THE FEDERAL CONSTITUTION AND AMENDMENTS[1]

We the People of the United States, in Order to form a more perfect Union, establish Justice, insure domestic Tranquility, provide for the common defence, promote the general Welfare, and secure the Blessings of Liberty to ourselves and our Posterity, do ordain and establish this CONSTITUTION for the United States of America.

ARTICE I.

Section 1. All legislative Powers herein granted shall be vested in a Congress of the United States, which shall consist of a Senate and House of Representatives.

Section 2. The House of Representatives shall be composed of Members chosen every second Year by the People of the several States, and the Electors in each State shall have the Qualifications requisite for Electors of the most numerous Branch of the State Legislature.

No person shall be a Representative who shall not have attained to the Age of twenty-five Years, and

---

1. The text of the Constitution in this chapter is a reprint of the pamphlet Constitution printed by the Government Printing Office in 1891, with later amendments added.

been seven Years a Citizen of the United States, and who shall not, when elected, be an Inhabitant of that State in which he shall be chosen.

Representatives and direct Taxes shall be apportioned among the several States which may be included within this Union, according to their respective Numbers, which shall be determined by adding to the whole Number of free Persons, including those bound to Service for a Term of Years, and excluding Indians not taxed, three fifths of all other Persons. The actual Enumeration shall be made within three Years after the first Meeting of the Congress of the United States, and within every subsequent Term of Ten Years, in such Manner as they shall by Law direct. The Number of Representatives shall not exceed one for every thirty Thousand, but each State shall have at Least one Representative; and until such enumeration shall be made, the State of New Hampshire shall be entitled to chuse three, Massachusetts eight, Rhode Island and Providence Plantations one, Connecticut five, New York six, New Jersey four, Pennsylvania eight, Delaware one, Maryland six, Virginia ten, North Carolina five, South Carolina five, and Georgia three.

When vacancies happen in the Representation from any State, the Executive Authority thereof shall issue Writs of Election to fill such Vacancies.

The House of Representatives shall chuse their Speaker and other Officers; and shall have the sole Power of Impeachment.

Section 3. The Senate of the United States shall be composed of two Senators from each State, chosen by the Legislature thereof, for six Years; and each Senator shall have one Vote.

Immediately after they shall be assembled in Consequence of the first Election, they shall be divided as equally as may be into three Classes. The Seats of the Senators of the first Class shall be vacated at the Expiration of the second Year, of the second Class at the Expiration of the fourth Year, and of the third Class at the Expiration of the sixth Year, so that one third may be chosen every second Year; and if Vacancies happen by Resignation, or otherwise, during the Recess of the Legislature of any State, the Executive thereof may make temporary Appointments until the next Meeting of the Legislature, which shall then fill such Vacancies.

No Person shall be a Senator who shall not have attained to the Age of thirty Years, and been nine Years a Citizen of the United States, and who shall not, when, elected, be an Inhabitant of that State for which he shall be chosen.

The Vice President of the United States shall be President of the Senate, but shall have no Vote, unless they be equally divided.

The Senate shall chuse their other Officers, and also a President pro tempore, in the Absence of the Vice President or when he shall exercise the Office of President of the United States.

The Senate shall have the sole Power to try all Impeachments. When sitting for that Purpose, they shall be on Oath or Affirmation. When the President of the United States is tried, the Chief Justice shall preside: And no Person shall be convicted without the Concurrence of two thirds of the Members present.

Judgment in Cases of Impeachement shall not extend further than to removal from Office, and disqualification to hold and enjoy any Office of honor, Trust or Profit under the United States: but the Party convicted shall nevertheless be liable and subject to Indictment, Trial, Judgment and Punishment, according to Law.

Section 4. The Times, Places and Manner of holding Elections for Senators and Representatives, shall be prescribed in each State by the Legislature thereof; but the Congress may at any time by Law make or alter such Regulations, except as to the Places of chusing Senators.

The Congress shall assemble at least once in every Year, and such Meeting shall be on the first Monday in December, unless they shall by Law appoint a different Day.

Section 5. Each House shall be the Judge of the Elections, Returns and Qualifications of its own Members and a Majority of each shall constitute a Quorum to do Business; but a smaller Number may adjourn from day to day, and may be authorized to compel the

Attendance of absent Members, in such Manner, and under such Penalties as each House may provide.

Each House may determine the Rules of its Proceedings, punish its Members for disorderly Behaviour, and, with the Concurrence of two thirds, expel a Member.

Each House shall keep a Journal of its Proceedings, and from time to time publish the same, excepting such Parts as may in their Judgment require Secrecy; and the Yeas and Nays of the Members of either House on any question shall, at the desire of one fifth of those Present, be entered on the Journal.

Neither House, during the Session of Congress, shall, without the Consent of the other, adjourn for more than three days, nor to any other Place than that in which the two Houses shall be sitting.

Section 6. The Senators and Representattives shall receive a Compensation for their Services, to be ascertained by Law, and paid out of the Treasury of the United States. They shall in all Cases, except Treason, Felony and Breach of the Peace, be privileged from Arrest during their Attendance at the Session of their respective Houses, and in going to and returning from the same; and for any Speech or Debate in either House, they shall not be questioned in any other Place.

No Senator or Representative shall, during the Time for which he was elected, be appointed to any civil Office under the Authority of the United States, which shall have been created, or the Emoluments whereof shall have been encreased during such time; and no Person holding any Office under the United States, shall be a Member of either House during his Continuance in Office.

Section 7. All Bills for raising Revenue shall originate in the House of Representatives; but the Senate may propose or concur with Amendments as on other Bills.

Every Bill which shall have passed the House of Representatives and the Senate, shall, before it become a Law, be presented to the President of the United States; If he approve he shall sign it, but if not he shall return it, with his Objections to that House in which it shall have originated, who shall enter the Objections at large on their Journal, and proceed to reconsider it. If after such Reconsideration two thirds of that House shall agree to pass the Bill, it shall be sent, together with the Objections, to the other House, by which it shall likewise be reconsidered, and if approved by two thirds of that House, it shall become a Law. But in all such Cases the Votes of both Houses shall be determined by yeas and Nays, and the Names of the Persons voting for and against the Bill shall be entered on the Journal of each House respectively. If any Bill shall not be returned by the President within ten Days (Sundays excepted) after it shall have been presented to him, the Same shall be a Law, in like Manner as if he had signed it, unless the Congress by their Adjournment prevent its Return, in which Case it shall not be a Law.

Every Order, Resolution, or Vote to which the Concurrence of the Senate and House of Representatives may be necessary (except on a question of Adjournment) shall be presented to the President of the United States; and before the Same shall take Effect shall be approved by him, or being disapproved by him, shall be repassed by two thirds of the Senate and House of Representatives, according to the Rules and Limitations prescribed in the Case of a Bill.

Section 8. The Congress shall have Power To lay and collect Taxes, Duties, Imposts and Excises, to pay the Debts and provide for the common Defence and general Welfare of the United States; but all Duties, Imposts and Excises shall be uniform throughout the United States;

To borrow Money on the credit of the United States;

To regulate Commerce with foreign Nations, and among the several States, and with the Indian Tribes;

To establish an uniform Rule of Naturalization, and uniform Laws on the subject of Bankruptcies throughout the United States;

To coin Money, regulate the Value thereof, and of foreign Coin, and fix the Standard of Weights and Measures;

To provide for the Punishment of counterfeiting the Securities and current Coin of the United States;

To establish Post Offices and post Roads;

To promote the Progress of Science and useful Arts, by securing for limited Times to Authors and Inventors the exclusive Right to their respective Writings and Discoveries;

To constitute Tribunals inferior to the supreme Court;

To define and punish Piracies and Felonies committed on the high Seas, and Offences against the Law of Nations;

To declare War, grant Letters of Marque and Reprisal, and make Rules concerning Captures on Land and Water;

To raise and support Armies, but no Appropriation of Money to that Use shall be for a longer Term than two Years;

To provide and maintain a Navy;

To make Rules for the Government and Regulation of the land and naval Forces;

To provide for calling forth the Militia to execute the Laws of the Union, suppress Insurrections and repel Invasions;

To provide for organizing, arming, and disciplining, the Militia, and for governing such Part of them as may be employed in the Service of the United States, reserving to the States respectively, the Appointment of the Officers, and the Authority of training the Militia according to the discipline prescribed by Congress.

To exercise exclusive Legislation in all Cases whatsoever, over such District (not exceeding ten Miles square) as may, by Cession of particular States, and the Acceptance of Congress, become the Seat of the Government of the United States, and to exercise like Authority over all Places purchased by the Consent of the Legislature of the State in which the Same shall be, for the Erection of Forts, Magazines, Arsenals, dock-Yards, and other needful Buildings;—And

To make all Laws which shall be necessary and proper for carrying into Execution the foregoing Powers, and all other Powers vested by this Constitution in the Government of the United States, or in any Department or Officer thereof.

Section 9. The Migration or Importation of such Persons as any of the States now existing shall think proper to admit, shall not be prohibited by the Congress prior to the Year one thousand eight hundred and eight, but a Tax or duty may be imposed on such Importation, not exceeding ten dollars for each Person.

The Privilege of the Writ of Habeas Corpus shall not be suspended unless when in Cases of Rebellion or Invasion the public Safety may require it.

No Bill of Attainder or ex post facto Law shall be passed.

No Capitation, or other direct, Tax shall be laid, unless in Proportion to the Census of Enumeration herein before directed to be taken.

No Tax or Duty shall be laid on Articles exported from any State.

No Preference shall be given by any Regulation of Commerce or Revenue to the Ports of one State over those of another; nor shall Vessels bound to, or from, one State, be obliged to enter, clear, or pay Duties in another.

No Money shall be drawn from the Treasury, but in Consequence of Appropriations made by Law; and a regular Statement and Account of the Receipts and Expenditures of all public Money shall be published from time to time.

No Title of Nobility shall be granted by the United States: And no Person holding any Office of Profit or Trust under them, shall, without the Consent of the Congress, accept of any present, Emolument, Office, or Title, of any kind whatever, from any King, Prince, or foreign State.

Section 10. No state shall enter into any Treaty Alliance, or Confederation; grant Letters of Marque and Reprisal; coin Money; emit Bills of Credit; make any Thing but gold and silver Coin a Tender in Payment of Debts; pass any Bill of Attainder, ex post facto Law, or Law impairing the Obligation of Contracts, or grant any Title of Nobility.

No State shall, without the Consent of the Congress, lay any Imposts or Duties on Imports or Exports, except what may be absolutely necessary for executing its inspection Laws; and the net Produce of all Duties and Imposts, laid by any State on Imports or Exports, shall be for the Use of the Treasury of the United States; and all such Laws shall be subject to the Revision and Controul of the Congress.

No State shall, without the Consent of Congress, lay any Duty of Tonnage, keep Troops, or Ships of War in time of Peace, enter into any Agreement or Compact with another State, or with a foreign Power, or engage in War, unless actually invaded, or in such imminent Danger as will not admit of delay.

ARTICLE II.

Section 1. The executive Power shall be vested in a President of the United States of America. He shall hold his Office during the Term of four Years, and, together with the Vice President, chosen for the same Term, be elected, as follows:

Each State shall appoint in such Manner as the Legislature thereof may direct, a Number of Electors, equal to the whole Number of Senators and Representatives to which the State may be entitled in the Congress: but no Senator or Representative, or Person holding an Office of Trust or Profit under the United States, shall be appointed an Elector.

The Electors shall meet in their respective States, and vote by Ballot for two Persons, of whom one at least shall not be an Inhabitant of the same State with themselves. And they shall make a List of all the Persons voted for, and of the Number of Votes for each; which List they shall sign and certify, and transmit sealed to the Seat of the Government of the United States, directed to the President of the Senate. The President of the Senate shall, in the Presence of the Senate and House of Representatives, open all the Certificates, and the Votes shall then be counted. The Person having the greatest Number of Votes shall be the President, if such Number be a Majority of the whole Number of Electors appointed; and if there be more than one who have such Majority, and have an equal Number of Votes, then the House of Representatives shall immediately chuse by Ballot one of them for President; and if no Person have a Majority, then from the five highest on the List the said House shall in like Manner chuse the President. But in chusing the President, the Votes shall be taken by States, the Representation from each State having one Vote; A quorum for this Purpose shall consist of a Member or Members from two thirds of the States, and a Majority of all the States shall be necessary to a Choice. In every Case, after the Choice of the President, the Person having the greatest Number of Votes of the Electors shall be the Vice President. But if there should remain two or more who have equal Votes, the Senate shall chuse from them by Ballot the Vice President.

The Congress may determine the Time of chusing the Electors, and the Day on which they shall give their Votes; which Day shall be the same throughout the United States.

No Person except a natural born Citizen, or a Citizen of the United States, at the time of the Adoption of this Constitution, shall be eligible to the Office of President; neither shall any Person be eligible to that Office who shall not have attained to the Age of thirty five Years, and been fourteen Years a Resident within the United States.

In Case of the Removal of the President from Office, or of his Death, Resignation, or Inability to discharge the Powers and Duties of the said Office, the Same shall devolve on the Vice President, and the Congress may by Law provide for the Case of Removal, Death, Resignation or Inability, both of the President and Vice President, declaring what Officer shall then act as President, and such Officer shall act accordingly, until the Disability be removed, or a President shall be elected.

The President shall, at stated Times, receive for his Services, a Compensation, which shall neither be encreased nor diminished during the Period for which he shall have been elected, and he shall not receive within that Period any other Emolument from the United States, or any of them.

Before he enter on the Execution of his Office, he shall take the following Oath or Affirmation:—"I do solemnly swear (or affirm) that I will faithfully execute the Office of President of the United States, and will to the best of my Ability, preserve, protect and defend the Constitution of the United States."

Section 2. The President shall be Commander in Chief of the Army and Navy of the United States, and of the Militia of the several States, when called into the actual Service of the United States; he may require the Opinion, in writing, of the principal Officer in each of the executive Departments, upon any Subject relating to the Duties of their respective Offices, and he shall have Power to grant Reprieves and Pardons for Offences against the United States, except in Cases of Impeachment.

He shall have Power, by and with the Advice and Consent of the Senate, to make Treaties, provided two thirds of the Senators present concur; and he shall nominate, and by and with the Advice and Consent of the Senate, shall appoint Ambassadors, other public Ministers and Consuls, Judges of the supreme Court, and all other Officers of the United States, whose Appointments are not herein otherwise provided for, and which shall be established by law: but the Congress may by Law vest the Appointment of such inferior Officers, as they think proper, in the President alone, in the Courts of Law, or in the Heads of Departments.

The President shall have Power to fill up all Vacancies that may happen during the Recess of the Senate, by granting Commissions which shall expire at the End of their next Session.

Section 3. He shall from time to time give to the Congress Information of the State of the Union, and recommend to their Consideration such Measures as he shall judge necessary and expedient; he may, on extraordinary Occasions, convene both Houses, or either of them, and in Case of Disagreement between them, with Respect to the Time of Adjournment, he may adjourn them to such Time as he shall think proper; he shall receive Ambassadors and other public Ministers; he shall take Care that the Laws be faithfully executed, and shall Commission all the Officers of the United States.

Section 4. The President, Vice President and all civil Officers of the United States, shall be removed from Office on Impeachment for, and Conviction of, Treason, Bribery, or other high Crimes and Mis-demeanors.

ARTICLE III.

Section 1. The judicial Power of the United States, shall be vested in one supreme Court, and in such inferior Courts as the Congress may from time to time ordain and establish. The Judges, both of the supreme and inferior Courts, shall hold their Offices during good Behavior, and shall, at stated Times, receive for their Services, a Compensation, which shall not be diminished during their continuance in Office.

Section 2. The judicial Power shall extend to all Cases, in Law and Equity, arising under this Constitution, the Laws of the United States, and Treaties made, or which shall be made, under their Authority;—to all Cases affecting Ambassadors, other public Ministers and Consuls;—to all Cases of admiralty and maritime Jurisdiction;—to Controversies to which the United States shall be a Party;—to Controversies between two or more States;—between a State and Citizens of another State;—between Citizens of different States,—between Citizens of the same State claiming Lands under Grants of different States, and between a State, or the Citizens thereof, and foreign States, Citizens or Subjects.

In all Cases affecting Ambassadors, other public Ministers and Consuls, and those in which a State shall be Party, the supreme Court shall have original Jurisdiction. In all the other Cases before mentioned, the supreme Court shall have appellate Jurisdiction, both as to Law and Fact, with such Exceptions, and under such regulations as the Congress shall make.

The Trial of all Crimes, except in Cases of Impeachment, shall be by Jury; and such Trial shall be held in the State where the said Crimes shall have been committed; but when not committed within any State, the Trial shall be at such Place or Places as the Congress may by Law have directed.

Section 3. Treason against the United States, shall consist only in levying War against them, or in adhering to their Enemies, giving them Aid and Comfort. No Person shall be convicted of Treason unless on the Testimony of two Witnesses to the same overt Act, or on Confession in open Court.

The Congress shall have Power to declare the Punishment of Treason, but no Attainder of Treason shall work Corruption of Blood, or Forfeiture except during the Life of the Person attainted.

ARTICLE IV.

Section 1. Full Faith and Credit shall be given in each State to the public Acts, Records, and judicial Proceedings of every other State. And the Congress may by general Laws prescribe the Manner in which such Acts, Records and Proceedings shall be proved, and the Effect thereof.

Section 2. The Citizens of each State shall be entitled to all Privileges and Immunities of Citizens in the several States.

A Person charged in any State with Treason, Felony, or other Crime, who shall flee from Justice, and be found in another State, shall on Demand of the executive Authority of the State from which he fled, be delivered up, to be removed to the State having Jurisdiction of the Crime.

No Person held to Service or Labour in one State, under the Laws thereof, escaping into another, shall, in Consequence of any Law or Regulation therein, be discharged from such Service or Labour, but shall be delivered up on Claim of the Party to whom such Service or Labour may be due.

Section 3. New States may be admitted by the Congress into this Union; but no new State shall be formed or erected within the Jurisdiction of any other State; nor any State be formed by the Junction of two or more States, or Parts of States, without the Consent of the Legislatures of the States concerned as well as of the Congress.

The Congress shall have Power to dispose of and make all needful Rules and Regulations respecting the Territory or other Property belonging to the United States; and nothing in this Constitution shall be so construed as to Prejudice any Claims of the United States, or of any particular State.

Section 4. The United States shall guarantee to every State in this Union a Republican Form of Government, and shall protect each of them against Invasion; and on Application of the Legislature, or of the Executive (when the Legislature cannot be convened) against domestic Violence.

ARTICLE V.

The Congress, whenever two thirds of both Houses shall deem it necessary, shall propose Amendments to this Constitution, or, on the Application of the Legislatures of two thirds of the several States, shall call a Convention for proposing Amendments, which, in either Case, shall be valid to all Intents and Purposes, as Part of this Constitution, when ratified by the Legislatures of three fourths of the several States, or by Conventions in three fourths thereof, as the one or the other Mode of Ratification may be proposed by the Congress; Provided that no Amendment which may be made prior to the Year One thousand eight hundred and eight shall in any Manner affect the first and fourth Clauses in the Ninth Section of the first Article; and that no State, without its Consent, shall be deprived of its equal Suffrage in the Senate.

490

ARTICLE VI.

All Debts contracted and Engagements entered into, before the Adoption of this Constitution, shall be as valid against the United States under this Constitution, as under the Confederation.

This Constitution, and the Laws of the United States which shall be made in Pursuance thereof; and all Treaties made, or which shall be made, under the Authority of the United States, shall be the supreme Law of the Land; and the Judges in every State shall be bound thereby, any Thing in the Constitution or Laws of any State to the Contrary notwithstanding.

The Senators and Representatives befose mentioned, and the Members of the several State Legislatures, and all executive and judicial Officers, both of the United States and of the several States, shall be bound by Oath or Affirmation, to support this Constitution; but no religious Test shall ever be required as a Qualification to any Office or public Trust under the United States.

ARTICLE VII.

The Ratification of the Conventions of nine States, shall be sufficient for the Establishment of this Constitution between the States so ratifying the Same.

DONE in Convention by the Unanimous Consent of the States present the Seventeenth Day of September in the Year of our Lord one thousand seven hundred and Eighty seven and of the Independence of the United States of America the Twelfth.

IN WITNESS whereof We have hereunto subscribed our Names,

GO: WASHINGTON—*Presidt.*
and deputy from Virginia

Attest WILLIAM JACKSON *Secretary*

	JOHN LANGDON
New Hampshire	NICHOLAS GILMAN
	NATHANIEL GORHAM
Massachusetts	RUFUS KING
	WM: SAML. JOHNSON
Connecticut	ROGER SHERMAN
New York	ALEXANDER HAMILTON
	WIL: LIVINGSTON
	DAVID BREARLEY.
New Jersey	WM. PATERSON.
	JONA: DAYTON
	B FRANKLIN

	THOMAS MIFFLIN
Pennsylvania	ROBT. MORRIS
	GEO. CLYMER
	THOS. FITZ SIMONS
	JARED INGERSOLL
Delaware	JAMES WILSON
	GOUV MORRIS
	GEO: READ
Maryland	GUNNING BEDFORD jun
	JOHN DICKINSON
	RICHARD BASSETT
	JACO: BROOM
	JAMES MCHENRY
	DAN OF ST THOS. JENIFER
	DANL CARROLL
Virginia	JOHN BLAIR—
	JAMES MADISON JR.
North Carolina	WM: BLOUNT
	RICHD. DOBBS SPAIGHT.
	HU WILLIAMSON
	J. RUTLEDGE
	CHARLES COTESWORTH PINCKNEY
South Carolina	CHARLES PINCKNEY
	PIERCE BUTLER.
Georgia	WILLIAM FEW
	ABR BALDWIN

ARTICLES

IN

ADDITION TO, AND AMENDMENT OF

THE

CONSTITUTION OF THE UNITED STATES OF AMERICA

Proposed by Congress and Ratified by the Legislatures
of the Several States, Pursuant to the Fifth
Article of the Constitution

[ARTICLE I.]

Congress shall make no law respecting an establishment of religion, or prohibiting the free exercise thereof; or abridging the freedom of speech, or of the press; or the right of the people peaceably to assemble, and to petition the Government for a redress of grievances.

[ARTICLE II.]

A well regulated Militia, being necessary to the security of a free State, the right of the people to keep and bear Arms, shall not be infringed.

[ARTICLE III.]

No Soldier shall, in time of peace be quartered in any house, without the consent of the Owner, nor in time of war, but in a manner to be prescribed by law.

494

[ARTICLE IV.]

The right of the people to be secure in their persons, houses, papers, and effects, against unreasonable searches and seizures, shall not be violated, and no Warrants shall issue, but upon probable cause, supported by Oath or affirmation, and particularly describing the place to be searched, and the persons or things to be seized.

[ARTICLE V.]

No person shall be held to answer for a capital, or otherwise infamous crime, unless on a presentment or indictment of a Grand Jury, except in cases arising in the land or naval forces, or in the Militia, when in actual service in time of War or public danger; nor shall any person be subject for the same offence to be twice put in jeopardy of life or limb; nor shall be compelled in any Criminal Case to be a witness against himself, nor be deprived of life, liberty, or property, without due process of law; nor shall private property be taken for public use, without just compensation.

[ARTICLE VI.]

In all criminal prosecutions, the accused shall enjoy the right to a speedy and public trial, by an impartial jury of the State and district wherein the crime shall have been committed, which district shall have been previously ascertained by law, and to be informed of the nature and cause of the accusation; to be con-

495

fronted with the witnesses against him; to have compulsory process for obtaining Witnesses in his favor, and to have the Assistance of Counsel for his defence.

[ARTICLE VII.]

In suits at common law, where the value in controversy shall exceed twenty dollars, the right of trial by jury shall be preserved, and no fact tried by a jury shall be otherwise re-examined in any Court of the United States, than according to the rules of the common law.

[ARTICLE VIII.]

Excessive bail shall not be required, nor excessive fines imposed, nor cruel and unusual punishments inflicted.

[ARTICLE IX.]

The enumeration in the Constitution, of certain rights, shall not be construed to deny or disparage others retained by the people.

[ARTICLE X.]

The powers not delegated to the United States by the Constitution, nor prohibited by it to the States, are reserved to the States respectively, or to the people.

[ARTICLE XI.]

The Judicial power of he United States shall not be construed to extend to any suit in law or equity, commenced or prosecuted against one of the United States by Citizens of another State, or by Citizens or Subjects of any Foreign State.

[ARTICLE XII.]

The Electors shall meet in their respective states, and vote by ballot for President and Vice-President, one of whom, at least, shall not be an inhabitant of the same state with themselves; they shall name in their ballots the person voted for as President, and in distinct ballots the person voted for as Vice-President, and they shall make distinct lists of all persons voted for as President, and of all persons voted for as Vice-President, and of the number of votes for each, which lists they shall sign and certify, and transmit sealed to the seat of the government of the United States, directed to the President of the Senate;—The President of the Senate shall, in presence of the Senate and House of Representatives, open all the certificates and the votes shall then be counted;—The person having the greatest number of votes for President, shall be the President, if such number be a majority of the whole number of electors appointed; and if no person have such majority, then from the persons having the highest numbers not exceeding three on the list of those voted for as President, the House of Representatives shall choose immediately, by ballot, the President. But in choosing the President, the votes shall be taken by states, the representation from each state having one vote; a quorum for this purpose shall consist of a member or members from two-thirds of the states, and a majority of all the states shall be necessary to a choice. And if the House of Representatives shall not choose a President whenever the right of choice shall devolve upon them, before the fourth day of March next following, then the Vice-President shall act as President, as in the case of the death or other constitutional disability of the President. The person having the greatest number of votes as Vice-President, shall be the Vice-President, if such number be a majority of the whole number of Electors appointed, and if no person have a majority, then from the two highest numbers on the list, the Senate shall choose the Vice-President; a quorum for the purpose shall consist of two-thirds of the whole number of Senators, and a majority of the whole number shall be necessary to a choice. But no person constitutionally ineligible to the office of President shall be eligible to that of Vice-President of the United States.

[ARTICLE XIII.]

Section 1. Neither slavery nor involuntary servitude, except as a punishment for crime whereof the party shall have been duly convicted, shall exist within the United States, or any place subject to their jurisdiction.

Section 2. Congress shall have power to enforce this article by appropriate legislation.

[ARTICLE XIV.]

Section 1. All persons born or naturalized in the United States, and subject to the jurisdiction thereof, are citizens of the United States and of the State wherein they reside. No State shall make or enforce any law which shall abridge the privileges or immunities of citizens of the United States; nor shall any State deprive any person of life, liberty, or property, without due process of law; nor deny to any person within its jurisdiction the equal protection of the laws.

Section 2. Representatives shall be apportioned among the several States according to their respective numbers, counting the whole number of persons in each State, excluding Indians not taxed. But when the right to vote at any election for the choice of electors for President and Vice-President of the United States, Representatives in Congress, the Executive and Judicial officers of a State, or the members of the Legislature thereof, is denied to any of the male inhabitants of such State, being twenty-one years of age, and citizens of the United States, or in any way abridged, except for participation in rebellion, or other crime, the basis of representation therein shall be reduced in the proportion which the number of such male citizens shall bear to the whole number of male citizens twenty-one years of age in such State.

Section 3. No person shall be a Senator or Representative in Congress, or elector of President and Vice-

President, or hold any office, civil or military, under the United States, or under any State, who, having previously taken an oath, as a member of Congress, or as an officer of the United States, or as a member of any State Legislature, or as an executive or judicial officer of any State, to support the Constitution of the United States, shall have engaged in insurrection or rebellion against the same, or given aid or comfort to the enemies thereof. But Congress may by a vote of two-thirds of each House, remove such disability.

Section 4. The validity of the public debt of the United States authorized by law, including debts incurred for payment of pensions and bounties for services in suppressing insurrection or rebellion, shall not be questioned. But neither the United States nor any State shall assume or pay any debt or obligation incurred in aid of insurrection or rebellion against the United States, or any claim for the loss of emancipation of any slave; but all such debts, obligations and claims shall be held illegal and void.

Section 5. The Congress shall have power to enforce, by appropriate legislation, the provisions of this article.

[ARTICLE XV.]

Section 1. The right of citizens of the United States to vote shall not be denied or abridged by the United States or by any State on account of race, color, or previous condition of servitude.

500

Section 2. The Congress shall have power to enforce this article by appropriate legislation.

[ARTICLE XVI.]

The Congress shall have power to lay and collect taxes on incomes, from whatever source derived, without apportionment among the several States, and without regard to any census or enumeration.

[ARTICLE XVII.]

The Senate of the United States shall be composed of two Senators from each State, elected by the people thereof, for six years; and each Senator shall have one vote. The electors in each State shall have the qualifications requisite for electors of the most numerous branch of the State legislatures.

2. When vacancies happen in the representation of any State in the Senate, the executive authority of such State shall issue writs of election to fill such vacancies: Provided, That the legislature of any State may empower the executive thereof to make temporary appointment until the people fill the vacancies by election as the legislature may direct.

3. This amendment shall not be so construed as to affect the election or term of any Senator chosen before it becomes valid as part of the Constitution.

ARTICLE XVIII.

Section 1. After one year from the ratification of this article the manufacture, sale, or transportation of intoxicating liquors within, the importation thereof into, or the exportation thereof from the United States and all territory subject to the jurisdiction thereof for beverage purposes is hereby prohibited.

Sec. 2. The Congress and the several States shall have concurrent power to enforce this article by appropriate legislation.

Sec. 3. This article shall be inoperative unless it shall have been ratified as an amendment to the Constitution by the legislatures of the several States, as provided in the Constitution, within seven years from the date of the submission hereof to the States by the Congress.

ARTICLE XIX.

The right of citizens of the United States to vote shall not be denied or abridged by the United States or by any State on account of sex.

Congress shall have power to enforce this article by appropriate legislation.

INDEX

ANALYTICAL INDEX

OF THE

CONSTITUTION AND THE AMENDMENTS THERETO

A.

505

INDEX TO CONSTITUTION

506

INDEX TO CONSTITUTION

507

INDEX TO CONSTITUTION

INDEX TO CONSTITUTION

INDEX TO CONSTITUTION

512

INDEX TO CONSTITUTION

513

INDEX TO CONSTITUTION

514

INDEX TO CONSTITUTION

515

INDEX TO CONSTITUTION

516

517

INDEX TO CONSTITUTION

INDEX TO CONSTITUTION

519

INDEX TO CONSTITUTION

INDEX TO CONSTITUTION

522

INDEX TO CONSTITUTION

523

INDEX TO CONSTITUTION

INDEX TO CONSTITUTION

INDEX TO CONSTITUTION

527

528

529

INDEX TO CONSTITUTION

530

INDEX TO CONSTITUTION

532

INDEX TO CONSTITUTION

533

INDEX TO CONSTITUTION

534

INDEX TO CONSTITUTION

535

INDEX TO CONSTITUTION

536

INDEX TO CONSTITUTION

INDEX TO CONSTITUTION

541

INDEX TO CONSTITUTION

542

INDEX TO CONSTITUTION

544

INDEX TO CONSTITUTION

INDEX TO CONSTITUTION

INDEX TO CONSTITUTION

R.

INDEX TO CONSTITUTION

553

554

INDEX TO CONSTITUTION

555

INDEX TO CONSTITUTION

INDEX TO CONSTITUTION

558

INDEX TO CONSTITUTION

559

INDEX TO CONSTITUTION

INDEX TO CONSTITUTION

INDEX TO CONSTITUTION

562

INDEX TO CONSTITUTION

563

564

INDEX TO CONSTITUTION

565

INDEX TO CONSTITUTION

567

INDEX TO CONSTITUTION

569

INDEX TO CONSTITUTION

TABLE OF CASES

573

577